Economics for Prophets

A Primer on Concepts, Realities, and Values in Our Economic System

by

Walter L. Owensby

WILLIAM B. EERDMANS PUBLISHING COMPANY
GRAND RAPIDS, MICHIGAN

255 Jefferson Ave. S.E., Grand Rapids, Mich. 49503

Printed in the United States of America

Reprinted, May 1990

Library of Congress Cataloging-in-Publication Data

Owensby, Walter L.
Economics for prophets : a primer on concepts, realities, and values in our economic system
by Walter L. Owensby.
p. cm.
ISBN 0-8028-0357-1
1. Economics—Moral and ethical aspects.
2. Economics—Religious aspects. I. Title.
HB72.094 1988
330—dc19 88-1402
CIP

Contents

Foreword

A living-room dialogue between Sydney Thomson Brown and Robert McAfee Brown, while finishing *Economics for Prophets*

STB (*after a long silence in which the two of them have been reading galley proofs*): Well, what do you think?

RMB: I like the methodology. He starts in right where people are, with what they hear all the time about how our economic system works, and then, thud, he shows us what is actually going on when "the reality destroys the theory." And only after that does he begin to theorize. It's been one of the liabilities of my professional life that people get put off when the theology comes on too early and too strong.

STB: As a layperson who resists those who begin with theological proclamations, I think his method worked: I wasn't put off. But what *I* liked best about the book was his specificity, his human examples, his avoidance of page after page of nothing but theory. A little ungrounded theory goes a long way with me.

RMB: But don't you agree that we need to know about "supply- side projection" and "conglomerate pyramiding" and "surplus value" and "aggregate demand"?

STB: You're bluffing and you know it.

RMB: Wrong. I would have been bluffing a week ago, but not now. Because the author explains all the forbidding terms the experts throw at us so we'll get confused and leave the field to them. [*After a little paper shuffling*] Just look on pages 93, 97, 93 again, and 90, in that order, and you too can know what I'm talking about.

STB: Very impressive. Considering your previous lack of exposure to economics, Owensby has done a marvelous job of communicating to you what "capital" really is.

RMB (*smugly*): Do you mean "real capital" or "finance capital" or "capital accumulation"? [*Quickly*] Pages 40 and 41.

STB: I'll save pages 40 and 41 until after this conversation. I'm much more interested in finding out what happens to real people when their lives are threatened by economic pressures they can't control than I am in an academic debate.

RMB: Like that professor of yours who said, "Economics is a perfect system; it's just that people muck it up"?

STB: Right. I'm concerned about the people, and what happens to them under capitalism—or any economic system, for that matter.

RMB: Well, it looks like Owensby is writing for you. The book is people-oriented all the way through—without, let me add, neglecting to weave theory into the human scene as well.

STB: And he goes on to make the point that the consequences of any economic system affect people not only domestically but internationally as well. People all over the world get hurt.

RMB: Is that what "plant closures" are all about?

STB: Yes. Whenever a plant closes down, the community spinoff is that three and a half other jobs disappear for every plant job lost. The community services take a terrific beating—the closedown affects supermarket clerks, librarians, nurses in the clinics, those who work at satellite industries in the area, and so on. And then, if the company relocates overseas, one of the conditions it demands from the overseas government is "stability."

RMB: You make that sound like a code word.

STB: It *is* a code word. It means a promise that the government won't tolerate strikes or union organizing, and won't inspect working conditions or insist on safety precautions—and so on. . . . Listen, you're a theologian; how does all this immediate and practical stuff strike you?

RMB: That's where Owensby's methodology works for me. He gives me a crash course in economics in the first two sections of each chapter, and then in section three he lays the theology all out for me, or at least raises the theological questions I have to struggle with. He certainly demonstrates that "religion and economics *do* mix," and no one who reads his book can deny it. That alone is worth the price of admission.

STB: What else?

RMB: I like the way he disposes of the assumption that economics is "value-free," as though an economic system could exemplify moral neutrality.

STB: Would you mind translating that into English?

RMB: Well, for example: what view of human nature is implied in the idea that "competition is the law of life"? If that slogan is true, a lot of people are going to get destroyed by the competition. If I come along and say that people shouldn't get destroyed, I'm making a positive value judgment about the worth of people. And if an economic system destroys them, I've got to make a negative value judgment about that system, since the system incorporates the "value" that it's all right for a lot of people to be destroyed so that a few people can succeed.

STB: Got it. And I like the fact that Owensby doesn't get preachy at that point and dump *his* value judgments on us coercively. He is content to describe what is really going on and then let us make up our minds about it.

RMB: Such as . . .

STB: Well, when he's describing the kind of world we live in, for example, he says, "The needs of the poor must bid against the wants of the rich." If somebody says that's stacking the evidence against the rich, Owensby can respond, "Well, isn't that what actually happens? Isn't that descriptively true?" And from my perspective it is.

RMB: I remember a well-known scientist who gave a lecture called "Physics for Poets," in which he tried to communicate across very difficult language barriers. It seems to me that that's what Owensby is up to here, with that neat twist in the title that a lot of people are going to miss: *Economics for Prophets* instead of *Economics for Profits*. [*Short pause*] Get it?

STB: As a matter of fact, that's the first thing I noticed about the book.

RMB (*hastily*): Well, getting beyond word play, he really has given us an economics for church types or ordinary people (if there's a difference), and church types and ordinary people surely need it. I hope they'll stay with the book and hear him through to the end.

STB: I think they will. After all, we did, and we're pretty typical ordinary people/church types when it comes to economics. And think of the side effects! Some people may think he's making a case for a critical capitalism, while others may think that the word "critical" makes him a socialist, or worse. That in itself should produce some good, healthy discussion.

RMB: So he must be doing something right. Here, listen to this . . .

Preface

First, a word to the prophets. The title of this work is not just a play on words—though I am sure the reader will not begrudge that. The spelling makes it clear that this is not a book for investors aspiring to impress their brokers or neighbors. It is intended for people who want to make an impact, not a killing. Neither is this book for the palm readers, futurists, and market analysts who claim to know what tomorrow holds. One of the measures of the failure of Christians to communicate is the degree to which even church people still think of prophets as foretellers of the future. The biblical emphasis is clearly much more on their being "forthtellers" of God's message in troubled times—which is to say our times and all times. Putting it that way makes it sound as though this is a book for preachers, pastors, and priests, whose job it is to speak out on the issues of faith and life. In part that is true, but only with the caveat that the corollary of the Protestant doctrine of the priesthood of all believers is the prophethood of all believers. To be a part of the believing community is to be among the forthtellers, those who share their concerns about the way the world is and ought to be as God gives them insight.

Much of the message of the biblical prophets had to do with how economic realities of the day affected the lives of people and the nation. In our own time as well, faith has something to say about such things. That does not mean posing as economists when we are not. It does mean knowing enough about the way our economic system functions to be able to identify the moral issues at stake within it and to be able to enter responsibly into the public debate about the economic choices that lie before us.

It is the goal of this work to help members of the biblical faith community take part more confidently and effectively in that dialogue on ethics and economics. At this point it is important to note the subtitle of the book. This is a *primer.* That is, it aims at being a starting point for reflection on economic issues and their ethical implications. It assumes no prior knowledge of economics on the part of readers and, on matters of economic theory, will be of only limited value to those with a significant background in the subject. Still, I hope that the review of basic concepts and the accounts of real-world issues will go far in demystifying the world of economists and economic policymakers.

To facilitate that, I've organized each of the following chapters according to the same general scheme. The first segment deals with a basic concept of market economics. The underlying question is, how does our system say this concept is supposed to function? This involves a bit of theory, a bit of history, the definition of some of the common terms to help make economic jargon more intelligible, and an encounter with some of the ideas of notable economists, past and present. The second segment of each chapter deals with a real-world issue that relates to the concept laid out in the previous section. Here the question is, what happens when theory meets the real world? The focus is upon the functioning and the malfunctioning of some element of our economic system. The third segment in each chapter deals with the values at stake in either the concepts or the practice of the system. Why is the biblical faith community concerned or even interested?

There is no guarantee that any two thoughtful people will agree on the soundness of the summary of concepts, the legitimacy of the concerns expressed, or the answers to the questions raised. But agreement is not the purpose of this book. The goal is to draw more people of the faith community into the dialogue on the issues presented.

Those who are looking for detailed answers to contemporary economic dilemmas will be disappointed. There are, of course, suggestions sprinkled throughout the book, and I hope that readers will find merit in some of them. But they are not systematic, and no argument is made that these represent the only possible or the best solutions.

Those who seek a well-elaborated alternative to our present economic system will be even more disappointed. This is not a work on comparative economic systems. It deals with the principles, problems, and moral implications of market capitalism. That is not because capitalism holds any special claim of allegiance for Christians, but simply because capitalism is the system under which we live, for which we have specific responsibility, and which, therefore, we must seek to understand, critique, and transform.

The perspective from which we do that is, in a sense, the main concern of this book. The third segment of each chapter is not usually the longest, but it is the most crucial in that it seeks to establish the biblical, theological, and moral ground from which we approach the dilemmas of economic thought and performance. The dialogue between faith and economic order is ongoing. Our concern is not to end a particular set of abuses by corporations or individuals or to alter the economic policies of a given governmental administration. Rather, it is to call this and all economic systems to their highest potential for assisting human fulfillment through bountiful production, just distribution, and careful stewardship of the world and its resources.

Introduction

It seems that economists never tire of telling jokes on themselves. What beginning student has not encountered in lectures or texts such self-deprecating humor as "If all economists were laid end to end, they would never reach a conclusion"—hinting not just that economists are verbose but that they are indecisive. A variant is "If all economists were laid end to end, it would probably be a good thing"—stressing their ultimate uselessness. Or "What the world needs is a good one-armed economist"—recalling the frequency of the phrase "On the one hand . . . but on the other hand" as the symbol of the economist's inability to make a commitment.

The derisive humor spills over into real life and betrays a deep suspicion of practitioners of the art (or is it science?) of economics. In speaking of former Labor Secretary John Dunlop, George Meany was able to say only, "Despite the fact that he is an economist, basically, I have great confidence in him." And in recent years the reputation of economists seems to have fallen to a new low. One suspects that in a public opinion poll they would probably rank in social esteem somewhere below used-car salesmen and discredited TV evangelists. President Reagan, for example, showed contempt for the profession by making a stockbroker, not an economist, Secretary of the Treasury and by leaving unfilled for over two years the post of Chair of the Council of Economic Advisors.

Nevertheless, despite the frequent bad humor, bad press, and bad treatment meted out to economists, few doubt the importance of economics in the social order. After all, *economics is the study of the principles by which society organizes itself to use scarce resources for the production and distribution of goods and services*. When it is put that way, economics sounds like a dull and distant academic discipline, but it really deals with the stuff of life: the food and shelter that existence requires, the comforts and conveniences that lie beyond need and make life pleasant, and less easily measurable benefits like education and national defense that make society viable. Economics deals with all the things we do to achieve those goals—working, spending, saving, paying taxes, planning for the future.

All societies need and have economic systems for production and distribution because most of the things we want are not freely available in nature. The briefest list of our daily activities and consumption makes it clear how little we do on our own and how much collaboration and organization lies behind the most common acts—living in a house or apartment building, taking a drink of water, eating, dressing, reading the newspaper. However private they may seem, each is a social act that presupposes an elaborate economic system.

But an economy is not only the way we organize for production and distribution; it is also the way we allocate resources. Since there is not enough of everything for everyone, there are choices to be made. How much of which goods will be produced? Whose wants will be satisfied first? Will the limited amounts be divided by lottery, by equal shares, or by the exchange of goods or money? Will such decisions be made by fiat, by election, by a price system where dollars determine outcome, or by some combination of these?

That series of questions brings us to a fundamental matter about the nature of economics: is economics a science? Economists have struggled since the earliest days of the discipline to make their projections more accurate. In the process, economic theory has become more and more abstract and in recent years has been dominated by elaborate mathematical formulas and models. Still, not even the greatest enthusiasts for this approach could claim that economics can be considered a science in the same sense as physics or chemistry. Its theories cannot be tested with the same rigor. Society is not as controllable as the laboratory environment. Human nature is not as manipulable as chemicals and compounds, lenses and levers. Whereas experimental science can isolate and regulate, economists must deal with the world all at once, as it is, always moving and changing, and with "elements" that make decisions of their own that are not always predictable.

If economics is a science, then, it is a social science, not an exact science. This distinction becomes very important when we evaluate the recent trends toward mathematical modeling and the extent to which an economy can be planned. The theories of economics are intertwined with the happenings of history, the wills of individuals, and the institutions of society, with family, religious belief, and law. Trying to deal with economic reality as though it were a separate and distinct area of life leads not only to sterile discussion but to wrong conclusions as well. For instance, it is nonsense to speak of increasing the output of peasant agriculture by introducing high-yielding seed varieties, chemical fertilizer, and machinery. Such an economic decision does not multiply the yields of traditional agriculture; it transforms peasant society into something wholly new. Similarly, though usually less dramatically, every economic decision changes the world—not only the world that is, but the world that will be. There are no pure economic realities because economic realities are also social realities.

Only within the past two or three generations has that distinction been blurred by the tendency to promote economics as a science. For more than a century after Adam Smith wrote, the most common designation for the discipline was *political economy.* That is a cumbersome name, but it has the advantage of reminding us of the human and institutional connections of economic decision-making. Given recent trends of attempting to detach economics from living, breathing reality, we might do well to return to that former title.

A part of the movement to make the discipline more predictive and more exact has been the tendency to focus on what is called *positive economics,* which limits concern to what is rather than to what ought to be. By such a definition, economics must necessarily be limited to matters of fact, excluding opinion and belief. The job of the economist is to generate hypotheses that can be proved or disproved by objective evidence. For example, if inflation rises, unemployment will fall; if investment is increased, the gross national product will rise; if the money supply grows while output remains unchanged, inflation will result. Most economists today have been taught that ethics have no place in the field. The standard declaration of this value-neutral approach is made by the professor to first-year students: "Let society tell us what sort of world it wants; the task of economics is to show how to achieve it."

There is another approach called *normative economics,* which concerns itself with ethics, value judgments, and beliefs about what ought to be rather than merely explaining what is or what might be if. . . . Normative propositions about economics take on a different tone, as the following examples show: unemployment is too high to tighten the money supply; income distribution in this country is too skewed; a progressive income tax is more fair than a sales tax. Normative economics is not an alternative discipline; it still casts theory and data in crucial roles. Normative economics is simply an acknowledgment that since economic decisions have moral effects, it is not only acceptable but inescapable that economists, policymakers, and citizens function with a particular set of values and a vision of a preferred future.

Many economists reject the value-neutral claims of their profession and embrace its social and moral effects as a great opportunity. That was the perspective of the renowned British economist Arthur Cecil Pigou:

> I would add one word for any student beginning economics study who may be discouraged by the severity of the effort which the study . . . seems to require of him. The complicated analyses which economists endeavor to carry through are not mere gymnastic[s]. They are instruments for the bettering of human life. The misery and squalor that surround us, the injurious luxury of some wealthy families, the terrible uncertainty overshadowing many families of the poor—these are evils too plain to be ignored. By the knowledge that our science seeks it is possible that they may be restrained. Out of the darkness light! The search for it is the task, to find it perhaps the prize, which the "dismal science of Political Economy" offers to those who face its discipline.

Such words go far in answering the question so often raised about books like this one: Why bring biblical faith into discussions about economics? Clearly, as long as economics is regarded as a value-neutral, technical field, faith has no place in it. Believers are not better equipped than others to devise or utilize mathematical formulas, or to determine how much the growth of the money supply should be reduced to bring inflation down by two percentage points. However, when it is recognized that economics is an arena of values and vision as well as of theories and data, there is a legitimate role for the faith community in the public dialogue on economic policy. The valuing of life, the structuring of a just human society, and the use of creation's resources are as much concerns of faith as they are of economics and policy. Accordingly, there are major biblical themes that constitute a mandate for economic reflection and action by the churches and all their members.

First, we are a people who believe in *stewardship*. The Old Testament teaching about the land portrays its attitude toward wealth and economic relationships in general. Land was the symbol of productive power. It was the resource from which all wealth came. It is no accident, then, that in biblical thought only God owned the land. "The earth is the Lord's and the fulness thereof" (Ps. 24:1, RSV). Thus land was not a possession to boast about but a gift to be received, used, safeguarded, and passed on to future generations.

Because they believed in the divine ownership of the land, the Hebrew people carefully designed their laws to prevent its control from passing into the hands of a privileged few. Land was not a commodity to be traded at will. It was a right of inheritance. If for very pressing reasons it had to be sold, other members of the same family had the first option to buy. Even if purchased by someone else, the land was not forever lost. At the end of fifty years, in the Year of Jubilee, it had to be returned to the original owners.

A strange law—one that perhaps never functioned in reality—but the implication is clear. It was designed to make forever impossible the permanent concentration of productive power and wealth in the hands of some elite group, resulting in the impoverishment of the many. Thus the structure of landholding became the symbol of concern for a just economic order. Today, we too are to be stewards of God's creation, not owners of it always manipulating it for personal wealth and advantage.

At the heart of biblical faith is the conviction that we are the managers of everything and the owners of nothing. The concept of stewardship builds economic order upon the responsibility of using all of God's resources to benefit all of God's people for all ages. There is no room for narrow maximization of self, class, nation, or generation.

A second element of biblical faith that shapes the way we think about economic issues is the Bible's *emphasis upon communities* rather than individuals. This presents a great dilemma for those of us reared in a culture where social contract theory has regarded society as the mere voluntary association of persons. The individual is viewed as the absolute value, prior to and superior to the community. The right to maximize personal benefits is seen as the cornerstone of the natural order.

A cartoon in the newspapers several years ago caught the spirit of this view. It pictured a middle-class family—father, mother, and three children—seated around the kitchen table. Before them were the bills and the checkbook. The father said, "I've called you all together to let you know that because of inflation, I'm going to have to let two of you go." That strikes us as funny because it is so ludicrous: families don't function that way, or at least they're not supposed to. Ideally, families face adversity together. Following biblical principle, we can imagine one member sacrificing self to make life better for the others. We cannot imagine one sacrificing others for the benefit of self.

This is the biblical perspective. The individual is of absolute value, but the individual finds highest fulfillment in community, not in isolation. To be sure, God's call is personal: it comes to each believer. But God's covenant is with a people, not with heroic individuals; God's plan is for the reconciliation of all humankind and the restoration of the whole created order.

Thus poverty is not merely a personal tragedy. It is an attack upon the solidarity of the people of God. The goal of an economic system, therefore, is not to guarantee the right of the individual to acquire and accumulate all that personal ability and drive make possible. The goal is to provide for the needs of the global human community in a way that will draw people and nations together rather than further divide them. We may endure systems at odds with that vision, but we must not celebrate them or defend them from challenge or change.

This relates closely to a third theme that impels us into the economic arena. *Justice is the responsibility of the community.* "What does the Lord require of you but to do justice, and to love kindness, and to walk humbly with your God?" (Mic. 6:8, RSV). Biblical faith goes beyond personal piety and acts of charity that soften the edges of poverty. It requires the shaping of a society that will prevent the inequities that cause the suffering. The Law and the Commandments, given as the sign of the covenant with God's people, made it clear that a right relationship with God entails a respect for the rights and needs of others. Accordingly, Exodus, Leviticus, Numbers, and Deuteronomy are filled with injunctions designed to help and protect those who were most endangered by injustice: widows, orphans, and foreigners. Today's list of victims may be different, but the biblical principle remains clear. It is the responsibility of the covenant community to help shape a society where the weakest and most vulnerable will be defended and uplifted.

Advancing one's own interests at the expense of others is a sin clearly condemned by biblical faith. Traditionally, however, we have tended to think of this only at the individual level. But when such traits are institutionalized and depersonalized, they do not become less matters of spiritual concern. The fact that a huge enterprise, rather than some identifiable individual, cheats in business is not one bit less odious to God. That our government arranges trade laws to advance our interest at the cost of the continued suffering of the poor in other countries is not less of a moral problem than if an individual committed this transgression. We understand when Jeremiah condemns employers for not paying fair wages: "Woe to him . . . who makes his neighbor serve him for nothing, and does not give him his wages" (22:13, RSV). It is not less of a human tragedy or a moral failing when modern corporations search the world over for countries where the lowest wages can be paid, even when all know full well that thirty or forty cents an hour is not enough to keep a family at a decent level of living—perhaps not even enough to keep all members alive.

In a world where human damage is being done by the impersonal economic decisions made in corporate boardrooms and government agencies, it is not enough that we content ourselves with a reading of the Bible that limits moral concern to the actions of individuals.

A fourth theme related to our economic involvement is the *belief in creation.* The second chapter of Genesis reminds us that human beings were given a definite task in the created order. We were designated the keepers, shapers, and perfecters of all that God has made. We inherit the world not as a finished product but as a possibility. How well we fulfill our responsibility of shaping the world will determine to some extent the success of the creation.

The Bible also closes with a creation story in the book of Revelation (21:1-7; 22:1-5). This new creation, the world that God envisions, will be one where pain, suffering, and deprivation have given way to abundance shared in equity and in peace.

From the biblical perspective, history stands between the garden of creation and the city of the new creation. Our task is to create a world order that mirrors as closely as possible God's original intent and God's ultimate purpose. But there are others who have alternate visions and are busily making tomorrow's world. The economic and political decisions of corporations and governments are creating one kind of future and closing doors to other possibilities. Whether the future that is being made incrementally is in keeping with the biblical hope is a deeply theological matter. We have a vision of what the world ought to be that needs to be shared.

Finally, we are thrust into the arena of economic concern because *biblical faith rejects idolatry.* "You shall have no other gods before me," we read in Exodus 20:3 (RSV). As Christians we make only one absolute commitment—to God as we know God in Jesus Christ. Everything else is negotiable. Any ideology, system, or nation that is made absolute is an idol. It has ceased to be a part of the dynamic, changing order of creation and is somehow set above it.

Yet those of us reared in the United States have almost unconsciously absorbed the idea that biblical faith and capitalism are inseparable realities, that any criticism of market economics is somehow a betrayal of God, country, and logic. Such an attitude is heresy. God did not invent capitalism—or socialism, communism, or feudalism. If an economic system is producing the kinds of human results that are helping to achieve the biblical vision of God's creation, then it deserves to be supported. If it is causing human tragedy or not meeting human needs, then it must be either transformed or abandoned.

For theological reasons quite apart from reasons of social performance, we as Christians must denounce frequently and clearly any system that tries to lay absolute claim to our lives and our loyalty—especially when we live under that system and it has treated us well. We must not consent to selling the birthright for either a mess of pottage or the promise of affluence.

For these reasons at least, and undoubtedly for others not stated, people of biblical faith have not only the right but the responsibility to reflect upon, comment about, and seek to transform our present system and all future economic systems. That is the invitation issued in the following pages.

Chapter One

Economics as Struggle, Freedom, and Responsibility

I. Concepts: Underlying Principles of Market Economics

Computer models, data printouts, regression analyses, charts, tables, and graphs make economics seem an arcane discipline. Yet it is likely that economic decisions are made less on the grounds of unquestioned laws and irrefutable evidence than upon the basic beliefs and preferences the economist or policymaker has about the way the world is and ought to be. Consequently, it is important to begin this inquiry into economic reasoning and reality by recognizing that deeply held, value-laden convictions underlie the seemingly objective theories, calculations, and policies of the capitalist economic system. Four of these deserve special mention.

A. Freedom: The Fundamental Virtue

Freedom is usually perceived as being related more to politics than to economics. But freedom is so crucial an economic concept that it has been enshrined in some of the names we use to describe our system—"the free enterprise system" or "the free market system." That is no accident. The heart of classical economic theory is that the individual, and the individual alone, has the right and the responsibility to decide whether or not to work, whether to buy or sell, whether to save or spend.

For those of us who have always lived in the reflected light of idealized freedom, this seems natural enough. Indeed, we tend to assume that it has always been this way. Not so. As a matter of fact, the concepts of free-market economics and the individual economic actor are relative newcomers to history, having burst onto the scene only three or four hundred years ago. To be sure, there had been buying and selling long before that, but there was nothing like the free market that Adam Smith described in 1776. For thousands of years before the seventeenth and eighteenth centuries, life had far different rhythms and structures. Land and its resources were owned by the few or held in common by tribes or clans. It was the source of wealth and power, a birthright to be protected and yielded intact to the next generation and, therefore, not normally for sale. People were often tied to the land. Slaves could never leave. Serfs rendered a whole life's work in exchange for a portion of the crop from a small piece of land and the promise that if the harvest failed, the lord of the manor would provide. Artisans created products for sale and were expected to remain in their trades for life. There were no hiring halls and few job changes. There was no credit system to encourage investment and innovation, and no banks as we know them, and their forebears—the moneylenders—were regarded as moral outcasts.

Then, over three or four generations, the tradition-bound Western economic world was transformed. Where previously order and mutual responsibility had characterized life, the new age stressed freedom and individual gain. Capitalism had dawned. Suddenly, everything was for sale—land, labor, capital. Children whose parents had lived almost entirely outside a monetary economy found a world where they survived by cash alone. The sense of freedom this change produced must have been simultaneously exhilarating and terrifying. People had the opportunity and the responsibility as never before to make real decisions about their own lives—opportunity, because now they could choose where and how to live; responsibility, because now they had to pay the rent. To choose not to do one job depended on finding another. Freedom to choose stew over gruel was not freedom unless the price difference could be paid. To leave the manor was to leave the landlord's grain reserve, which meant that hunger lay just a day's wages away. Riches beckoned the few, and poverty stalked the many. Yet the new system regarded them all as free.

Today the threats of economic freedom have been ameliorated somewhat through welfare, unemployment compensation, job retraining, and government hiring programs. But none of those has anything to do with *classical* capitalism. They are all the result of government intervention that Adam Smith's model did not allow. The freedom proclaimed by the theory itself is still a two-edged sword: individuals are indeed free to choose but also free to accept the consequences of that choice. They are free to accumulate as much as ability allows and forced to assume the risks of failure. The consumer is free to choose from a panoply of goods but only to the extent that he or she has the money with which to pay. For the poor of the earth, the market offers as much frustration as freedom.

B. Scarcity and Efficiency: The Keystones of Economics

Scarcity is the unavailability of enough resources to satisfy all of the wants of all of the people. Scarcity creates economic value. People have enough air to breathe without a government agency to plan it, a corporation to manufacture it, or a system to deliver it. That is why air never figures into the calculations of economists. It is what they call a *free good.* It has no economic value. Economic scarcity, then, is the fundamental reality faced by all societies. "How can that be?" we ask, in the face of stories of a grain glut that makes farmers poor, and the memory of government storage costs for surplus products, and the occasional slaughter of dairy herds because of a massive oversupply of milk, cheese, and butter. The answer, of course, is not that all desires have been satiated, nor even all needs met. Rather, it is simply that there is no one who wants such products who also has money to pay. The clearest indication of scarcity—that there is not enough for everyone—is that something has a price. Dollars are the ration stamps of capitalism.

Notice that economics deals with *wants,* not *needs.* Plenty of people want sports cars, but almost no one needs one. Yet a twenty-thousand-dollar car has the same economic value as twenty thousand dollars' worth of grain that could feed a thousand people for a month. The point is that the list of things required to sustain life is a short one: a couple of thousand calories of food per day; enough clothing to shield against the dangers of exposure to sun or cold; some shelter from the elements. As many as half the world's people are preoccupied with life at such a level. There is no doubt that if the resources of the earth and the resourcefulness of humanity were fully harnessed for the task, all such needs could be met with a considerable margin of surplus. In that sense there is no shortage. There is scarcity because *need is not an economic category.* While objective needs are modest and relatively constant, wants are infinite and constantly changing. When the need for calories is met, the desire for filet mignon is close at hand. When the fear of frostbite has been eliminated, the lure of a new designer label every year seems irresistible. Indeed, because desire and not need determines what is produced, no whim will be ignored if a profit can be made. Thus it is that economic scarcity can and does exist amid a profusion of products and a glut of supply.

Economic systems exist to manage this problem of scarcity. They must make choices: *who will receive how much of which goods, at what price, and how will they be produced?* One approach to answering these questions is through planning committees or plebiscites. Capitalism has chosen another, more efficient way: the price system. Its focus is not need but *effective demand*—that is, desire plus enough money to do something about it: They shall receive who want and who can pay. In theory the free market knows no discrimination or favoritism. It is pure economic democracy, and goods are allocated according to a simple principle—one dollar, one vote. The problem, of course, is that some people have more votes than others.

The evangelists of free enterprise have always proclaimed the efficiency of the market mechanism in allocating goods: there can be neither shortages nor surpluses because price is set at precisely the level necessary to insure that all units of a good are bought. The more scarce the resource, the higher the price at which it will be supplied, and the fewer the people who will be able to afford it. This efficiency is achieved by creating a moral trap in which wealth, not need, determines what goods are produced and who gets them. As a result the needs of the poor must bid against the wants of the rich for limited supplies. Surely this is the most serious shortcoming of the market mechanism: its structural inability to allocate scarce resources on the basis of human need.

C. Competition: Goad to Plenty, Limit to Greed, Guarantor of Efficiency

Scarcity, for all its pain, is perceived by classical economics as having its benefits. It is the goad first to survival and then to plenty. Scarcity in capitalism forces individuals to look to their own benefit first, to seek gain, to work, produce, sell, profit, and invest for themselves.

All of this sounds terribly self-centered. But it should be said in defense of Adam Smith that when he wrote about the principles of the new economic order that he saw unfolding in the eighteenth century, he did not write a tract called "Ten Easy Steps to Personal Riches." Instead, he wrote a scholarly treatise on wealth—not the wealth of individuals but the wealth of nations. In the world he described in *An Inquiry into the Nature and Causes of the Wealth of Nations,* social benefit did not depend upon the good intentions of individuals and much less upon the generous actions of government. Instead, the system relied solely upon people doing what came naturally—aggressively seeking their own advantage. According to Smith, the self-interested striving of the individual was guided by an "invisible hand" in such a way that it actually produced social benefit. The social duty of every individual was not to do good but to do well. The human tendency toward greed that religious faith had long denounced was baptized and made a virtue. The fear of loss and the constant search for gain became the driving force of the new order.

How could the free play of these forces lead to social benefit? First, Smith observed, aggressive action in the hope of personal gain unleashes tremendous productive energies. Capitalism is first and foremost a production-oriented system. As more is produced, more can be shared. This drive of self-interest is kept in check by the competing demands of all other self-interested actors. It is this *competition*, then, that keeps avaricious individuals from holding society ransom. The market sets people free to obtain whatever they can, but at the same time it ensures that no one individual gains too much power over the system. Competition should not be thought of too narrowly, however. It is not just a force between two sellers of the same product or even between a buyer and a seller. At the heart of the system is the notion that all producers, all workers, all sellers, and all buyers are mutually in competition, each against all others. In capitalism, conflict is presumed to be natural and good because in the long run the interests of all are best served.

The mechanisms by which all this happens are what come closest to being laws in the inexact science of economics—*supply and demand.* Though not laws in the sense of the laws of the physical sciences, these concepts are so fundamental to economic analysis that it is worth seeing what they mean and how they may be expressed.

There are very few things the consumption of which will not be affected by the price. When the price falls, the amount purchased will almost always increase. In some cases that will occur because the people who have been buying all along will increase their consumption. (Chocolate lovers would gorge themselves all the more if chocolate were half its current price.) In other cases a low enough price will draw new consumers into the market. (A frugal couple who always thought of a trip to Europe as a vacation for the rich might well make reservations tomorrow if the airfare were cut in half.)

But how much will consumption change when the price changes? That is the question economists try to answer by drawing a *demand curve*. Pictured in Figure 1.1 (below) is a hypothetical demand curve for

Figure 1.1—Demand Curve for Ski Sweaters

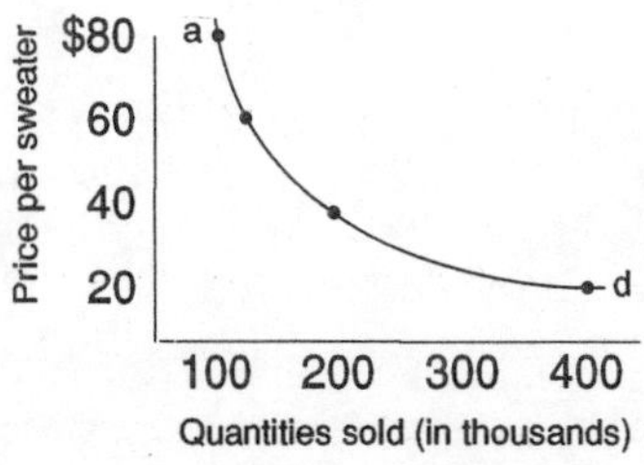

Figure 1.2—Supply Curve for Ski Sweaters

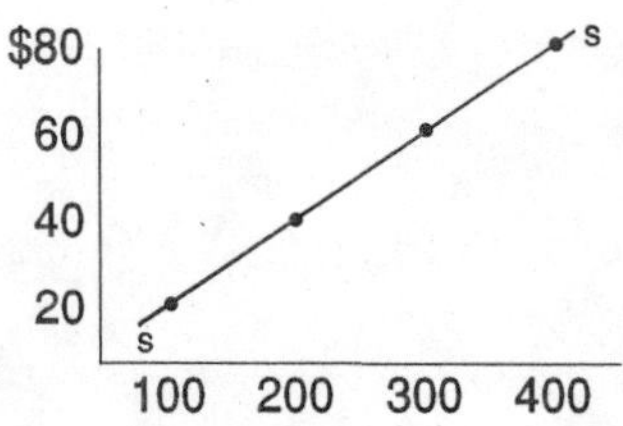

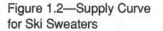

a purely imaginary line of ski sweaters. It tells us that at a price of $80, only 100,000 would be sold. If the price were lowered to $60, there would be a small increase in sales to 125,000 units. At $40, sales would jump to 200,000, and at $20, the public would be glad to buy 400,000.

As one would expect, Figure 1.2 (on page 5) depicts a *supply curve* showing that the producer reacts in just the opposite way from the buyer. At a price of $20, no new sweaters will be made because it costs the company more than that to manufacture and distribute the product. So the firm would simply liquidate the present stock at $20, take the loss, and turn its attention to something more profitable. However, if the sweaters can be sold at $40, the company can supply 200,000 of them under ordinary working conditions. At a price of $60, the firm can make 300,000 sweaters by pressing employees into overtime, even though that is more costly. And if the product can be sold at $80, the producer will be glad to supply 400,000 of the garments by having the firm go to two shifts.

Out of the various possibilities, what will be the sustainable price of these ski sweaters in the store? Figure 1.3 (below) answers that question by putting the demand curve and the supply curve together in a single graph. The point at which they intersect is called the *equilibrium point*. It designates the only combination of price and quantity that can be maintained on a regular basis. Of course, the firm can produce 400,000 sweaters if it so chooses and attempt to sell them at $80. But it will quickly find that there are only 100,000 customers who are willing to pay that much. With a surplus of 300,000 garments, the supplier must choose between cutting the price and destroying or giving away the sweaters. On the other hand, consumers may try to hold out for a price below $40, but they will find that if the price is too low, no sweaters will be produced at all. If the sweaters are produced, would-be buyers find that there are enough customers willing to pay $40 that the company has

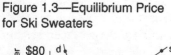

Figure 1.3—Equilibrium Price for Ski Sweaters

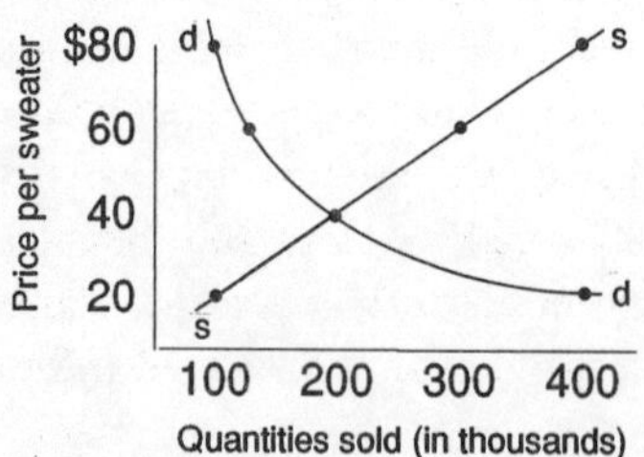

no incentive for selling them for less. Thus consumers who want the sweaters will simply have to pay the price.

The competition that is built into the market system between the producer and the consumer and among the various buyers is clearly evident from what has been said so far. You may have noticed, however, that in the example given the manufacturer is in a very nice position. The firm finds that it can sell 200,000 sweaters at $40 when the actual cost of production and distribution is somewhere above $20. Obviously there is a profit to be made. Here another dimension of competition enters in. The profitability of producing this type of ski sweater may draw another firm into the market. With a greater supply of the same or an equal product, the buyers are now in the driver's seat. The price will be forced below the former equilibrium point of $40 because supply and demand are no longer in balance.

A crucial element of classical economic theory is that in a perfectly functioning market in which producers are free to enter whenever profit can be made, competition will keep pushing prices lower and lower until there is no longer any attraction for new suppliers to join in. Thus, in theory, profits cannot exist over the long run. They will continually be undercut by new suppliers who are convinced that they can market goods more efficiently (i.e., more cheaply) than producers who are presently reaping the benefits of an undersupplied or overpriced market. This theory of *pure* or *perfect competition* (as contrasted with the imperfect competition of big business discussed in Chapter Four) is the economic profession's equivalent of the popular idea of *free enterprise*.

Competition promises other benefits than low prices to consumers, however. Entrepreneurs, restless in their constant search for gain, will goad one another to the highest *productivity;* in classical economic theory, shortages cannot exist. As much of a product will be produced as people are able and willing to afford, or until all resources—land, labor, and capital—are fully employed. Hence the argument for *efficiency:* competition rewards the clever, the careful, and the hardworking to the point that the less efficient are finally driven from the market. All resources are utilized until all demand is met, and nothing is wasted because that would increase costs and open the door to competitors. *Quality* is guaranteed because if someone else can deliver a better product or service at the same price, business and profits will flow to him or her. Furthermore, endless *variety* is guaranteed. Because desire, not need, is the relevant boundary, no demand, no whim will be ignored if a profit can be made. No taste is too bizarre or too jaded for the truly free market to satisfy.

Even in the theory of Adam Smith, however, this bonanza of benefits is available only in the hypothetical world of perfect competition. How far we have moved from that world, if indeed it ever existed, will be the subject of a later chapter that focuses on economic life dominated by big business and shaped by governments.

D. Growth: The Necessary Good

It would be fair to say that prior to the advent of capitalism, economic relationships tended to be defined in terms of static realities. The size of the population, the kind and quality of goods available, the way in which crops were grown and items were produced—none of these variables changed much from generation to generation or, for that matter, from century to century. Economic issues tended to focus on how to distribute what was regarded as an essentially fixed quantity of goods. It was in large part to answer that question that the rigid hierarchies of feudalism were developed and maintained for over a thousand years.

Capitalism, by contrast, requires continued economic growth. This is not the charge of irresponsible critics outside the system. It is the consensus of virtually all standard texts, and none is more standard than that written by Paul Samuelson. In *Economics* he notes, "[A] prosperity period may come to an end, not simply because consumption sales have gone down, but merely because sales have *leveled off* at a high level (or have continued to grow, but at a lower rate than previously). Like an airplane that falls once it loses its motion, the economic system plummets downward."[1]

Why this happens involves a long and complex explanation. The summary version is as follows. When growth stops, producers are left competing for a fixed amount of business. That drives down profits. Because business is not growing, firms do not enter the market, and marginal firms drop out. Investment decreases, jobs are not created, and unemployment increases. Income to consumers is thereby reduced, sales drop even further, and the whole cycle is repeated, pushing the economy lower still. In short, the only way for business to avoid falling into recession—and perhaps depression—is to experience perpetual growth. Free enterprise, it seems, cannot survive where everyone has enough and where population growth has leveled off. This is a serious structural weakness in the system if long-term growth cannot be sustained in the future.

II. Realities: The Moral Dilemma of Economic Growth

Economic growth lies at the very heart of what our culture calls success. If this seems doubtful, we need only recall that the person who admits to having the same real income today as five years ago will likely be judged deficient in either drive or ability. And the company that slips a few rungs on the Fortune 500 list, even if sales and profits have remained constant, is likely to be referred to as "stagnant." Likewise, among nations it is no mere happenstance that in the lexicon of social change, the terms "economic growth," "development," and "modernization" are treated virtually as synonyms.

Common sense tells us that because populations increase, there is a demand for some expansion in the *gross national product* (GNP)—the total output of goods and services in society. However, the natural orientation toward growth has become an addiction for most countries—including our own—leading to what some economists have labeled "GNP fetishism." The goal is not only that the national income should increase with the population but that the *rate* of GNP growth should increase. Goods and services must continue to cascade in ever-greater volume into the life of the nation. Accordingly, growth, if not the *summum bonum* of the modern world, becomes good in itself—something pursued for its own sake. This mind-set was expressed very clearly a number of years ago by President Nixon's Council of Economic Advisers, which concluded that "if it is agreed that economic output is a good thing it follows by definition that there is not enough of it."[2]

A. The Social Utility of Growth

Lest we be tempted to dismiss economic growth as nothing but a textbook name for avarice, however, we would do well to remember that it has had great social utility. Indeed, it would not be too much to say that to a very large extent, personal happiness, national tranquility, and international development have been based on the fact of relatively continuous economic expansion.

First, there is the simple fact that it has helped to meet physical needs. It is estimated that there were about 250 million people on earth in the time of Jesus. Not until 1830 did the global population reach one billion. It took only a hundred years to add the second billion. We now number more than 4.5 billion, and with a population growth rate of almost 2 percent per year, the world's population will double before the year 2020.

In human terms this means that every thirty to forty years the world economy must produce twice as much food, clothing, and shelter as it produced previously just to meet human need at current levels. Without this increase in production, human needs could be met only if population levels were held in check—most likely by starvation or war. No degree of generosity or sharing could meet such increasing demand for more than a generation.

A growing economy also has a second effect: it enables society to avoid or at least postpone painful choices about human values and the distribution of goods. It is no mere accident of history that the United States has been more successful than most nations in avoiding the social stress of class conflicts. Despite the gap between rich and poor in this country—the top 20 percent of the population receives over eight times as much of the national income as the bottom 20 percent—the economic pie has been growing fast enough to keep even those near the bottom reasonably content with their ever-growing slices. Thus it is that society can have guns and butter, color televisions and anti-poverty programs, higher taxes and higher disposable incomes. Little wonder, then, that in this country and elsewhere, economic growth has increasingly been looked upon as a social and political necessity.

When continued economic growth in the advanced nations began to require more resources from the less developed countries and increased sales to their people, this project was undertaken with enthusiasm and a clear conscience out of the conviction that growth would do for them what it had done for its proponents. Having the character of a universal good, the model was thought exportable. Consequently, for the past quarter century, the gurus of international development have devoted their efforts primarily to answering one question: "How do you make the economy of a nation grow?" It was assumed that where there was poverty, growth would sow plenty; where there was discord, harmony; where there was hopelessness, hope; where there was backwardness, progress.

Only in recent years has it become clear that the formula is not working. Brazil had an annual growth rate of 10 to 13 percent for the better part of a decade, and yet 85 percent of the population did not significantly benefit. Similarly, in Mexico, an oil-rich country that is no longer officially classified as "less developed," not only are there widening gaps between the rich and the poor, but the lowest economic groups are worse off in absolute terms than they were a decade ago.

The stated premise of international development efforts has been that there is plenty for all. This has proved a salve to the conscience of those of us in the rich nations. If progress has not been as rapid as we might have hoped, we have still been able to counsel patience to the poor on the assumption that growth will eventually work its miracle, and the benefits will ultimately trickle down to all people in all places.

B. The Limits to Growth

This hopeful view that all countries can become affluent through untended growth seemingly has splintered on the rocks of nature. For a great many, the shattering came over a decade ago with the publication of a slender volume entitled *The Limits to Growth,* a book that, according to one reviewer, "may be as important to mankind as the Council of Nicaea and Martin Luther's 95 Theses. It is a revolutionary new way of looking at man and society."[3]

What makes the book so important is its conclusion that "if the present growth trends in world population, industrialization, pollution, food production, and resource depletion continue unchanged, the limits to growth on this planet will be reached sometime within the next hundred years. The most probable result will be a rather sudden and uncontrollable decline in both population and industrial capacity."[4] This in effect means the collapse of industrial civilization and massive numbers of deaths due primarily to starvation.

While the study has been criticized as being unduly pessimistic about human nature, social institutions, and the prospects of technology, little data has been generated to counter the general argument. Indeed, a more recent study confirms the basic conclusions of the first, with the added note that since the world is not an integrated system, we can expect regional catastrophies well before the hundred-year limit is reached.[5]

Having invested at least the last two hundred years in promoting economic growth as the nostrum of the human condition, we quite understandably feel that someone has changed the rules in the middle of the game when we are told that growth cannot continue as it has in the past. In the optimism and innocence of the 1950s and 1960s, the basic moral dilemma for Christians was how far we could baptize affluence and economic growth in the name of Christ. Where the potential for wealth seemed limitless, the moral question lay merely in controlling its use and abuse. The issue before us today is quite different and far more complex: What do we do when economic growth may threaten the very existence of humanity?

The first natural reaction of many deeply concerned people was to cry, "Stop the growth so that the population and the resource consumption will slow!" By itself, this solution would condemn today's poor and their descendants to eternal poverty. Having ascended to the heights of economic well-being, we would pull the ladder up behind us.

Consider, for instance, those who see the population explosion as the primary or sole cause of our present and future problems. Amid the comforts of affluence, they often propound population-control programs that fall just short of genocide while ignoring the poverty, inequality, and class structure that underlie the alarming numbers. To be sure, birth rates must fall dramatically and soon if we are to avoid immense human suffering, but when affluent nations look the other way as millions in poor countries go hungry, and when population control becomes the only or even the principal strategy, we fly in the face of all historical precedent.

None of the present economically advanced nations achieved or even attempted a reduction in population growth until an economic base had been established that provided the possibility of a better life for the masses of its people. And once a base existed, no economically advanced country failed to show a concomitant reduction in birth rates. This was true even before there were major advances in birth-control technology. To urge major population reduction as the prerequisite to development is to urge the opposite of all that has succeeded in the past. The social critics in Third World countries can hardly be blamed for assuming that the upper-class people of their own societies and the advanced nations who favor this approach do so as a way of avoiding social change that would threaten their affluent positions.

It should also be noted that consumption in the developed countries has risen far more rapidly than the population in less developed countries. It is estimated that a newborn American will place about the same strain on the world's resource base and environment as ninety Indians or Indonesians. Thus increased consumption by the rich has continued to place more pressure on world resources—including food—than the growth rates of the poor. We are not by nature more afflicted than others with avarice or an excessive appetite for things. We have simply learned to consume as we do. In 1984 we spent $376 in advertising for every adult and child in the United States—more than the per capita income of half the world's people.

It may be that at some point in the future the great dilemma of humankind will revolve around the question of lifeboat ethics—that is, the realization that there are not enough resources for all to survive and that some will be left behind. But moral sensitivity demands that we not make that decision while so many are still cruising about on a luxury liner. There is no justification for lifeboat ethics while there is still a chance that an ethic of sharing and planning will keep the ship afloat.

Sharing has never been easy within the human community. Even under conditions of unprecedented plenty such as we have known in this country for more than a quarter century, we have found it difficult to bridge the gaps of income and opportunity in our own society. We can only imagine how much more difficult it will be to address the far greater international inequalities. Yet imagine we must, for the relevant question is not whether we should have growth, but rather what sort of growth, where, toward what end, and for whose benefit? These are questions not only of economics but of values. The matter was succinctly put by the Second Report to the Club of Rome (an informal international association that funds research and publishes materials on global issues): "No doubt the real limits to growth are social, political and managerial, and finally reside within the nature of man."[6]

Economic growth as the blind, undifferentiated addition to the gross national product must end. Growth that widens the income gap between countries and classes must stop. Instead there must be economic growth focusing on the areas of greatest human need rather than on those of greatest profit, growth in poor countries rather than in rich countries, and ultimately growth in ways that will foster a cooperative spirit so that limited resources may become the impetus for an ethic of sharing.

III. Values: Protestantism and the Capitalist Way

Having to face the dilemmas of human demand amid the constraints of nature's resources and society's institutions has always nudged economics close to philosophy and sometimes toward theology. An example of this is George Gilder's call to faith in the closing chapter of his book *Wealth and Poverty:*

> These problems and crises are the new frontier. . . . The tale of human life is less the pageant of unfolding rationality and purpose envisioned by the Enlightenment than a saga of desert wanderings and brief bounty, the endless dialogue between man and God, between alienation and providence, as we search for the ever-rising and receding promised land, which we can see most clearly, with the most luminous logic, when we have the faith and courage to leave ourselves open to chance and fate.[7]

Gilder makes clear his opinion that such openness to God and logic can lead to only one economic form—capitalism: "the only appropriate system for a world in which all certitude is a sham."[8]

In the end, Gilder's god is chance. He and others who hold that laissez-faire principles provide the only economic hope are not conservatives, nor are they careful builders or investors; they are gamblers. They are willing to risk all creation on the assumption that there need be no limits on the freedom to acquire and consume, on the assumption that human ingenuity and technology will respond correctly before the biosphere—that thin veneer of air and soil and water that nurtures all life—is irrevocably damaged, earth's resources are depleted, and humanity is condemned to slow extinction. The fanfare for a special link between God and the capitalist order may have reached a new crescendo in our day, but it is far from new.

A. Max Weber's Reconstructed Reformation

For the two hundred years before Adam Smith wrote, the Reformation and capitalism were two of the primary fibers in the tapestry of post-medieval, pre-modern Europe. The two have been so entwined that some have postulated a causal relationship. This approach was formalized in Max Weber's essay entitled *The Protestant Ethic and the Spirit of Capitalism.*[9] His principal thesis is that modern capitalism required for its development a spirit so unnatural to human experience that it could not have grown into a dominant force without the support of Protestant doctrine and practice, particularly that of Calvinism. Weber summarized, "As far as the influence of the Puritan outlook extended, under all circumstances . . . it favoured the development of a rational bourgeois economic life; it was the most important, and above all the only consistent influence in the development of that life. It stood at the cradle of the modern economic man."[10]

For over three-quarters of a century, the case has been argued so often and with such force that, for many, Christianity and capitalism are inseparable. To question the present economic order is tantamount to heresy. Even those who have never read Max Weber know the popularized outline of the argument:

- The Reformation rejected the rigid distinction between the holy life of priests and monks and the common life of ordinary people. Instead, the Reformers spoke of each person as having a divine calling.
- Work became something the believer did for God, not just for gain for self or employer. Thus it was a Christian's duty to work hard.
- Hard work, of course, produced greater income, but the religious life demanded frugality.
- This produced savings, which led to investment.

- Greater investments coupled with hard work and continued frugality produced greater profits. Thus capital continued to accumulate.

This scenario draws a straight line from Protestant Christian faith to the system of market capitalism. What are we to make of such an argument?

First of all, Weber did not set out to prove that John Calvin was a precursor of Adam Smith. His essay was only part of a wide-ranging inquiry into the impact of religious thought and life on economic order.

Weber argued that Protestantism, and especially its Calvinist variant, was *one very important factor* in the development of the *spirit* of capitalism. He argued that religious factors were a source of the attitude toward life that made such an economic system possible. He readily acknowledged that "capitalism existed in China, India, Babylonia, in the classic world and in the Middle Ages. But in all these cases . . . this particular ethos was lacking."[11] The ethos of which he spoke, the spirit of capitalism, developed when the making of money was transformed from a means to achieve certain needs or pleasures and became an end in itself. "The *Summum Bonum* of this ethic," Weber maintained, is "the earning of more and more money, combined with the strict avoidance of all spontaneous enjoyment of life."[12]

In stark contrast to those like Milton Friedman, who see freedom as the basis of capitalism, Weber found the genesis of the capitalist spirit in the Calvinist doctrine of predestination. According to Weber's reading of Calvin, only God was free to choose between salvation and damnation for individuals. Unable to know their destinies, human beings were reduced to seeking signs that they were among the elect. Calvinists found inklings of divine election in an individual's ability to live by a standard of conduct unmistakably different from the ordinary—one of restraint and discipline.

This "worldly asceticism" is the key to Weber's theory. Reasoning that God would not torment his chosen with the pains of poverty, Calvinists began to look upon financial well-being as a sign of salvation. Under this form of Calvinism, people were not simply allowed to enter into economic life for gain but were impelled to do so as a religious duty. Weber maintained that such a religious spirit made two major contributions to the emerging economic order. First, it allowed the legal acquisition of money with a good conscience. Second, it laid the groundwork for justifying a profit-oriented economic ethic:

- Entrepreneurs could be conscious of being in God's grace and visibly blessed.
- People were free to follow pecuniary interests as if fulfilling a divine duty.

- There was the assurance that an unequal distribution of the world's goods was a divine dispensation, not something that had to be corrected. In this regard Weber noted, "Calvin himself made the much quoted statement that only when the people, i.e., the mass of labourers and craftsmen, were poor did they remain obedient to God."[13]

The work of Max Weber has had a powerful influence on ecclesiastical thought, social science, and public policy. However, it has serious shortcomings that cannot be overlooked. First, while Weber acknowledged that various forms of capitalism existed both prior to and apart from Protestantism, he tended to dismiss such expressions as being different in character from the fully rationalistic capitalism that developed in the seventeenth century. But it is hard to see how the "capitalist spirit" of Roman Catholic Venice or Florence in the fifteenth century was less genuine than that of England or Holland two hundred years later.

Weber also tended to slight other factors that helped create the modern entrepreneurial spirit. The impact of secular philosophy was significant. Dramatic changes in the business environment called forth new actions and therefore new attitudes quite apart from the influence of religious doctrine. The discoveries of the New World, dramatically increased trade with the Orient, and a torrent of inventions created opportunities for investment and speculation that simply never existed in the same measure before.

In addition, Weber used the term "Calvinism" in a way that tends to confuse both history and the reader. The attitudes that he described are really applied only to seventeenth-century Calvinists. Indeed, Weber specifically exempted Calvin and his personal doctrine from the generalizations of his thesis.[14] Instead, Weber focused mainly on the "worldly asceticism" of various strains of seventeenth-century Puritanism—Calvinists, the Reformed, Zwinglians, Baptists, Mennonites, and Quakers primarily—a relatively small proportion of the population of Europe at that time. In other words, his empirical base was very narrow, yet he generalized from it very broadly.

Whatever its shortcomings, the Weberian thesis still continues to be a useful tool in assessing the relationship between Christian faith and market capitalism. R. H. Tawney's conclusion is undoubtedly the right one:

> What is true and valuable in his essay is his insistence that the commercial classes in seventeenth-century England were the standard-bearers of a particular conception of social expediency, which was markedly different from that of the more conservative elements in society—the peasants, the craftsmen, and many landed gentry—and that that concep-

tion found expression in religion, in politics, and not least, in social and economic conduct and policy.[15]

B. Rescuing Calvin

So central was Calvin's doctrine to Weber's thesis that there is a tendency to forget that Calvin was driven primarily by theological and religious motives, not commercial ones. Assuredly he differed with theologians before him who had been deeply suspicious of commercial relationships, for he viewed trade as a way of sharing goods that God has provided for the world and as a sign of the human solidarity God intends. "The life of the godly is justly compared to trading," Calvin explained, "for they ought naturally to exchange and barter with each other . . . because the use and end which they have in view is to promote mutual intercourse among men."[16]

Yet Calvin did not idealize the world of commerce. He recognized its dangers and pointedly condemned profit-making when it was regarded as the only or even the chief end of enterprise. "It is not enough when one can say, 'Oh, I work, I have my trade, I set the pace.' This is not enough; for one must be concerned whether it is good and profitable to the community and if it is able to serve our neighbors. . . . It is certain that no occupation will be approved by him which is not useful and that does not serve the common good and that also redounds to the profit of everyone."[17] Whatever impetus Calvin may have given the enterprise of capitalism, unchecked freedom and individual gain were far from his mind. Economic activity had to benefit the whole community, not merely the acquisitive instincts of the individual.

The difference between Calvin and the latter-day Calvinists is most clearly illustrated by the issue of usury. The common perception that Calvin eagerly embraced the practice of making money by charging interest is a serious misreading of his thought. A sixteenth-century observer remarked, "Calvin deals with usurie as the apothecarie doth with poyson."[18]

The practice of lending money at a profit was not born in Geneva. Princes, popes, and the pious had been paying interest on loans for centuries. Long before Calvin, the Franciscan order in Italy had established small banks and pawnshops so that the poor might have a more humane alternative to the 20 to 50 percent rates on petty loans charged by non-Christian money handlers. The 5 to 10 percent rate charged by the monks themselves was regarded not as interest but as a service charge to cover the cost of operation.[19] But while medieval theologians acknowledged the payment of interest as a practical necessity and even paid and charged interest themselves, none was willing to give it theological justification. That task fell to Calvin. This he undertook, not with glee but with the resignation of his very pragmatic spirit. "It would be wished," he wrote, "that all usury, and even the name, were banished from the earth. But since this is impossible, it is necessary to concede to the common good."[20] Acknowledging that there were strong scriptural prohibitions against usury, Calvin nevertheless concluded that "usury must be judged, not by any particular passage of scripture, but simply by the rules of equity."[21]

Toward that end, he hedged the right to lend at interest with a series of prohibitions and warnings:

- The poor were not to be charged interest.
- Charity was not to be neglected in order to have money to lend.
- The loan should benefit the borrower at least as much as the lender.
- Mere legality was not sufficient moral justification for an action. A loan arrangement must be measured by the word of God, not just by civil law.
- What was legal might be prohibited to the Christian.
- The public good took precedence over private benefit.[22]

Nevertheless, with all of his hedges, Calvin was able to make peace with the modern world—including its new economic forms—in a way that his predecessors had been unable to. The difference lies not in Calvin's notion of predestination, as Weber and others have supposed, but in Calvin's fundamental doctrine—the sovereignty of God. Because God is sovereign, Calvin felt no need to defend the old order or lament its passing. Because God was sovereign over the emerging order, Calvin could see in it positive values and legitimate opportunities for the exercise of the Christian calling. Peace could be made with market forces, although only an uneasy peace, full of caution. Calvin dealt with capitalism not so much by embracing it as by holding it at arm's length, because in the end he fully embraced only the sovereign God.

Thus Calvin's key contribution to economic life and thought is the principle that no economic system is to be regarded as permanent or absolute. His twentieth-century heirs are not those who defend laissez-faire as divine doctrine, but those who are pragmatic in their insistence that new opportunities and new dilemmas require new approaches and structures in the social and economic order. The Calvinist can never regard the economy as more than a tool to be used to fulfill the unending responsibility of humankind to glorify God through the achievement of God's purposes for all of life and creation.

C. Recasting Reformation Principles for a Modern World

Despite Calvin's high intentions, most of Protestantism and, later, Roman Catholicism have followed the aberrant Calvinism exalting liberty above responsibility, individual above community, and property above piety. While the Weberian hypothesis presents a "Protestant ethic" that is more caricature than description, it nevertheless suggests the manner in which traditional religious values and perspectives have been subordinated to the needs of an emerging economic order.

In the melding of economic, social, and religious thought that characterized nineteenth-century liberalism, it was only fitting that the statement of the moral rationale for capitalism should shift from European theologians to American religious practitioners. Wealth, no longer regarded with theological suspicion, was sanctified as the instrument of divine benevolence. In the last quarter of the nineteenth century, a popular text on Christian ethics argued, "By the proper use of wealth man may greatly elevate and extend his moral work. It is therefore his duty to seek to secure wealth for this high end, and to make a diligent use of what the Moral Governor may bestow upon him for the same end. . . . The Moral Governor has placed the power of acquisitiveness in man for a good and noble purpose."[23]

Another religious pundit held that the capitalist economic system promised not only more goods but better people. Toward the end of the last century, Bishop Lawrence of Massachusetts declared, "In the long run, it is only to the man of morality that wealth comes. . . . Godliness is in league with riches. . . . Material prosperity is helping to make the national character sweeter, more joyous, more unselfish, more Christ-like."[24]

The belief that harmony and tranquility were the sure future of a world directed only by the competitive instincts of individuals did not survive long into the twentieth century. Economic panics persisted in the face of bright promises; World War I took its toll in hope as well as lives; labor strife demonstrated that not all shared in the plenty; and the decade-long Great Depression made the perfectionism, optimism, and liberalism of the 1920s seem grimly naive.

The theological tone changed. Many began to question the nature of a system that would allow vast inequities to persist. Reinhold Niebuhr expressed his concern that "laissez-faire theory did not realize that human freedom expresses itself destructively as well as creatively. . . . Once it is fully understood that there are no natural harmonies and equilibria of power in history, as there are in nature, and that advancing civilization tends to accentuate, rather than diminish, such disproportions of power as exist in even primitive communities, it must become apparent that property rights become instruments of injustice."[25]

Still, Niebuhr acknowledged the need for private property. He joined classical Christian theory in the belief that because of human sin, private property is a necessary evil. He perceived it as the most effective way yet devised to limit the claims of some over others and over the creation, but stressed that it is not absolute, and is always subject to a higher purpose than self-aggrandizement.

In a similarly pragmatic vein, Niebuhr argued that the economic order must harness rather than suppress self-interest for two reasons. First, it is simply too powerful to suppress. Second, there is no individual—and therefore no institution—wise enough and good enough to determine how the infinite variety of human skills is to be turned to the common good, or how such labor may be properly rewarded.[26]

All this sounds like a grudging endorsement of free-enterprise capitalism and a ringing denunciation of communism. Niebuhr's thought was more incisive and threatening, however. "The contradictory dogmas about property can most easily be dissolved if the utopianism which underlies both of them is dispelled," Niebuhr claimed. "In communities where Marxist dogma has never developed the power to challenge the bourgeois dogma, *the primary requirement of justice is that the dominant dogma be discredited*" (emphasis added).[27]

Increasingly in the past decade, Americian churches have undertaken this task. Many denominations, from Lutheran and Methodist to Presbyterian and Roman Catholic, have published studies and statements questioning some of the most hallowed convictions of capitalism. In 1986 the Catholic Bishops' Conference issued its long-awaited pastoral on the U.S. economy, a statement that has sent shock waves through corporate boardrooms and the halls of Congress. Until about a decade ago, there was little indication that churches were giving much thought to the principles of capitalism itself. But now that such critique has become commonplace, many proponents of the market system feel that the church has betrayed the economic system it helped foster.

Not surprisingly, a counterattack has begun with forces that are as diverse as those who criticize—from conservative think-tank analysts to vested preachers of the Bible Belt, from born-again economists to Catholic social philosophers and Jewish businessmen. The denunciation of the new critics of capitalism is shrill. The goal of the critics appears to be to solidify a union between biblical faith and market economics that is presumed to have existed in the past but now seems threatened.

George Gilder, a conservative social critic, sees economics as a choice between an ideal type of capitalism and a centralized, state-ordered, bureaucratic socialism. Thus Gilder concludes, "I think that [Jesus'] teachings cannot be fulfilled in a socialist society. . . . [It] is inherently hostile to Christianity and *capitalism is simply the essential mode of human life that corresponds to religious truth*" (emphasis added).[28] There we have the essence of the gospel according to Gilder: God can and will work only through capitalism. Much of evangelical Protestantism has embraced this perspective. In his book *Listen, America!* evangelist Jerry Falwell assures us that "the free enterprise system is clearly outlined in the Book of Proverbs." Most of the noted religious defenders of capitalism would be less specific and simplistic but no less fervent in their insistence that it has a special relationship to biblical faith. This view is often motivated less by any detailed knowledge of the system than by a desire to make a strong statement against the totalitarian aspects of Soviet-style socialism.

This view is not monolithic, however. For committed Christians, especially those of a Calvinist bent who take very seriously the sovereignty of God, only God is absolute. The attempt to place an economic system beyond history, to give it eternal significance, must at some point create a crisis of faith for those who are theologically more reflective than George Gilder. A brief comment by Carl F. H. Henry, someone with unimpeachable credentials as a theological conservative, makes it clear that exaggerated claims for capitalism cannot go unquestioned in these circles: "Free enterprise at least intrinsically incorporates certain economic values, notably a certain legitimacy of self-interest and the propriety of private property [that] can become idolatrous if taken out of [a] larger moral context."[29]

In this larger moral context, there is a mismatch of values between the biblical economy and the market economy. One exalts consumption that the other can only regard as hedonism. The market lives by self-interest while faith honors self-sacrifice. Economists praise the freedom that capitalism both grants and requires, while theologians dwell on the responsibilities that faith entails. It is not that the values of the two systems are mutually exclusive. They are more like gears that do not quite mesh; in the attempt to force them together there is frightful noise and violent shaking that makes us realize that something is wrong at the point where the two systems touch.

Michael Novak, a Roman Catholic moral philosopher and lay theologian, argues that all such apparent conflicts are washed away by one great historical fact—capitalism works.[30] In his view, traditional Christian economic ethics were elaborated over centuries in which insufficiency was the chief economic reality. It is understandable that the rules of distribution should have become the primary ethical concern. But Novak maintains that capitalism has broken through the logjam of stagnation by providing incentives for such productivity that plenty for all is historically realizable. In such a world the moral imperative of economic ethics is not distribution but production. Oddly, Novak attributes the success of capitalism not to individualism but to what he sees as the fundamental communitarianism of the modern capitalist economy.

The symbol of this communitarianism is the large business corporation, which, Novak maintains, requires more coordinated human activity for production and distribution than past economic institutions. For Novak it is part of a system that has as its vision nothing less than the interdependence of all people. "The fundamental nature of capitalism . . . ," Novak reminds us, "is not the wealth of individuals . . . but the wealth of nations—all nations, without exception. The driving force of capitalism is social, indeed, universal."[31]

It is easy to be swept along by such rhetoric. We would all like to believe in a system so universal in its spirit and so capable of prodigious production that all concern about sharing would be eliminated. Wishing, however, doesn't make it so.

In the real world, everyday experience tells us that a laissez-faire economic system will not fairly and fully address the needs of all those who live under it. It therefore has no absolute claim on the loyalties of those of biblical faith. This does not mean accepting the absolutist claim of some other system instead. Nor does it mean that there are not useful elements in capitalism. What it does mean is that we are under no obligation to defend all or any elements of capitalism for their own sake. Rather, we are obligated by faith to stand in judgment of this and all economic orders, insisting always that they produce a society as nearly in accord with the biblical vision as possible. There is no Christian economics. But there is a Christian critique of all economics.

Notes

1. Samuelson, *Economics,* 8th ed. (New York: McGraw-Hill, 1970), p. 247.
2. *Fortune,* May 1974, p. 24.
3. *National Observer,* n.d., as quoted in Donella H. Meadows et al., *Limits to Growth* (New York: Signet Books, 1972), p. i.
4. Meadows et al., *Limits to Growth,* p. 29.
5. Mihajlo Mesarovic and Eduard Pestel, *Mankind at the Turning Point* (New York: E. P. Dutton, 1974).
6. Mesarovic and Pestel, *Mankind at the Turning Point,* p. 204.
7. Gilder, *Wealth and Poverty* (New York: Bantam Books, 1982), pp. 314-15.

8. Gilder, *Wealth and Poverty*, p. 311.

9. Weber, *The Protestant Ethic and the Spirit of Capitalism* (New York: Scribner's, 1958).

10. Weber, *The Protestant Ethic and the Spirit of Capitalism*, p. 174.

11. Weber, *The Protestant Ethic and the Spirit of Capitalism*, p. 52.

12. Weber, *The Protestant Ethic and the Spirit of Capitalism*, p. 53.

13. Weber, *The Protestant Ethic and the Spirit of Capitalism*, p. 177.

14. Tawney, *Religion and the Rise of Capitalism* (1926; New York: Mentor Books, 1947), p. 262.

15. Tawney, *Religion and the Rise of Capitalism*, pp. 262-63.

16. John Calvin's commentary on Matthew 25:20, quoted by W. Fred Graham in *The Constructive Revolutionary: John Calvin and His Socio-Economic Impact* (Atlanta: John Knox Press, 1978), pp. 77-78.

17. From a sermon by John Calvin on Ephesians 4:26-28, quoted by Graham in *The Constructive Revolutionary*, pp. 80-81.

18. Quoted by Tawney in *Religion and the Rise of Capitalism*, p. 89.

19. Graham, *The Constructive Revolutionary*, p. 89.

20. Calvin, quoted by Graham in *The Constructive Revolutionary*, p. 91.

21. Calvin, quoted by Graham in *The Constructive Revolutionary*, p. 92.

22. Graham, *The Constructive Revolutionary*, p. 92.

23. From D. S. Gregory's *Christian Ethics*, as quoted by J. Milton Yinger in *Religion, Society and the Individual* (New York: Macmillan, 1957), p. 218.

24. Bishop Lawrence, quoted by Yinger in *Religion, Society and the Individual*, p. 218.

25. *Reinhold Niebuhr on Politics*, ed. Harry R. Davis and Robert C. Good (New York: Scribner's, 1960), pp. 216-17.

26. *Reinhold Niebuhr on Politics*, p. 221.

27. *Reinhold Niebuhr on Politics*, p. 222.

28. Gilder, "Where Capitalism and Christianity Meet," *Christianity Today*, 3 Feb. 1983, p. 27.

29. Henry, *God, Revelation and Authority: God Who Speaks and Shows*, vol. 6 (Waco, Tex.: Word Books, 1983), p. 476.

30. Michael Novak is a seminary-trained Roman Catholic layman and social ethicist whose perspective on economic issues has more in common with Weberian notions than with the church fathers or papal encyclicals. In his book *Freedom with Justice: Catholic Social Thought and Liberal Institutions* (New York: Harper & Row, 1984), Novak says,

> I hold that the liberal society [read "a capitalist economy and a democratic policy"] . . . best uplifts the poor, institutionalizes the dignity of the human person, makes possible the growth and manifold activities of human associations of every sort and conspires to establish a more voluntary and open and communitarian form of life than any society of the past, present, or foreseeable future.

The popularized version of the Protestant economic spirit has been ecumenized!

31. Novak, *The Need for Theory and Vision: The Religious Foundations of Democratic Capitalism* (Washington: American Enterprise Institute, n.d.), p. 77.

Chapter Two

The Role of Capital in the Market System

I. Concepts: Property and Capital

A. Private Property

One foundation stone of our economic system is its commitment to the private ownership of property. Both the concept and the debates about it are ancient. Roman law absolutized private property, but for millennia before the Caesars, tribal groups held far more in common than they claimed individually, and nomadic peoples tended to live and move, feast or starve together. Even when settled agriculture became the norm, absolute individual ownership was seldom the practice. Feudalism reigned after the fall of Rome, and for a thousand years no one owned the land individually and absolutely. Whether serf, lord, or king, each had only use rights, and then only with the permission of and with responsibility to some superior. Even the claims of royalty were limited theologically because ownership by divine right also theoretically acknowledged responsibility to God, who alone was the true owner.

Economists have frequently distinguished two quite different kinds of value. Each good has a *use value*. That is, it satisfies a particular need or desire of the person who produces it. Thus the first pair of shoes the cobbler makes for himself may be of immense value. A second pair may be useful, a third bring pleasure. But at some point, at the fourth or the tenth pair, producing more will not increase the cobbler's utility or pleasure. After this point is reached, he will make no more shoes unless they can be traded for something more useful or enjoyable. This is commonly called *exchange value*.

In subsistence economies, where goods are few and used almost entirely by the producers, where one body effectively consumes what two hands can produce, conflicting private-property claims are few. But where some margin above subsistence is produced, where the potential for satisfying other wants through exchange becomes common, the attempt to claim the *surplus* becomes almost irresistible. *Private property,* which began as a concept to guarantee individuals the right to the product of their own labor, easily slips into the concept of the right to claim from the labor of others the output beyond subsistence. As societies have moved toward more exchange, claims of private property have been more pronounced, specific, and absolute.

Thus we arrive at a current definition: "The right to own property means the right to use it, to save it, to invest it for gain, and to transmit it to others."[1] Such rights of property are integral to the concept and practice of capital accumulation and utilization in our present economic system.

B. Capital

Until the mid-eighteenth century, capital as a concept received scant attention from those who wrote about economic matters. The word did not even exist in the English language before about 1600, and at first it was the functional equivalent of the older word "stock," something you had to have on hand before production could begin.[2] In those early days, land and labor were the key economic categories. The technologies of production were ancient, well-known to all, and, most important, relatively inexpensive.

With the advent of the Industrial Revolution in the late eighteenth century, all that changed. New discoveries, inventions, and techniques began to come in a kind of technical-social avalanche. Harnessing these new ideas to the productive process involved bringing natural resources and labor together with sometimes prodigious amounts of machinery. The ability to marshal the financial resources necessary to do that became the basic limiting factor in the productive process. Capital was rather suddenly king.

When economists speak of capital, they generally mean *real capital,* physical goods that have been produced and are in turn used to produce other goods. The inputs necessary for the production of real capital are land (natural resources) and labor. Both of these inputs are prior to the economic system (that is, they cannot be generated at will), although their output can be affected by investment and technology. Capital, on the other hand, is the one factor that the economic system itself produces.

Capital is anything that increases the productive power of people for economically useful ends. A sharpened stone on the end of a stick is capital to the traditional hunter. So too is a hoe in the hands of a peasant who previously has used only bent sticks as agricultural tools. Factory buildings, drill presses, computers, and highway systems are all capital goods to modern industry. Even the know-how of technicians and managers becomes a kind of capital in today's technological society.

The term "capital" can also be used to mean money, or *finance capital*. The connection is obvious. Real capital is costly to produce. Money must be saved and set aside for productive investment if the increased output that technology promises to provide is to be realized.

C. Myths about Savings and Capital Accumulation

Saving is a key issue in capitalism and in all economic systems. It is a universal truth that what is consumed today cannot be invested for tomorrow. Even a hungry farmer will not eat the seed corn—at least not until all other hope of survival is gone. In order to create capital, then, it is necessary to restrain present consumption.

There is a familiar and well-elaborated mythology about how the saving was accomplished that thrust Europe into the Industrial Revolution. The mythic heroes of capitalist ideology are the craggy individualists who so longed for a better future that no measure of personal sacrifice seemed too great. While such persons worked hard, they perhaps worked no harder than their compatriots. The difference was that, with gritty determination, these individuals refused to consume all that they produced. Of the meager income they received from land or labor, they managed to save a small amount. Hard work and voluntary restraint of consumption over a period of time produced funds that could be put into a plow or a bellows or some other device that increased production and income. When a critical mass of such rugged individualists came together at one time and place, the whole society began to rise under their influence, and the Industrial Revolution got its start.

Myths persist because they contain a measure of truth. There were undoubtedly many such individualists whose voluntary sacrifice and savings promoted their economic advancement. But this does not explain the realities of capital accumulation in the eighteenth century or since. It was certainly true in England and elsewhere that the landed gentry and the urban manufacturers "saved" in the sense that they diverted significant portions of their income from immediate consumption to investment in production. Their life-style, however, could hardly be described as sacrificial. They served a useful social purpose of gathering and channeling funds, but their goal was to saddle others with the burden of sacrifice whenever possible.

The *enclosure movement* was in a sense a kind of capital "savings" program in England that extended over several hundred years. By feudal custom the lord had ancestral rights to large tracts of land and corresponding responsibilities for all the people who lived there. Most of the land was not held exclusively. In exchange for their labor, peasants were guaranteed some portion of the land and were allowed to graze their livestock on the common land. But as the price of wool rose, tradition bent to profit. The common lands were privatized, hedgerows were planted, sheep were added in large numbers, and peasants were evicted.

The economic and human results of the enclosure movement were mixed. On the one hand, land was more productively employed. Supplies were guaranteed to the burgeoning textile industry, the consumer price of wool was kept down, and profits from the land became available as capital for business expansion. On the other hand, those who reaped the profits and made the investments were not the ones to make the sacrifices. It was the peasants whose consumption was reduced so that capital savings could accumulate. Tens of thousands of them were displaced and made their way to urban centers, where they joined the industrial labor force.

Factory workers were also forced savers. They had no savings accounts, of course, but they did have their labor power to sell. The problem was that the massive influx of people from the countryside during the last half of the eighteenth century drove wages so low that most workers could barely survive on their earnings.[3] Even children became savers. They were a source of cheap labor as they worked from dawn to dusk for a pittance in factories and mines. Abuses abounded. An 1832 committee of the British parliament found that young girls were laboring in the textile mills upwards of nineteen hours a day in busy seasons, with a total of only an hour off for breaks. Many were maimed, and injury brought neither medical care nor unemployment compensation.[4]

The point is not that working conditions were brutal in those early days of capitalism. The condition of urban factory workers may have been no worse than that of the society's peasants. The point is that wages and benefits paid bore little relationship to the economic value the workers created. It was such forced savings that remained in the accounts of the factory owners that became one of the streams of investment capital for the Industrial Revolution.

Of course, not all capital accumulation of industrial societies came even from their own people. Significant amounts were extracted from far-off lands through piracy, plunder, and profits from all manner of investments. Sir Francis Drake was knighted for his success in stealing gold from Spanish galleons.

Drake's expedition in the ship *Golden Hind* was a business venture launched at a cost of £5,000, half of which was put up by Queen Elizabeth. The booty of one excursion is estimated to have been between £500,000 and £1,500,000.[5] All that from a single expedition! The total economic impact of all piracy, however, was much greater. Such adventures added £12 million to British coffers during the reign of Queen Elizabeth alone.[6] It is estimated that in 1688 the total capital value of land and buildings in England was only £234 million and the liquid asset value of the country, including livestock, was just £86 million.[7] Thus the £12 million in capital that piracy added amounted to 5 percent of the total capital stock of the country and almost 15 percent of the liquid assets.

If we consider the even larger amounts that flowed into Europe from the slave trade and other only slightly more legitimate international business ventures, we begin to see that the vast distance separating today's more developed countries from less developed countries is not to be explained merely by luck or by the assumption that Europeans worked harder and saved more than Asians, Africans, or Latin Americans.

Our cultural myth about the role of voluntary, individual sacrifice and savings in capital formation has a certain inspirational value, but it does not explain what really happened. It is clear that the early capital base of our economic system came less from the voluntary savings of the frugal than from the ability of the few—both individuals and nations—to force savings upon the many and use the funds for their own benefit in a system that had exalted private ownership at the expense of conceptions of human community.

D. Making Capital in Modern Corporate Society

Generally speaking, it is fair to say that in our society, people save and businesses invest. To be sure, most of us spend far more of our income than we save. Over the years we Americans have usually spent about 95 percent of everything we take in and saved only about 5 percent. Others are far more thrifty than we. The West Germans, for instance, save nearly 15 percent of their income, and the Japanese save 20 percent. That does not mean that they are by nature more frugal than we, or that they would not like to spend more on consumer items. Different social expectations about retirement and how it is financed, the cost and availability of credit, the tax benefits of interest payments, and the payment of educational expenses are just a few of the factors that determine the savings rate of whole societies.

The universal reality is that people do not save unless they benefit from doing so. Thus banks pay us for the privilege of using our money on deposit, and businesses pay the banks a slightly greater interest rate for borrowing. Or businesses may avoid the middleman banker altogether and try to get direct access to people's savings by selling bonds or stock. To do that, they have to convince savers that such investments will be personally profitable. The profit motive is not reserved to individuals of high finance. It is the implicit expectation of every saver as well.

In the market system, money is treated like any other commodity. It is ruled by supply and demand. If savings are low so that money available for investment is in short supply, and if businesses have many projects requiring capital expenditure that they are waiting to start up (in other words, if demand for money is high), the rate of interest for savings will be high. On the other hand, if sales are slow and the future looks dim, and if people have increased their savings expecting "a rainy day," then the interest rates will be lower.

Of course, no rate of interest will be paid, no money borrowed, no investment made unless the business believes there is a profit to be made. It is this search for gain that drives capitalism. Large corporations borrow enormous amounts from banks, and they seek capital from individual and institutional investors through the sale of bonds and new stock issues. But, from management's point of view, it would be risky business to trust the basic operations of the firm to such mechanisms. This would mean that each major decision would have to be submitted not only to the board of directors but also to the independent investment community in a kind of financial plebiscite. Crucial plans of the company might be delayed during periods when money is tight, or worse yet, there simply might be no money available at acceptable interest rates. Such veto power over corporate plans is looked upon as an infringement on the prerogatives of management.

It is not surprising, then, that large corporations have changed the way most saving for industrial expansion is handled. Part of the firm's profits are withheld for reinvestment rather than paid out in dividends. Normally, only about half of a large firm's earnings are distributed to stockholders. The stockholders may complain, but the control of major corporations was long ago wrested from their token owners and placed securely in the hands of managers. Stockholders can always sell out, but there are few large companies to which they can turn that do not operate in the same fashion. When buying stock in today's huge enterprises, what one is investing in more than anything else is the presumed expertise of the firm's technical-managerial corps.

According to John Kenneth Galbraith, "The decisions which provide three-quarters of the community's supply of savings are made not by individuals but by authority, in the main by the management of a few hundred corporations. And from these savings comes the major wherewithal for the growth of the economy."[8] Thus the power of capital in modern U.S. society is not only concentrated in a few percent of the population who own it but further concentrated in the almost autonomous decisions of a few thousand individuals who manage it. One of the questions that haunts modern capitalism, however, is whether the investment decisions based on profit-seeking for the few can at the same time serve the needs and interests of the many—workers, consumers, and communities.

II. Realities: The Youngstown Story

Some economists still regard capital in a physical sense, perceive it as being embedded in productive facilities—buildings, equipment, tools. Increasingly in the real world of business, however, capital has been made abstract, monetized. Profit often has more to do with financial manipulations than with production efficiency. This shift in thinking about capital, its rewards, and its concentration in the hands of ever fewer decision-makers has led to a growing perception of basic conflict between owners and communities, managers and workers. This in turn has led to calls for new approaches to the questions of ownership, worker participation in management, and the responsibilities of firms to the communities in which they operate. Nowhere is this more clearly documented than in the case of the closing of the Youngstown Sheet and Tube steel plant.

Youngstown, Ohio, rests in the Mahoning Valley, better known around the state as "Steel Valley." Youngstown Sheet and Tube started production there in 1909 and grew up with the automobile industry, which took most of its production. The company was founded by local entrepreneurs, and for sixty years it was run by local managers who lived in the community. The investment strategy was to modernize steelmaking facilities near their marketplace. When the marketplace began to move west, the company followed and built a second plant in Chicago. The plan had been to use the profits from the new facility to upgrade the mill and the technology in Youngstown.

But that never happened. Instead, on a Monday in September 1977, just fifteen minutes before the day shift ended, the management sent down word that the plant was to be closed. Five thousand people lost their jobs at the company—the largest number of Americans ever affected by the closing of a nondefense industry. Estimates are that another ten thousand people—suppliers, vendors, and local businesses—experienced drastic cuts in income because of the shutdown. In all, some fifty thousand people were directly touched.

The beginning of the end for Youngstown Sheet and Tube came in 1969, when it was acquired by the Lykes Corporation. Originally a shipbuilding firm based in New Orleans, Lykes sought to diversify its operations. Like the growth of many other companies in the 1960s, its expansion was not dictated by need for raw materials, by logic of geography, or by technological expertise, but stemmed simply from the desire to grow larger. To do that involved borrowing huge sums of money for which banks and investors required real assets and sound businesses as security.

Youngstown Sheet and Tube was just the sort of firm a conglomerate looked for. It had a cash flow of about $100 million a year,[9] and it owed the banks relatively little. In 1968, just before the merger, the combined debt of Lykes and Youngstown Sheet and Tube was only $192 million. By 1970 it stood at $609 million. Instead of modernizing the Youngstown facilities, Lykes used steel money to buy other businesses. This cash milking of healthy companies was a favorite tactic of conglomerates undertaking expansion in the 1960s.

Although there was a boom in the steel business in 1973-1974, Youngstown Sheet and Tube did not benefit fully from it because the plant and the equipment had been allowed to deteriorate. The upgrading of facilities that the original owners had projected never happened. Without it, Youngstown Sheet and Tube was not able to compete against the more efficient Japanese and European plants.

The Lykes Corporation had not come to Youngstown to make steel. They had come to make money. And when Youngstown Steel and Tube could not be used any longer to produce cash for growth, Lykes left Youngstown to die, or to live as best it could. On a Sunday afternoon in September 1977, Lykes's top management met at the Pittsburgh airport and decided that the mill should be shut down. The owners and managers of Lykes did what seemed most natural. They looked at columns of figures and decided that more money could be made elsewhere. Capital exercised its right to decide. Without consulting with workers, unions, or the community, Lykes announced the next day that the plant would close.

One chronicler of the events sums the matter up in this way:

> Urban dwellers are familiar with landlords who buy sound buildings with borrowed money and then collect the rents for several years, refusing to provide adequate maintenance and services or to make needed repairs. When the building has fallen into disrepair and [he] can't borrow

> on it further, the landlord walks away. When Lykes acquired it, Youngstown Sheet and Tube was a healthy company. In the ensuing eight years, Lykes' policies of heavy borrowing, siphoning off assets, mismanagement and neglect . . . left Youngstown Sheet and Tube an expendable part of a sick conglomerate.[10]

Similar stories could be told by dozens of communities around the United States. What was different in Youngstown was that people tried to do something about the situation. They decided to have the community and the workers jointly buy the plant and run it.

The leaders of the local religious community organized what was called the "Save Our Valley Campaign." It brought together an ecumenical coalition of representatives from the Steelworkers Union and business and community groups. An extensive study funded by a grant from the United States Department of Housing and Urban Affairs concluded that "given certain reasonable actions on the part of the federal government, the Works can be reopened and operated as a profitable basic steel manufacturer under community/employee ownership."[11]

The plan called for putting 1,600 employees back to work after only a few months of repairs. A second stage would have upgraded facilities, added a new electric furnace, and recalled a thousand more workers. Community Steel, Inc., was the proposed name for the new enterprise that was to have fifteen directors—six chosen by private investors, six by labor, and three by the community of Youngstown. Former managers of Youngstown Sheet and Tube were deeply involved in the planning since they as well as factory workers were suddenly without jobs.

To show enthusiasm for the new pattern of ownership and faith in the plan, local individuals and groups, along with national religious organizations, deposited $3.5 million in Youngstown banks as a pledge against the purchase of stock. Of course, the project required much more money than that. Feasibility rested upon an anticipated $30 million in private investment, $27 million in grants from the state and from federal agencies, and federal loan guarantees of $245 million.[12]

This was an ambitious and imaginative plan, and there was sufficient expert testimony about its workability to justify the effort. But the opportunity never came to test its validity. Both government and business resisted any such social-economic experimentation.

When first approached by the religious coalition about the possibility of loan guarantees, a high official of the Carter administration indicated that such guarantees should be no problem.[13] But after almost a year of deliberation, and in the face of strong lobbying by big steel companies against federal involvement, the government in 1979 declined to provide the necessary loan guarantees. The official reason given was that the request exceeded the Department's $100 million limit on such activities.

From the beginning, Lykes maintained that it would not sell the facilities to any group that depended upon government grants or loan guarantees. Its position was that such involvement would be anticompetitive and a threat to the free enterprise system. After the Commerce Department finally declined to make the necessary guarantees, Lykes sold the Youngstown Sheet and Tube facilities to the LTV Corporation, which destroyed them in 1981, ending all hopes of their passing to worker-community control.

Why was a plan that offered such a measure of hope to an economically devastated city rejected so vehemently by business and abandoned by government?

The answer goes to the heart of our consideration of the nature of capital ownership and its role in our economic society. To have allowed the community (i.e., as a political entity) to appoint directors would have challenged the right of investors and managers to make business decisions in the privacy of the boardroom and on only the narrowest definition of profitability. To have allowed workers to become the majority shareholders in a plan financed by borrowed money would have threatened to create a system in which capital owners would simply put their money out at interest and have neither the power nor the profitability of ownership. To have allowed workers equal power in the decision-making of the firm would have attacked the mystique of modern management. As one analyst put it, "Much of the power of U.S. capitalism rests on the carefully cultivated myth that the economy will fall apart without capitalist management. Fear that this myth would be shattered is a significant motivation behind Big Steel's opposition to the Youngstown plan."[14]

In the end, both business and government opposed the Youngstown plan, fearing that the concept of worker-community ownership and management might spread to other cities and other firms. It might have been the beginning of a new way of thinking about economic organization in our society. That was the real threat of Youngstown.

III. Values: Biblical Faith and Capital Accumulation

We have lived and even thrived for two hundred years in an economic world characterized by industry, commerce, increasingly complex financial exchanges, borrowing, lending, and interest. The rights of capital have grown, have been defined and refined, and have tended to dominate the economic scene. In such a world the accumulation of capital and the associated concentration of power have become so logical, so much a part of social reality, that it is difficult for many in the modern faith community to imagine why prophets in the eighth century B.C. or medieval monks might have objected. Yet it is clear that neither biblical faith nor church tradition rests easy with the concept of money concentrated in the hands of the few.

Our economic system rests upon the concept of privatizing creation. It assumes that everything of economic value should belong to a particular individual whenever possible. It is the right of that individual to accumulate as much as energy and opportunity make possible and to do with those goods whatever he or she chooses. This is not the biblical perspective.

A. The Old Testament Witness

The Bible does recognize the legitimacy of private ownership. Otherwise, what would be the significance of "Thou shalt not steal" or of Jesus' words to the rich young man in Mark 10:21 (RSV)—"Go, sell what you have, and give to the poor"? But possession is always conceived of in the larger context of responsibility. What belongs to the individual belonged first to God and does not cease to belong to God. Stewardship rather than ownership is the primal category.

Implicit in the biblical narrative are limits to the accumulation of goods and wealth. The story of Israel in the wilderness demonstrates God's bias against unrestricted accumulation. As a practical matter, accumulation simply increased the burden of nomadic existence. When the very life of the community was threatened by starvation, God provided manna for the people to eat (Exod. 16). Yet part of God's merciful provision was the prohibition against gathering more than one day's ration at a time—except before the Sabbath. Unrestricted accumulation would have had profound theological and social significance. Socially, the amassing of food by some and not by others would have brought disequilibrium to a fragile society by endorsing the concept of individual above community security. Religiously, it could have led the people of Israel to conclude that God was now superfluous, that they could make it on their own.

When the years of wandering ended and Israel became a settled, property-owning people, the endless accumulation of goods and wealth still was not easily accepted. Deuteronomy warned that even kings were not to amass for themselves horses, wives, or silver and gold (17:16-17).

Even so, the egalitarianism of nomadic existence gave way to a stratified society centered in a glittering court life under Solomon. There was pride in the glory of the kingdom: "Once every three years the fleet of ships of Tarshish used to come bringing gold, silver, ivory, apes, and peacocks. . . . And the king made silver as common in Jerusalem as stone" (1 Kings 10:22, 27, RSV). Yet it was this policy of accumulating wealth that led to the downfall of the kingdom.

The prophets inveighed against the wealthy of Israel:

> You have plundered vineyards, and your houses are full of what you have taken from the poor.
>
> A day is coming when the Lord will take away from the women of Jerusalem everything they are so proud of. . . . He will take away their veils and their hats; the magic charms they wear on their arms and at their waists; the rings they wear on their fingers and in their noses; all their fine robes, gowns, cloaks, and purses; their revealing garments, their linen handkerchiefs, and the scarves and long veils they wear on their heads. (Isa. 3:14, 18-23, TEV)

The harsh judgment pronounced on accumulated wealth extended beyond Israel itself to include the surrounding nations as well.

> Tyre has built herself a rampart,
> and heaped up silver like dust,
> and gold like the mud of the streets.
> But lo, the Lord will strip her of her possessions
> and hurl her wealth into the sea. (Zech. 9:3-4, RSV)

The Old Testament recognized as one of the dangers inherent in accumulated wealth the temptation to use it as leverage over poor and powerless people. Thus the Pentateuch set stringent limits on lending money at interest. In Exodus 22:25 (TEV) we read, "If you lend money to any of my people who are poor, do not act like a moneylender and require him to pay interest." And in Deuteronomy 23:20 (TEV) we read, "You may charge interest on what you lend to a foreigner, but not on what you lend to a fellow Israelite." Obviously the fear was that the need of individuals might become the occasion for profit-making that would permanently impoverish many and lead to class divisions in Israel, thus endangering the solidarity and viability of the nation.

B. New Testament Variations

Jesus and the New Testament writers were far more adjusted to a monetized society and to its more complex financial transactions. The investment of funds and the payment of interest were accepted as part of social reality. (See, for example, the parable of the talents in Matt. 25:14-30.) However, there was still hesitancy about and harsh judgment pronounced on accumulated wealth. "Do not lay up for yourselves treasures on earth" (Matt. 6:19, RSV).

James simply assumes that there is no way wealth can be amassed that does not depend on injustice (5:1-6). It should not surprise us that Mary interpreted the meaning of the child she was to bear in terms of economic upheaval: "[God] has brought down mighty kings from their thrones, and lifted up the lowly. He has filled the hungry with good things, and sent the rich away with empty hands" (Luke 1:52-53, TEV).

The point of the New Testament is not that wealth should not exist, only that it should not be accumulated to guarantee the power, privilege, and pleasure of the holder. Distribution of wealth to end misery, not endless accumulation, is the biblical ideal. It was the commitment to these principles that caused the Christian community in Jerusalem to enter into a radical form of common life where goods were shared and money was derived from the sale of assets divided. An entry in *A Companion to the Bible* offers this explanation of the New Testament viewpoint: "The condition of misery is not agreeable to God. On the contrary, God wishes it to cease, and that is why he forbids the accumulation of possessions in the hands of the rich. That accumulation announces the ruin of the rich man, who puts his confidence not in God but in his riches themselves."[15]

Such biblical concepts about the accumulation of wealth and property ownership were ultimately based upon the recognition that God is the true owner of all things and that human claims are contingent upon stewardship responsibilities. This perception, inherited by the early church, ran headlong into the definition of Roman law, which recognized absolute and exclusive individual ownership over virtually all property and the right to acquire all that ability, opportunity, and privilege afforded. This confrontation of perspectives became the background for significant theological comment by the early church fathers.

C. Patristic Perspectives

Clement of Alexandria (late second century) did not reject wealth in itself; poverty was no ideal. But he did attack the vast differences in wealth within society. While he accepted the right to private ownership, he maintained that property was to be used, not accumulated for prestige or power. Two principles determined his understanding of ownership. The first was *autarkeia,* or self-sufficiency, by which he meant possession of goods sufficient for a life of human dignity but not of excess. He asked, for instance, "Does a table knife refuse to cut if it be not studded with silver or have a handle of ivory?"[16] The second was *koinonia,* or community. Property should be used to abolish the distinction between rich and poor: "He who holds possessions . . . possesses them for his brothers' sake rather than his own" (p. 44).

Basil the Great (fourth century) took a harder line by regarding the accumulation of goods as robbery from the poor: "Who is a robber? One who takes the goods of another. . . . That bread which you keep belongs to the hungry; that coat which you preserve in the wardrobe, to the naked; those shoes which are rotting in your possession, to the shoeless; that gold which you have hidden in the ground, to the needy" (p. 50). He maintained that since land, seeds, rain, and beasts of burden are gifts of God for all humanity, wealth that stems from them should be available to all as a right of creation. The accumulation of wealth based upon deriving private benefit from public goods is robbery.

While Basil focused on the question of how poverty generates wealth, Ambrose of Milan (fourth century) took the more radical step of noting how wealth generates poverty. He believed that "the poverty of the many *is caused* by the accumulated wealth, the ever-expanding wealth, of a few" (p. 63, emphasis added). Authentic needs, not mere desire, set the limits of ownership. Beyond that, Ambrose concluded, "avarice . . . must be the cause of our need" (p. 73). He argued that "God has created everything in such a way that all things be possessed in common. Nature therefore is the mother of common right, usurpation of private right" (p. 74).

Ambrose's principle of economic reorganization can be summarized in a line: "If you claim as your own anything of that which was given to the human race . . . in common, you should distribute at least a part among the poor" (p. 74). That is a clear and advanced social principle, but it still appeals to voluntarism. No guidance is given as to how much wealth should be transferred, nor is any force implied beyond that of moral conviction. Ambrose clearly preferred common property over private property, but he conceived of no social mechanism beyond moral suasion to achieve that goal.

The old adage says that "possession is nine-tenths of the law." John Chrysostom (fourth century), archbishop of Constantinople, rejected that notion. He refused to recognize mere possession as giving any legitimate claim of ownership. Far more crucial in his view was the question of how one obtained possession and how the property was used. Was it obtained by robbery, by honest labor, or by inheritance? If by robbery—either personal or ancestral—there were no rights. The burden of proof of legitimate ownership lay with the possessor, not with those who challenged the possession. "Can you, ascending through many generations, show the acquisition just? It cannot be. The root and origin of it must have been injustice. Why? Because God in the beginning did not make one man rich and another poor" (p. 94).

If one's own labor was the source of claims to ownership of wealth, there was still the question of other claims to the same property that went unrecognized. What of others whose labor was also mixed in the creation of the goods? Was it fairly and fully rewarded? Even if one labored alone, there were still the claims of God. That which was now claimed individually and absolutely by one person was nevertheless derived from that which God created. And "the possessions of one Lord are all common," Chrysostom declared (p. 95).

John Chrysostom was the first of the church fathers to address the matter of inheritance as a moral issue. He maintained that amassing wealth and leaving it to one's children had a double negative effect. It robbed the poor of what was theirs, and it encouraged laziness on the part of the heirs of wealth. Chrysostom held that Paul's injunction that "Anyone who does not work should not eat" applies to the rich as well as to the poor. "If you wish to leave much wealth to your children . . . ," he advised, "do not leave them riches, but virtue and skill" (p. 89). Chrysostom ultimately rejected absolute and exclusive right of ownership as being against nature and opposed to God's intentions in creation.

Augustine (fourth century), bishop of Hippo, dealt with the problem of property from two perspectives. At the purely functional level, he acknowledged the existence of laws governing ownership. But his concern and comment dealt largely with the moral issues. That is, he was more concerned with what ought to be than with what is. The monastic communities of common sharing that he established represent the bridge between the two. Ownership, he maintained, had its genesis in human law, not in divine or natural law. And in the process of privatizing property, a system had resulted that actually diminished the benefits of creation.

Augustine argued that ownership should be determined not by possession but by right use of property. "The one who uses his wealth badly possesses it wrongfully, and wrongful possession means that it is another's property" (p. 110). On that basis Augustine argued that "gold and silver *therefore* belong to those who know how to use gold and silver." The individual "must be said to possess something [only] when he or she uses it well" (p. 116). Thus Augustine was the first of the early church fathers to move toward an ethic of accumulation tied to concepts of productivity. Right use, however, never meant merely increasing one's private wealth. It meant meeting the needs of others.

Augustine regarded private property as the principle source of strife in the world. "For, on account of the things which each one of us possesses singly, wars exist, hatreds, discords, strifes among human beings, tumults, dissensions, scandals, sins, injustices, and murders. . . . Do we fight over the things we possess in common?" (p. 120). Certainly not in his estimation.

"Those who wish to make room for the Lord," Augustine declared, "must find pleasure not in private, but in common property" (p. 120). Augustine's call to the faithful was "Let us therefore abstain from the possession of private property." But, almost as though despairing of that possibility, he added, "or from the love of it, if we cannot abstain from possession" (p. 120).

We now have before us the basic outline of patristic reflection on the issue of private property. Material goods are not evil but rather the good gifts of God for all humankind. Evil arises when what God intends to be shared in common is seized by the few for their own power and privilege. Ownership should be determined by need and by the ability to use resources appropriately—that is, in meeting the need of others. The concentration of wealth through inheritance is denounced. Not even labor power expended gives absolute property rights to the individual, since the resources with which labor is mixed are the gifts of God. God does not abandon a prior claim, and thus Christian faith can honor no absolute, individual right to private property.

Such a message represented a direct challenge to the Roman laws regarding property and to the self-interest of the privileged groups addressed by the early church fathers. It should not surprise us, then, that in emerging economic systems, self-interest won out over the concept of stewardship in defining the relationship of people to property.

Clearly our present system of economic organization, based on concepts of individual property rights that tend toward absolute claims, owes more to secular Roman law than to biblical faith or patristic precepts. It derives more from the driving self-interest of the privileged than from the anguished and angry sermons of the prophets and the writings of early bishops and theologians.

God is the Sovereign of history, and history is dynamic. Therefore, we cannot look to biblical faith or its early interpreters for a blueprint for contemporary social and economic organization. The specific structures and laws suitable for a nomadic people, a subsistence-level agricultural environment, or the trading activity of a barely monetized society can hardly be expected to suffice for the intricacies of today's complex transnational economy. But the underlying concerns of that faith tradition are still relevant and put its followers at odds with much of what classical and contemporary economists have assumed about the absolute character of rights of accumulation and ownership.

There is simply nothing in biblical tradition that even remotely accepts the concept of the right of the individual to acquire any quantity of goods or wealth in blind indifference to the condition and needs of others. Nor does the biblical tradition exhibit any inclination to trust in the good will of individuals or in supposedly automatic mechanisms (e.g., invisible hands or trickle-down theories) to achieve a God-envisioned economy of justice where the needs of all are met. The voice of the prophets and of the early church fathers is avowedly interventionist in economic affairs.

Biblical faith acknowledges individual property rights, but only within the context of a stewardship ethic that regards the whole of creation as God's capital on loan to each generation to meet the needs of all of God's people. It is out of character with our faith to accord autonomy to capital owners in the economic decision-making process. However efficient, however profitable for enterprise, investment decisions made in the absence of concern about the larger arena of labor, consumer, and community are not acceptable to the norms of our early faith tradition.

Savings and investment are crucial factors in modern economic society, but neither capital as an abstraction, nor business enterprises as capital users, nor individuals as capital owners, nor capitalists as a class can be accorded any absolute right by those who adhere to biblical faith. God lays a prior claim upon all of the resources of the earth and upon all human systems in order to achieve an envisioned world of plenty shared in justice and in peace.

Notes

1. Paul L. Poirot, "Guaranty Survey," Guaranty Trust Company, Oct. 1952, as reprinted in *Free Market Economics: A Basic Reader*, ed. Bettina B. Greaves (Irvington-on-Hudson, N.Y.: Foundation for Economic Education, 1975), p. 23.

2. John W. McConnell, *Ideas of the Great Economists* (New York: Barnes & Noble, 1980), p. 65.

3. Maurice Dobb, *Studies in the Development of Capitalism* (New York: International, 1963), p. 239.

4. Robert L. Heilbroner, *The Making of Economic Society* (Englewood Cliffs, N.J.: Prentice-Hall, 1980), p. 83.

5. Dobb, *Studies in the Development of Capitalism*, p. 192.

6. Ernest Mandel, *Marxist Economic Theory* (New York: Monthly Review Press, 1962), p. 108.

7. Dobb, *Studies in the Development of Capitalism*, p. 191.

8. Galbraith, *The New Industrial State* (New York: Signet Books, 1967), pp. 51-52.

9. Gerald Dickey, "Youngstown Sheet and Tube—A Classic 'Takeover' Case," *The Center Magazine,* Nov./Dec. 1979, p. 33.

10. John Collins, "What Does a Community Do When Industry Leaves It to Die?" in *Must We Choose Sides?* ed. Harry Strharsky (Oakland, Calif.: Inter-Religious Task Force for Social Analysis, 1979), p. 118.

11. Martin Carnoy and Derek Shearer, *Economic Democracy: The Challenge of the 1980s* (Armonk, N.Y.: M. E. Sharpe, 1980), p. 361.

12. Collins, "What Does a Community Do When Industry Leaves It to Die?" p. 120.

13. From a personal interview with Philip R. Newell regarding his recollections of a White House conference he attended in late 1978.

14. Collins, "What Does a Community Do When Industry Leaves It to Die?" p. 121.

15. R. Mehl, "Money," in *A Companion to the Bible,* ed. J. J. von Allmen (New York: Oxford University Press, 1958), p. 272.

16. Clement of Alexandria, quoted by Charles Avila in *Ownership: Early Christian Teaching* (Maryknoll, N.Y.: Orbis Books, 1983), p. 37. Subsequent references to this source will be made parenthetically in the text.

Chapter Three

The Role of Labor in the Market System

I. Concepts: Labor, Workers, and Employment

A. Labor as Economic Creator

For most people, "labor" is a verb. It conjures up images of tasks being done, products being turned out or services being performed by sweat of brow or by intense concentration. But for economists, "labor" is more often a noun. It does not focus on the work accomplishments of individuals. Instead, labor is conceived of as the homogenization of a vast variety of human skills, intellectual powers, and physical efforts into a production force. Economically speaking, labor is not a human endeavor but a depersonalized factor of production.

This is not to say that economists undervalue the importance of labor. Indeed, the early classical school held that the value of all items was determined solely by the amount of human effort that went into their creation. Goods were viewed economically as nothing more than their total labor-time. Although this *labor theory of value* is usually associated with Karl Marx, it has its roots in Adam Smith and was formally elaborated by David Ricardo. The logic of the theory is both simple and compelling. If it takes three days to fashion a wagon wheel and only one day to make a chair from the same amount of raw lumber, then wagon wheels would naturally be valued at three times the rate of chairs. Or if a farmer working by himself for a season can produce either 1,500 pounds of corn or 1,000 pounds of wheat on the same land, then wheat might be expected to be valued half again as much as corn.

However logical such calculations, most of us see almost intuitively that items can be valued solely by the labor time it took to make them only in a world where everything else is freely available—land, water, resources, raw materials, and necessary tools. The moment any of these factors becomes scarce, value begins to be determined by something more than the number of labor hours an item embodies. This is particularly true when human labor is brought together with ever greater amounts of tools and equipment (capital goods) in order to increase output.

The growing importance of capital goods has dramatically changed the character of labor in human society. It is the ability to organize human energy and multiply human output through tools and technology that has changed labor from a verb to a noun, from the more or less isolated effort of individuals and families to the highly complex structures of a labor force. Central to the development of industrial society was the shift from labor as a means of producing goods for direct consumption to labor as a commodity employed in the production of goods for sale. The labor power of the individual, be it physical or intellectual, makes the person an element in a process, a companion of machinery, the temporary possessor of skills not yet automated or of judgment not yet duplicable by computers. One of the enduring features of industrial capitalism has been the attempt on the part of capital owners to minimize the power and prerogatives of labor and to maintain for themselves the absolute right to direct the production process.

B. Dividing the Work and the Workers

The key to the power to direct the production process has been the *division of labor* in modern economic society. From the ancient division of labor between the sexes, to the medieval division of artisan guilds, to the narrow tasks of twentieth-century assembly lines, people have understood that specialization and cooperation in creating certain goods may allow a superabundance of that item to be produced. The surplus can then be traded for some other good, also produced by specialists, in superabundance. By this division of labor the variety and quantity of goods and services can be dramatically increased.

One of the often-quoted illustrations from economic literature is the passage in which Adam Smith describes the tremendous increase in the output of a pin factory brought about by the specialization of cooperative worker activity:

> One man draws out the wire, another straits it, a third cuts it, a fourth points it, a fifth grinds it at the top for receiving the head; to make the head requires two or three distinct operations; to put it on is a peculiar business; to whiten it another; it is even a trade by itself to put them into paper. . . .
>
> I have seen a small manufactory of this kind where ten men only were employed and where some of them consequently performed two or three distinct operations. But though they were poor, and therefore but indifferently accommodated with the necessary machinery, they could

> when they exerted themselves make among them about twelve pounds of pins a day. There are in a pound upwards of four thousand pins of middling size. These ten persons, therefore, could make among them upwards of forty-eight thousand pins in a day. . . . But if they had all wrought separately and independently . . . they could certainly not each of them make twenty, perhaps not one pin in a day.[1]

Of course, the degree of specialization in Adam Smith's pin factory is rudimentary in comparison with that of today's facilities. Indeed, John Kenneth Galbraith argues that the division of labor is the modern world's substitute for brilliant individuals: "The real accomplishment of modern science and technology consists in taking ordinary men, informing them narrowly and deeply and then through appropriate organization, arranging to have their knowledge combined with that of other specialized but equally ordinary men. This dispenses with the need for genius. The resulting performance, though less inspiring, is far more predictable."[2]

The oft-made promise of specialization combined with highly mechanized technology is that difficult, dirty, and dangerous work will be done by machines, leaving human beings with easier and more challenging tasks. This promise is not without its dark side. Karl Marx spoke of the dangers of narrow specialization and of the *alienation* that is its natural result. In the continual drive for the division of labor necessary to maximize output, Marx argued, workers are separated from the tradition of independent production for self and family and brought into a depersonalized work environment over which they have no control. They are assigned such small tasks that they are unable to recognize their unique contribution in the creation of the product. Indeed, they can often do their job in total ignorance of what the final product is. In Marx's view, work is thus robbed of any creative function, workers are denied pride of accomplishment, and human labor is reduced to a routine in which the person is little more than an adaptable machine utilized in production. Even Adam Smith worried that constant repetition of a few mechanical functions over a long period of time might cause the worker to lose the capacity for intelligent thought.

The fears of Marx and Smith may already have been realized. We need only think of the waitress who cannot perform simple addition without a cash register, or the grocery checkout clerk whose function has been reduced to dragging items across a scanner that reads the price and calculates the bill.

Unfortunately, the division of labor has not delivered on its promise to free human workers for more challenging tasks. Instead, for a large segment of the work force it has done the opposite, condemning them to low-skill jobs that make them all but unemployable when their little niche is finally taken over by a machine. Where will these people go? To be sure, machines will have to be produced, and computers will have to be programmed and serviced, but that is the work of a few specialists, not of the mass of skilled and semiskilled employees that the new systems replace.

A study by the International Metalworkers Federation concludes that within thirty years only 2 to 10 percent of the world's current industrialized labor force will be needed to produce all the goods necessary to meet total demand. Anyone who doubts the possibility need only imagine how it would have amazed someone in the 1920s to have heard that only 2 percent of the population would be necessary to produce all the food this country needs to eat and to export. After all, at that time between one-half and one-third of the population still lived in the rural sector. Nevertheless, within half a century, that is the transformation that took place. There is little reason to doubt the possibility that the industrial sector will experience the same kind of transformation.

Displaced rural workers of a generation ago were able to find better jobs in the still labor-intensive industrial sector. Society's need for large numbers of skilled and semiskilled workers—who were well-paid—helped to create America's middle class as the country moved away from a rural-based population during the past century. Job mobility and the opportunity to increase skills and income gave society a sense of openness and made people feel confident about the future. The economic transition to the postindustrial age may not be so felicitous. Many social scientists and policymakers fear that the new technologies may be moving us toward a highly polarized labor force and a more stratified and less upwardly mobile society. A small percentage of highly trained professionals and technical people will be eagerly sought and well-paid, while a growing mass of workers will be required only for mundane, low-paying tasks.

Only the most pessimistic would speak of a new economic dark age. Still, it seems likely that the future can no longer be regarded as automatically better and brighter. Slipping real wages and high levels of unemployment will likely be increasing concerns in the emerging economy and its new stages in the division of labor.

C. The Employment Dilemma

The threat of unemployment does not hang equally over all workers. Groups are affected very differently by unemployment patterns. The following table compares what happened in 1979 with what happened in

Table 3.1

Unemployment Rates by Population Groups

	1979		June, 1986	
GROUP	**Official**	**"Real"**	**Official**	**"Real"**
Total	5.8%	9.7%	7.0%	12.7%
Whites	5.1	8.7	6.1	11.2
Blacks	12.3	18.9	14.8	23.2
Hispanics	8.3	13.6	10.4	18.0
White Teens	14.0	21.3	15.6	31.9
Black Teens	36.5	47.2	42.6	56.5

Sources: Bureau of Labor Statistics, U.S. Department of Labor

1986. The data report both official rates of unemployment and "real" rates that are adjusted by taking into account those people who have become so discouraged in job-hunting that they have stopped looking and those who want to work full-time but can find only part-time employment.

Nineteen seventy-nine was a bad year economically. Petroleum prices leaped, inflation was in double digits, and stock prices were in the doldrums. By contrast, 1986 continued a four-year economic recovery: prices were stable, corporate earnings were high, and stock prices were up. Nevertheless, comparing the official statistics from the two periods, overall unemployment jumped 31 percent. Both whites and blacks experienced a 20 percent increase in joblessness, but that seemed moderate compared with the 25 percent rise among Hispanics. Although it started at a much higher level, the rate of unemployment among black teenagers grew over 50 percent more than that of their white counterparts.

These data document some rock-hard realities of work in America. In good times or in bad, black Americans are more than twice as likely to be without a job as white Americans. The case of Hispanics is somewhat less desperate, but they are still over half again as likely to be unemployed as whites. Meanwhile, black teenagers represent a special situation of despair. Their unemployment rate is more than twice that of their young white counterparts and five times the national average.

Clearly there is a strong racial bias in the employment structure of the United States. It would be difficult to deny the conclusion reached by the National Urban League in reviewing these and other data: "Black males and females are losing ground to whites in every age category in terms of their labor force participation. Black unemployment is higher than that of any other period between the Great Depression and the start of the recession early in 1982. Blacks as a whole show no sign of holding steady or gaining ground vis-a-vis whites in their ability to maintain employment."[3]

The employment challenge facing the nation is formidable. Today's unemployed teenagers who are not learning job skills will be tomorrow's breadwinners looking for work. Just over half of all adult women are presently in the labor force. By the end of the century, 63 percent of all females will hold or seek employment. Meanwhile, the economic transformation of the world continues so that American business and labor competes against companies and workers in dozens of other countries. It is in this context that unemployment must be resolved.

In order to provide a job for everyone who wants to work, it will be necessary to create twenty million new jobs between 1987 and 1994—a seven-year period. That is no mean task; the previous seven years produced only 2.2 million new jobs.

The benchmark for *full employment* in recent years has officially been 4 percent unemployment. Many economists have maintained that at that level the only people without jobs are those who choose to be temporarily unemployed or who are in transition to other employment. The United States last experienced such a low rate of unemployment in 1969.

Because of the persistence of higher levels of unemployment, some economists—and public officials resisting further government involvement in the economy—have sought to redefine "full employment" upward. They now speak of it as 6 or 7 or 8 percent unemployment. The grounds cited are various but often include certain observations.

One is that unemployment benefits have become so extravagant that they undermine the incentive to seek employment. Instead of taking a lower-paying job immediately, people tend to wait longer in hopes of landing a better one. While there is always episodic evidence of this claim, studies give little credence to the idea that this is a major factor in maintaining present high levels of unemployment. There are few situations in which people are economically better off by not working.

Another observation commonly used to explain higher levels of unemployment is that in recent years women have flooded the labor market, many of them in search of second income streams that raise the level of family consumption but are not strictly necessary to survival. What such an argument ignores is that the supposed spur for greater family consumption income that has driven many women into the labor force is not necessarily avarice. Instead, it represents the most viable way for many families to compensate for the dramatic loss in real income brought about by inflation in recent years. Neither does this line of reasoning account for the fact that many women have entered the labor pool because they are heads of families and the chief or sole source of income.

Finally, the rapid growth of teenage employment is often cited as a prime cause for high unemployment in the labor force as a whole. The unspoken assumption of this view is that a teenager's income is discretionary and not necessary. Unquestionably some employers prefer teenage labor to adult labor. This is particularly notable in sales positions and in fast-food restaurants. The attraction of young workers is that they will work for minimum wages and only part-time. This enables the employer to staff for peak-period needs while avoiding offering fringe benefits (e.g., health insurance, vacation pay, unemployment compensation, and pension programs) commonly associated with permanent, full-time employment.

While the entry of women and youth into the labor force has undoubtedly contributed to the employment dilemma, it is scapegoating to focus on them as primary factors. A study of the recession of 1974-1975, when unemployment reached 8.5 percent, provides an interesting parallel.[4] The data indicate that even if there had been no increase in the number of women in the labor force, unemployment would still have reached 8.25 percent—a mere one-quarter-point difference. The number of teenagers seeking employment during that period actually fell, thereby keeping the overall unemployment rate from being worse.

Whether we are speaking of young workers or adults, women or men, blacks, whites, or Hispanics, ultimately what is at stake is whether the U.S. economy is capable of providing employment opportunities for all those who want to work. To say no is to admit a basic failing in our economic system. To attempt to mask the failing by semantic redefinitions of full employment will only delay the creative thinking necessary to make labor more than a factor of production and instead a full partner with capital in the economic process.

II. Realities: Women in the Labor Force

One of the groups in our society that has been systematically excluded from full partnership in the economy is women. In every working-age category, women constitute a majority in the population, but they function in society like an economic minority: categories of employment have been restricted for them, their wages have remained low, and progress in changing past patterns has been slow at best.

The production demands created by both the First and the Second World Wars established a practical and patriotic justification for greater numbers of women entering the labor force. The tendency in much of society until then had been to think of them only as a reserve labor pool that was temporary and disposable. While the numbers of women at work diminished somewhat each time the troops came home, many refused to return to the narrow role of homemaker assigned them by tradition. By 1929, just before the Great Depression, 25 percent of women sixteen years and older were employed. That rose to 35 percent by 1950. Today, more than half of all women of working age are employed or looking for work, and that is expected to rise to 63 percent by the end of the decade. If that occurs, the Department of Labor estimates that women will make up more than half of the nation's labor force.

While the image persists that women are temporary or occasional workers, the average woman now expects to spend twenty-eight years in the labor force as compared with thirty-eight years for men. Clearly the old stereotype of women working from time to time to buy a new Easter dress or to achieve some other limited financial goal is not appropriate—and it never was. Most women work for the same reason that most men do—perceived economic need.

Increasingly, "the American dream" is financed by women at work. The average household now has one and one-half workers. Many families have been able to offset the effects of inflation only by having two incomes. Overall, working wives contribute about 26 percent of their families' income. Among minority families, that percentage rises to fully one-third.

The need or desire for more of what money will buy has brought most women into the workplace, and in the process they have changed many social attitudes about gender roles and expectations. It is fair to say that the American economy has been doubly dependent on women at work. On one side of the economic equation, they provide a large, growing, and crucial segment of the labor force. On the other side of the equation, their earnings increasingly provide both relief from poverty and the measure of comfort most families enjoy beyond subsistence. In addition, the two-income family, probably more than any other single factor, is responsible for the level of consumption that fuels the American economy.

Because women have made steady progress in joining the labor force, there has been the tendency to assume that things are getting better on all fronts. "You've come a long way, baby" was more than a television commercial directed at female consumers. It became a statement of confidence about where things were headed for women. In some economic areas, however, women have not made much progress at all.

In 1939 women who worked year-round and full-time earned 61 percent of what their male counterparts earned. By 1977 women earned only 57 percent as much as men—a relative loss of 7 percent from forty years before.[5] Not until 1987 did women's pay regain the 1939 proportion of the male average. Anyone who calls that progress has to be a male chauvinist—regardless of sex. Of course, the take-home pay for both groups is now more than it was in 1939, but the gender gap in the economy seemingly has remained the same.

This is so for three related reasons. First, the labor market is highly segmented. According to the Bureau of Labor Statistics, 80 percent of employed women work in only 20 out of 420 occupations listed. These are predominantly what have traditionally been called "women's occupations"—secretary, nurse, teacher, retail clerk—and tend to be at the lower end of the pay scale. Thus women are typically paid less than men in any job category, at any educational level, and in any age group. Women sales workers make only 52 percent of the earnings of their male counterparts; clerical workers, 68 percent; service workers, 72 percent; professional and technical workers, 74 percent. Neither does better education guarantee income advantage for women. On average, women who have graduated from high school (but not college) earn less than men who have not completed elementary school, and women college graduates receive less than men who are high-school dropouts. Finally, there is the age factor. While men typically continue to increase their earning power until their mid-fifties, wages for women begin to decline after the age of thirty-four.[6]

Such differentials are justified and maintained in large part by the segmentation of labor into men's and women's jobs. While the division is not absolute, it is the predominant and entrenched reality. With women concentrated in a few employment categories, wages can be paid that have little relationship to the economic value contributed. Even the "equal pay for equal work" concept has not changed the basic relationship of the income stream of men and women because women have such difficulty entering so many higher-paying job categories. Thus in recent years feminist organizations have begun to press the new concept of "equal pay for *comparable worth.*" The goal is to force employers to evaluate and compensate all jobs on the basis of points assigned to each for the skills demanded, the exertion or risk required, and the level of responsibility involved. The concept has received the support of many individuals and some unions, including the AFL-CIO. The state of California has established a "state policy of setting salaries for female-dominated jobs on the basis of comparability of the value of the work."[7]

While it is not clear that comparable-worth formulas can be developed with enough specificity to equalize incomes in the short run, they at least begin to address seriously the skewed character of the income structure based on the sex discrimination implicit in our division of labor.

III. Values: Work as Doctrine and as Practice

When Christianity broke the bonds of its Palestinian cradle, it invaded a world dominated by Roman administration and Greek philosophy. There were many differences between Greco-Roman and Christian views of the world. One of the most prominent of these was in the attitude toward work. For the Greek philosophers physical labor was demeaning. Aristotle's perfect man would not have had soiled or callused hands. Ideally, hard work was left to slaves. Since the Hebrews had few slaves, it is not surprising that they had a different doctrine. Social reality frequently defines religious and philosophical perspectives.

It is of more than passing significance that the Bible introduces work as a part of the creation narratives. God is first known in the work of creation, and the human being, made in the image of God, also works—the human task in Genesis was to till and keep the garden. Work is the way that we are seen to share in God's creativity. The Bible goes on from there to portray human labor as the normal condition of life. To be sure, rest on the Sabbath is equally a part of the rhythm of nature, but the idea that leisure might be an alternative life-style to work is inconceivable. Not only is idle consumption condemned (Amos 4:1-3), but prophets were frequently chosen from the ranks of ordinary people who worked for a living: Elisha, Amos, and Micah are examples. Likewise, the disciples came from the ranks of the working class, and Paul took pride in his periodic labor as a tentmaker. Even in the Incarnation, Jesus became a carpenter before he became a teacher or the Savior.

There is a high doctrine of work in the Scriptures, but there is no idolatry of it. That came later and perhaps reached its peak in the Reformation church, which sought to accommodate the needs of an emerging capitalism for a disciplined labor force at the unquestioned service of entrepreneurs. In the Zurich of 1525, Zwingli feared a relaxing in the incentive to work and thus wrote as a reminder to the populace, "Labor is a thing so good and godlike . . . that [it] makes the body hale and strong and cures the sicknesses produced by idleness. . . . In the things of this life, the laborer is most like to God."[8]

This is quite a different perspective from that of biblical faith, which sees work as having no meaning in itself. It has value only insofar as it contributes to God's purposes in creation and in community. One of the results of humankind's fall into sin was that what God intended as creative and fulfilling activity was transformed into tiresome toil. The difference must be understood not in the increased amount of work to be done after the Fall, but in the fact that what was originally to have been done for God's glory and creative purposes was turned by sin into pursuit of individual glory and gain.

Biblical faith proceeds from the notion that creation, not consumption, is the goal of work. That is not to say that adequate consumption is unimportant. Rather, it is assumed as the rightful outcome of labor, not its end. The purpose of work is to create and maintain a certain kind of world, not to "lay up for yourselves treasures on earth."

Work has meaning in the context of God's vision and God's justice.

> They shall build houses and inhabit them;
> they shall plant vineyards and eat their fruit.
> They shall not build and another inhabit;
> they shall not plant and another eat;
> for like the days of a tree shall the days of my people be,
> and my chosen shall long enjoy the work of their hands.
> (Isa. 65:21-22, RSV)

Reflecting that same spirit, liberation theologian Gustavo Gutiérrez wrote, "The work of man, the transformation of nature, continues creation only if it is a human act, that is to say, if it is not alienated by unjust socio-economic structures."[9] Work has no absolute value. Its value lies in its being a means for a person to meet his or her needs within the context of a society where labor is not deprived of its just rewards by powerful individuals or insensitive systems.

From the biblical faith perspective, work has three primary purposes. First, it is a creative outlet for human beings who are made in the image of the creative God. Human labor continues the creation. Second, work provides for the consumption needs of individuals and families—"In the sweat of your face you shall eat bread" (Gen. 3:19, RSV); "If any one will not work, let him not eat" (2 Thess. 3:10, RSV). Since life is sustained by work, not to work is to live by the sweat of someone else's brow rather than by one's own. That is unconscionable. Third, work provides for the consumption needs of the community. The passage from Isaiah just quoted captures the degree to which the biblical vision is communal rather than individual. The labors of production and the joys of adequate consumption will be experienced not in isolation but in community.

Theological convictions like these translate into economic attitudes that bring the faith community into direct conflict with many of the labor perspectives and practices of our economic system. These attitudes are spelled out in the assertions that follow.

1. Labor Is Supreme over Capital

The creation narratives proclaim, "God created man in his own image, in the image of God he created him; male and female he created them. And God blessed them, and God said to them, 'Be fruitful and multiply, and fill the earth and subdue it; and have dominion over . . . every living thing'" (Gen. 1:27-28, RSV).

This text has gotten a cold reception in the age of ecological concern. Its purpose, however, is not to say that we should regard the earth with indifference or use its resources with reckless abandon. Rather, its intent is to make clear the conviction that human nature, made in the image of God, is not to be sacrificed to any *thing* in all creation. And, as Pope John Paul II has so succinctly summarized the matter, "Everything in the concept of capital in the strict sense is only a collection of things."[10]

It becomes idolatry, then, to structure an economic system in such a way as to give absolute status to some nonhuman element. As the pope has noted, "The hierarchy of values and the profound meaning of work itself require that capital should be at the service of labor and not labor at the service of capital."[11] Specifically this means rejection of any economic system that regards labor as a commodity to be bought and sold. Such an attitude reduces humanity to the status of a mere factor of production and robs people of the full sense of participating in the creative process of production.

Recognizing the supremacy of labor also implicitly rejects a wage structure in which the returns to workers bear no relationship to the value created. This allows a disproportionate share of the returns to accrue to capital owners as profits or to consumers as falsely low prices. In either case, the true value of the people providing labor in the productive process will be understated, human dignity depreciated, and, in extreme cases, human life imperiled.

2. Full Employment Is the Only Acceptable National Labor Policy

For most people, having enough to survive and having the sense of being a contributor to life are very much tied up with employment. Living by the sweat of one's own brow is the norm. However, some people who are unable to work are unable to provide enough for themselves and their families. Societies have almost always had safety nets for these unfortunate ones. But in this country in recent years we have seen a determined effort to reduce the role of government in society and force a greater sense of individualism. Accordingly, the social safety net has been narrowed, and the ideology has been nurtured that the individual must be prepared to face economic reality alone. However one feels about the morality of such a social vision, it clearly rests upon the ability of people to find jobs that will sustain them and their families. Yet in recent years we have seen unemployment rise to the highest levels since the Great Depression. Perhaps even more significant is the ratchet effect of unemployment. Very high "temporary" levels of joblessness related to the business cycle seldom fall to their previous low when the economy recovers. (Throughout a five-year economic recovery, official unemployment has hovered near 7 percent.) We seem to be heading toward a situation where perhaps 10 percent of the labor force will be regarded as superfluous to the normal functioning of the economy.

The much-discussed productivity crisis in American manufacturing has raised entirely different questions about employment. Under the pressure of competition from Japanese productivity, American firms are beginning to discover that part of Japan's success lies in gathering groups of workers together and listening to their concerns about the workplace and their ideas about how to solve product and production problems. "Quality circles" and "participatory management" have become catch phrases in the corporate attempt to improve relations with workers while also improving output levels. It is a definite improvement to hear an executive say, "There's no longer management turf and worker turf."[12]

Thus far there has been a happy convergence of management interest in productivity and labor interest in a more participatory employment environment. Whether there has been any basic change in management's ideas about what workers can and should do remains to be seen. When the humanization of work no longer increases profitability, the moral issue will be posed more clearly.

Christian faith offers no unique technical solutions to labor issues, but it does hold up a vision of work and humanity that keeps workers from being regarded as mere resources in production. There is implicit in the concept of work as creativity the conviction that workers have a right to participate in the decisions about the way in which their labor will be rendered.

3. "Bread-and-Butter" Unionism Is Not Enough

Traditionally workers have sought to have an impact on the conditions of employment through labor unions. By the late 1950s, fully one-third of the U.S. labor force were union members, and the unions achieved for them higher salaries, better working conditions, and a more secure place in society than ever before. Along with their growing numbers and newly found position, unions also achieved increased political leverage in the two-party system.

In large measure, American unions have fulfilled the vision Samuel Gompers had for them when he organized the American Federation of Labor about a hundred years ago. When asked to define the philosophy of the AFL, he answered, "More!" European unions have often sought a role in the decision-making apparatus of companies and a voice in the national political structure through organized labor parties. They have wanted not just a better contract but a greater sense of participation in the enterprise and in the governance of society. The American labor movement has generally been content to leave the visioning and the driving of enterprise and society to others. Unions have been willing to trust the business acumen of management and the social direction of politicians as long as they could get higher wages, better benefits, and a safer work environment *for their own members.*

Such "bread-and-butter" unionism fits well with laissez-faire philosophy. It accepts the concept that an economy is best run by having each segment seek its own narrow advantage, trusting the invisible hand to meet the needs of society as a whole through the controlled conflict of these competing interests.

This philosophy of unionism continues to produce impressive benefits for its members. Union mine, steel, auto, and construction workers, for example, still have levels of benefits that are the envy of the unorganized and the unemployed. But organized workers are a shrinking portion of the labor force. Down from a high of over one-third in the 1950s, less than 20 percent of workers are now represented by a union—virtually the same proportion as in 1929. A determined Reagan administration defeated the Air Traffic Controllers Association and eliminated it as an effective union. With this as a signal to employers to resist unions, and under the pressure of a weak economy, the deregulation of several industries, and foreign competition, almost all unions have hit hard times. Instead of more lucrative agreements, "give-backs" are now negotiated with employers. Benefits hard won over decades are being deleted from contracts. Some companies are using the bankruptcy laws to break contracts with unions. The very existence of some unions is being challenged as some plants vote for decertification of union representation.

It may be that a biblical principle is being played out: "Where there is no vision, the people perish" (Prov. 29:18, KJV). But beyond the practical matter of survival, there are moral dilemmas in bread-and-butter unionism. Biblical faith does not endorse the notion of the narrow search for gain—whether by entrepreneurs or union members. Both capital and labor are to look upon the world and their part in its economy as a matter of stewardship, not as an opportunity to gain leverage and a privileged position over others.

Labor unions have been and continue to be an important mechanism by which to challenge and correct the excess and greed of laissez-faire capitalism. But the movement falters when it seeks only "more" for its members without seeking also a larger transformation of society that will provide meaningful work for all, with compensation that is fair and under working conditions that are humane. To have such things for the 20 percent of the labor force who are members of unions is not enough. Morality requires a larger vision.

Notes

1. Smith, *The Wealth of Nations* (New York: Modern Library, 1937), pp. 4-5.
2. Galbraith, *The New Industrial State* (New York: Houghton Mifflin, 1967), p. 73.
3. *The State of Black America 1984*, National Urban League, Inc., 19 Jan. 1984, p. 5.
4. James S. Henry, "Lazy, Young, Female and Black: The New Conservative Theories of Unemployment," *Working Papers*, May 1978, p. 58.
5. Lester C. Thurow, *The Zero-Sum Society: Distribution and the Possibilities for Economic Change* (New York: Basic Books, 1980), p. 187.
6. "Women Workers," *Economic Notes*, Feb. 1982, Labor Research Association, Inc., p. 4; and *Work and Family in the United States: A Policy Initiative* (New York: United Nations Association, 1985), p. 48.
7. "Women Workers," p. 7.
8. Zwingli, quoted by R. H. Tawney in *Religion and the Rise of Capitalism* (1926; New York: Mentor Books, 1947), p. 101.
9. Gutiérrez, *A Theology of Liberation*, trans. Inda Caridad, Sr., and John Eagleson (Maryknoll, N.Y.: Orbis Books, 1971), p. 173.
10. *On Human Work*, Encyclical Letter (Boston: St. Paul Editions, 1981), p. 31.
11. *On Human Work*, p. 31.
12. *Business Week*, 11 May 1981, p. 86.

Chapter Four

Big Business and the Transformation of Capitalism

Until about a century ago, the economic history of an age could be written essentially as a series of biographies of wealthy and powerful individuals who owned and headed large family firms. During the last hundred years, however, corporations have dominated the business world and transformed capitalism. How that happened and what it means for economic theory and practice are important elements in our inquiry.

I. Concepts: Imperfect Competition in an Imperfect World

Adam Smith's perspective on economic reality was that we should not try to do good but let good emerge as the by-product of selfishness. He was convinced that through the endless competition among individuals pursuing personal gain, the greatest good would result.

Of course, the invisible hand of the market would work its miracle only under the conditions of perfect competition—in an idealized world where firms have no control over prices, where the products produced by competitors are identical, where all firms have equal knowledge, where there are no barriers to entering the market, no labor unions, no collusion among competitors, and no government intervention.

While the mythology of contemporary economics continues to pay homage to these precepts of classical theory, it is clear that we do not live in such a world of pure competition. Instead, ours is a world of *imperfect competition,* an economy where firms make the same or similar products and compete with one another for customers, but in ways that Adam Smith would hardly recognize.

A. From Entrepreneurs to Corporations

The key to the unfolding economic life that Adam Smith observed and described in the last half of the eighteenth century was the entrepreneurial firm. Typically it was a business owned by one individual who more than likely opened the shop in the morning and closed it at night. In the meantime, he oversaw the work and probably did some of it himself. The distinction between owner, manager, and worker would have seemed strange and inefficient to these small entrepreneurs.

Size at first was limited by technology: it was difficult to make large quantities of goods when production rested on vast amounts of human labor. Even more important in determining factory size was the small market available. Shipping goods long distances by wagon over rutted roads was neither easy nor reliable, and very expensive. Thus local producers could charge less than distant competitors who had to transport goods to the area.

Two things dramatically transformed this tight little world of semi-isolated markets. First, with new technologies, craft production gave way to mass production. *Economies of scale* became possible. By using fewer people and more machines, manufacturers were able to reduce the unit cost of each item produced. This was a double blessing in a labor-short economy like nineteenth-century America. But the full advantage of such volume production depended on having a market large enough in which to sell all that could be produced. And this points to the second factor that made big business possible: mass transportation emerged to match the economic opportunity created by mass production. First canals and then railroads linked more parts of the country in a production-consumption network. For the first time, firms were able to think and plan for a market that stretched from coast to coast and included all the people of the nation.

But these advances created a crisis for entrepreneurs. As the scale of business grew, the huge amounts of money required for modern machinery and railroads outran the resources of even the wealthiest individuals.

Partnerships of entrepreneurs provided an alternative, but they had their drawbacks. Partnerships were not very efficient in managing rapid growth; massive fixed investments require a long-term commitment, yet partners were always free to withdraw and take their share with them. Each time a new partner was added, or one died or withdrew, the partnership had to be dissolved and reconstituted. Since major decisions required unanimity among partners, the least venturesome had veto power. But the most critical characteristic of partnerships was that each partner was financially liable for the actions of the firm to the full extent of his or her personal fortune. If sued, the individual could lose everything.

The business corporation emerged to meet these concerns, and within the past century it has become the chief way of organizing a large business enterprise. Conceptually, corporations were not new. For centuries monarchs and legislators had granted charters to groups of investors to engage in businesses that were in the government's interest as well as in the interest of private profit. The great trading enterprises like the East India Company are the best examples. What was new in the nineteenth century is that the royal privilege to so band together became the right of any group wanting to pool their money to engage in business.

Legally, the *corporation* is a fictitious person. It is immortal—unless dissolved. It exists independently of the investors who own it; it survives their entry and their withdrawal and even their death. It can enter into contracts, incur debt, and claim most of the rights accorded to the individual in society, regardless of who chairs the board or manages the operation. The corporation provides a unique and efficient method of accumulating capital. It makes ownership of the firm available in small units, or shares. Investors can buy one share or a million shares, depending on how much money they have. Investors do not have to risk their whole fortune in one enterprise; they can be partial owners of many corporations in many business fields. Finally, the investor has only a limited liability for the actions of the firm. Financial loss cannot exceed the value of the shares he or she owns. Thus the investor's personal fortune invested elsewhere is safe even if the corporation goes bankrupt.

Since the large corporations began to dominate the economic scene a hundred years ago, people have regularly wondered if bigness may also be badness. Moral judgments aside, it is clear that large corporations have radically transformed market structures and concepts. The system is still capitalist but in a sense different from the entrepreneurial capitalism of classical economic theory.

With this move from partnerships to corporations, there was still competition, but the dynamics were different. As several aggressive producers in an industry installed the most productive equipment, abundance became superabundance, often more than the market could absorb. Under the old craft-type production system, which depended primarily on human labor, a temporary glut could be dealt with by slowing production and laying off workers until they were needed again. The price of the goods produced was little affected. In the new age of mass production, however, businesses faced a greater problem. Machines cannot be laid off. They can be turned off, but the owner must continue to pay the interest on the loan with which they were purchased. Cutting production means using a machine capable of producing six thousand items an hour to produce three thousand items, which effectively raises the unit price. These *fixed costs* of machinery made steady revenues necessary. To assure a steady stream of revenue, one competitor might lower prices to lure customers away from another competitor. Predictably, the other competitor who was in the same situation would reduce prices still further. While such cutthroat competition greatly benefited the consumer, it threatened to make a shambles of whole industries.

B. The Classical Model Outgrown

Not surprisingly, businesses began to search for ways to avoid competition. *Cartels* were formed by rival firms that agreed to set prices and production quotas. Far more effective were the *trusts* established in many industries at the end of the nineteenth century. Stockholders of competing companies placed their shares of stock in the hands of a board of directors in exchange for a similar percentage share of the new trust company. The individual firms continued to function under their own names, but for all intents and purposes they were run as a single enterprise—with no competition. Trusts and cartels were the first inkling of *imperfect competition.*

The threat of *monopoly*—the domination of a market by a single producer—was initially avoided by antitrust legislation passed around the turn of the century. These laws, however, have not checked the growth of business. Of the fourteen million businesses in the United States, there are only two million corporations. But these two million take in almost six times as much money as the other twelve million enterprises. At the very top are the Fortune 500, the largest industrial corporations that own about one-third of all this country's productive assets, make two-thirds of all industrial sales, and chalk up three-fourths of the profits.

The size of Fortune 500 corporations inspires awe. The total sales of the sixteen largest U.S. industrial firms are greater than the total income of the forty poorest countries that are home to over half the world's population. In a sales-to-national-income comparison, Exxon is larger than Indonesia, Ford greater than Egypt, and IBM more important than Portugal.

While such comparisons are crude, they do give some sense of the great power these entities have. How did they become so large?

Most of today's giant corporations began by achieving some breakthrough in the production process (e.g., Ford Motor Company and the assembly-line technique) or by getting in on the ground floor of some emerging technology or product line (e.g., IBM and computers). They grew with expanding markets, often crushing their rivals ruthlessly. As this initial advantage eroded, many of these giants acquired or merged with rival companies to secure their powerful place in the market.

Indeed, many of today's huge corporations did not *grow large;* they *became large* through *merger*—combining into one company two or more previously independent firms. This is another concept important for understanding imperfect competition, because the merger of competitors is anticompetitive.

There have been three rather distinct periods of great merger activity in this century.[1] Generally, they have been associated with business cycles, so that when times have been good, there have been a lot of mergers, and when times have been bad, there have been fewer, today's wave being a possible exception.

The first merger wave came at the turn of the century. Standard Oil used the merger route to become the world's largest corporation, and United States Steel drew eleven firms together to become the second largest. A second great merger wave occurred in the 1920s. Between 1897 and 1902 there were 2,684 mergers; by contrast, from 1925 to 1930, 4,682 mergers were recorded. More often than not, these simply strengthened the dominant position of firms already made large earlier in the century. The one new field in which giants were created was the food industry. The Borden Company, General Foods, General Mills, Beatrice, and others emerged as food-processing giants in the 1920s.

These first two merger movements reshaped the structure of American business. According to professor Willard Mueller,

> The first two merger movements established the main contours of many industries as they are known today. In the main, the same "big three" or "big four" companies still occupy the top positions in such basic industries as steel, automobiles, petroleum, tires, and copper, as they did when the second merger movement was choked off by the Great Depression.
>
> Fully seventy-five of the one hundred largest industrial corporations of 1929 owe most of [their] relative size to mergers. Most of these companies, excepting those which themselves were subsequently acquired, are still among the top enterprises today.[2]

These movements were driven by firms' desire for both *horizontal integration* and *vertical integration.* To integrate horizontally, the firm extends its main business activity to another area or geographic market. For instance, a tire company might build a new tire plant or buy out a competitor nearer an automobile factory. To integrate vertically, a firm seeks increased control over its productive process. Thus a steel company might "integrate backward" by buying a coal company to assure a stable source of a key raw material. Or a bakery might "integrate forward" and acquire a trucking firm to guarantee its ability to deliver fresh goods to retail outlets.

The third merger movement occurred in the 1960s and was characterized by *conglomerate* expansion. Firms did not so much attempt to enlarge the market share of their traditional products or to control their productive processes. Rather, they sought to bring diverse manufacturing and service companies under one corporate banner. Consider the case of ITT. For over fifty years the firm functioned as the owner and operator of telephone companies outside the United States. By 1961 ITT had become the thirty-fourth largest U.S. industrial corporation. Not big enough, thought its new chairman, Harold Geneen. Consequently, over the following decade, ITT acquired 140 firms in various businesses and countries with a total value of $10 billion. It jumped from thirty-fourth to ninth on the Fortune 500 list and became the world's third-largest employer with nearly half a million workers. In its 67-country conglomerate collage, ITT at its height owned or controlled hundreds of companies in dozens of product areas selling under scores of brand names. In the transcripts of hearings before the United States House of Representatives in 1969, it took nine full pages simply to list the firms controlled by ITT.

The primary justifications for conglomerate acquisition are financial. One company's business losses can become another's tax shelter. Even more important, many firms are acquired because they have large assets and few debts. Their financial situation makes it possible for a management bent upon growth to use the borrowing capacity of such firms to buy still other companies. Growth thus becomes an end in itself. Finally, not all the eggs are in one basket, making the overall investment more secure.

Conglomerate pyramiding represents a marked shift in business philosophy. In the classical model, the entrepreneur identified an unmet demand and set out to render the product or service required as efficiently as possible. The product was the goal of the business, and it was assumed that a profit would be made in the process. Conglomerate organization inverts the formula. It assumes that the true product of enterprise is profit, not goods or services. It is oriented toward financial manipulations and the logic of accounting rather than toward the logic of production. Many of the dilemmas of American business and thus of the American economy can be traced to this shift. The situation is not likely to improve until the production and operations people wrest control of corporations from accountants, lawyers, and financial wizards.

The conglomerate merger movement subsided during most of the economically troubled 1970s. Now a fourth major merger movement is underway, largely because of the strongly pro-business policies of the Reagan administration. The Justice Department has given clear signals that there will be minimal antitrust enforcement, and that by and large the market will be allowed to determine what is necessary and efficient. The result has been a dramatic increase in mergers. Those in 1981 virtually doubled the value of those in 1980. By 1983 there were 2,533 mergers recorded, with a total value of $73.1 billion, and banks either extended or earmarked over $50 billion in credits for such mergers in just the first quarter of 1984.[3]

Unlike the conglomerate mergers of the 1960s, the present merger movement seems to be characterized by horizontal and vertical integration, as the earlier movements were.

The companies involved are some of the nation's largest. Texaco, the fourth-largest U.S. industrial company, bought Getty Oil, the twenty-sixth largest. Standard Oil of California, the fifth largest, merged with Gulf Oil, the seventh largest, to become the second-largest petroleum company and the third-largest industrial firm in America. Merger activity has begun to spread into other areas as well—computers, financial institutions, railroads, steel companies, and broadcasting.

C. Should We Worry about Size?

Does it really matter if corporations grow larger? Adam Smith thought so. He and most other economists since have worried greatly that large firms may become monopolies that would disrupt the supposed benefits of a perfectly competitive market. The last fifty years, however, have produced a voluminous body of economic literature that indicates that free markets and monopolies are not the only alternatives. For instance, in an *oligopoly,* a few producers or sellers dominate a market and because of their size and position are able to influence the price of their inputs, the price of their product, or both.

The merger movements have led not only to larger firms but also to more concentrated markets—that is, to markets where a few firms have a large percentage of the sales. In 1909, after the first wave of mergers was completed, the largest 100 industrial corporations controlled less than 18 percent of all industrial assets. By 1971 the top 100 firms held 49 percent of the assets. Economic studies suggest that when the top four firms make less than 40 percent of the sales of a given product, vigorous competition is maintained, but above that level of concentration, competition lessens. Fully one-third of the sales of manufactured goods in the United States are made in product lines where four firms or fewer make over half of the sales. Economists worry that the increasing size of companies and the increasing concentration of markets will diminish competition.

Oligopolists, for example, need not conspire to fix prices. Most industries have a dominant firm that acts as *price leader*. That firm establishes a price in the market, and others follow suit without meeting to set prices. The price leader must be careful to set the price at a level that allows for what would be an acceptable profit margin in the industry, even for the less efficient major producers. Those who produce efficiently, then, will have even greater return on their investment.

Of course, oligopolists are not free to charge whatever price they choose or even what the traffic will bear in the short run. If the price is too high, customers might change their consumption habits—eat eggs for breakfast instead of cereal. If profit margins are too high, new producers might come into the market, destabilize the industry, and reduce profits to all. Nonetheless, oligopolies remain a problem. Consumers are hurt by higher prices: fewer people can buy the good produced by the oligopoly because production is restricted. Society is hurt because there is misallocation of resources caused by inefficient firms remaining in the industry, and because costs are not driven down to their minimum.

D. What—if Anything—Should Be Done?

Both economists and policymakers disagree about what should be done regarding the growth of corporations and the concentration of markets. Some insist that greater government involvement will only make matters worse. Such people are convinced that trusts and cartels are self-destructive and that eventually competition will return to even the most distorted markets.

In theory they may be right. The problem, in the words of John Maynard Keynes, is that "in the long run we are all dead." The fact that price-rigging or market manipulation ends in one product line or industry does not mean that it will not be repeated in another. Nor does the fact that such an arrangement finally breaks down under the pressure of market forces reduce the financial loss of those who have been victimized, sometimes over a very long period of time.

A second approach to the issue of market concentration is to increase the use of antitrust legislation and enforcement mechanisms. The chief problem is that litigation is so costly and time consuming. Cases can drag on for years, giving a great advantage to large corporations. They can often outwait and outspend smaller rivals and even the government. Consider the implications of one well-known court case. In 1974 a private monopoly suit was brought by Control Data Corporation against IBM. IBM finally settled out of court and agreed to reimburse Control Data $15 million for legal fees in addition to the much larger settlement figure. At that time $15 million was more than the total annual budget of the Antitrust Division of the Justice Department. That was just one of dozens of cases the government might have taken to court if it had had the resources.

A third alternative would involve a different and larger role for government in the economy. This is a topic that will be considered in greater detail in the final chapter. Here it is sufficient to say that many economists doubt that competition is an absolute good and that it leads to the most rational, efficient, and humane economy.

Competition is an efficient and useful mechanism in many sectors of the economy; history has proved it so. The dilemma we face is whether the U.S. economy, in the closing years of the twentieth century, will respond best to the attempt to widen the competitive arena. Certainly the reviews on the deregulation of certain industries are mixed at best. Cutthroat competition has driven airfares down on the high-density routes between major cities, but service has been drastically reduced and prices have been increased in many secondary markets. The breakup of AT&T has created competition and at least temporarily lowered rates for long-distance calls but has resulted in higher rates for local service. Bank deregulation has multiplied services and perhaps has helped to reduce interest rates, but some claim that it has increased a kind of risk-taking that tends to destabilize the global financial structure.

While competition has been championed in recent years as never before, so too has it been questioned more deeply. Thus it may be that government-controlled monopolies and oligopolies will receive more favorable attention than they have in the recent past.

II. Realities: Transnational Corporations and Less Developed Countries

Most large corporations long ago overflowed the bounds of the nation that was their first home. National borders have become one of the irrationalities that big business feels it must overcome. Some argue that the transnational enterprise has embarked upon the first serious attempt to rationalize the world economy, to integrate it into a single, functioning unit that responds to the vision and logic of enterprise.[4]

One of the most serious consequences of this effort is that a system of production and distribution designed by and for the economically advanced nations is being transferred virtually intact to so-called less developed countries. The fact that this system is administered to a large extent by foreign interests has deep social and political as well as economic impacts on less developed nations.

A. The Economic Impact

In the years since World War II, we have been beguiled by the hope of rapid economic expansion as the primary way to help the poor of the earth. Since the un-poor live predominantly in the highly industrialized Western nations, the industrial mode of production and pattern of life have been accepted and promoted by academic experts, international bankers, government planners, and commercial interests as the only relevant model for economic development. The problem of development has been confined to asking one question: How is such modernization and industrialization to be implemented? Our country has seen private enterprise as the chief tool of economic development. For over a decade, various U.S. government administrations have stressed to the developing world that it must depend on private loans and investments, not on official aid, for its capital needs. In today's global setting that means reliance on the transnational corporation (TNC).

1. The Capital Flow

It is commonly assumed that when U.S. companies invest abroad, they infuse vast amounts of new funds into less developed countries. That is not normally the firm's intention. Since most Third World investment is deemed a high risk, the company ordinarily tries to bring in as little capital as necessary and to rely as much as possible on local sources of funds—basically retained earnings, depreciation accounts,* and local borrowings. In 1982, for example, retained earnings alone accounted for 60 percent of the total increased equity of U.S. firms in their affiliates in less developed countries. Such data lead many critics to conclude that Third World people are bankrolling their own underdevelopment.

The problem is not just that capital fails to flow in through the corporate conduit; it actually flows out. Between 1950 and 1965, for instance, U.S. firms put $3.8 billion into Latin America. But in the same period $11.3 billion was taken out in profits, royalties, dividends, and

---

**Retained earnings* represent profits not paid out to investors but reinvested by the firm. *Depreciation accounts* record funds accumulated for the replacement of plants and equipment. But since the productive life of such items may be much longer than the somewhat arbitrary depreciation period declared, the earmarked funds may be available for other investment for a considerable period.

service fees.[5] Thus the poor nations of Latin America made a net contribution of $7.5 billion to the wealth, comfort, and continued development of the United States. A 1975 study by Nobel prize-winning economist Wassily Leontief showed net capital outflow from less developed countries through multinational corporations to be $5.3 billion in one year. More recent data for U.S. companies indicate that in 1982 they received a net capital inflow of $3.7 billion from their Third World affiliates.[6]

The important thing to note is that what is true in the aggregate is the ultimate goal of every corporation. The goal of each firm is to risk as little as possible while setting up a permanent stream of profits for the shareholders back home. If the business is successful, the "take-out" will always be greater than the "in-put," and the more successful the business, the greater the differential.

It should be stressed that there is nothing illegal about this process. In addition, there is no malevolent intent. It is simply good business. Nevertheless, it is hard to escape the conviction that it is morally repugnant. One is reminded of the parable Nathan told David about the rich man who had large flocks and herds of his own but who, when a visitor came, chose to take the only lamb of the poor man—a family pet—to prepare for the feast. That the corporate powers of rich nations should appropriate for themselves the limited financial resources of poor nations is only the same social tendency raised to a new level. And it is one that has been condemned by three thousand years of biblical tradition.

In summary, we find that global companies, instead of making a major capital contribution to less developed countries, actually create a long-term capital outflow, compete with national interests for limited financial resources, and tend to denationalize the economy. It is hard to judge those as positive contributions.

2. The Employment Perspective

Unfortunately, not all economic effects can be conveniently measured in cash flow. The less developed country, in a situation where 30 percent of the its force is unemployed, has looked upon the foreign corporation that comes promising to create new jobs as something of a savior. While such firms have indeed created some employment, their long-run impact may very well be negative. How can that be? Quite simply because the global corporation is a marvelous misfit in the Third World. It is capable of doing great things, but all too often they are the wrong things, and they are done in the wrong way in light of the needs and resources of less developed nations.

Virtually all of the techniques and equipment used by such corporations were developed in advanced industrial societies, where capital is abundant and labor is scarce and expensive. Quite naturally, this leads to a form of production that substitutes machines for people wherever possible. The situation in less developed countries is the opposite. Labor is the abundant and cheap factor. This should lead to forms of production that use many people and few machines. Unfortunately, that is seldom the result. American managers have not generally been trained in the use of labor-intensive systems, and even if they had been, they would still normally opt for the capital-intensive systems because the companies they represent own those technologies and there is no additional cost for using them. Furthermore, machines do not go on strike, demand wage increases, or carry away company technology. They simply are less troublesome than people.

The employment problem would be bad enough if only foreign companies employed such techniques. But national companies using labor-intensive methods cannot compete against foreign firms using the latest machinery. As a result, the national enterprises invest in mechanization also, and more jobs are lost.

The corporation that plans and seeks to maximize its profits at a global level simply cannot be concerned about its secondary impact on the people and institutions of any one country in which it operates. Even when those who manage the enterprise wish that it were possible, it is not.

B. The Social Impact

Following from the obvious economic impact of transnational corporations on Third World nations are social impacts that touch the lives of millions.

1. The Manufacturing of Need

It would not be too much to say that the chief product of modern corporations is not chemicals, automobiles, energy, food, entertainment, or any of the thousands of other goods and services that they make and market. Rather, desire itself is. The manufacturing of perceived need is the goal. According to sociologist Erich Fromm,

> Twentieth century industrialization has created [a] new psychological type, *homo consumens,* primarily for economic reasons, *i.e.*, the need for mass consumption which is stimulated and manipulated by advertising. But the character type, once created, also influences the economy and makes the principles of ever-increasing satisfaction appear rational and

> realistic. Contemporary man, thus, has an unlimited hunger for more and more consumption.[7]

To date, this new person for the new age has been confined largely to the few industrially advanced countries. The goal of TNCs, however, is to establish "homo consumens" throughout the world.

For all intents and purposes, development has meant becoming—consciously or unconsciously—like Japan or West Germany or the United States. But it has become increasingly obvious that neither the physical resources nor the economic mechanisms exist to make possible such imitation by a hundred other countries of the world. Yet that is precisely the goal of corporate investment in the Third World. As one business analyst has put it, "Every individual [in Latin America] whose productivity can be raised above the subsistence level is a potential customer, and every person with a peso in his pocket after providing for minimum living needs can, with others of his kind, broaden the markets for American goods."[8]

The important thing to note is that the corporate approach to the poor of the world is not to attempt to determine their peculiar needs and find ways of meeting them but rather to promote its present line of goods, whatever that may be. It is no accident that almost all of the major American advertising firms have followed their clients abroad. Consequently, the mass media in less developed countries have taken on an American look—especially television. Commercials are liberally sprinkled among the programs, which themselves are predominantly American-made. The program content as well as the advertisements serve to sell not only a given product but the very concept of consumerism itself. Not too subtly the message is communicated that a modern society looks like "Dallas" or "Miami Vice" and the value of an individual is measured by the products purchased.

Christian faith has always been concerned about the images of humanity because of the conviction that we are made in the image of God. When investment goals set out to transform the image of personhood and thus the values of a society, it is no mere commercial matter. It is a theological concern.

The commitment of TNCs to the consumption ethic is felt at the societal as well as the individual level. A nationally based market economy must achieve a delicate long-run balance between two interdependent factors. On the one hand, it must achieve savings out of income sufficient for investment needs. On the other hand, it must create a demand for products that is large enough to attract investment. When there is a premature shift of underdeveloped economies toward conspicuous consumption, such as is promoted by most TNCs, people spend more and save less. The constant pressure of sophisticated advertising calling forth ever greater levels of consumption undermines attempts by the government to take the short-run austerity measures necessary for economic growth and the long-term well-being of the people.

It is not only the amount of consumption encouraged by the private sector that has social impact. The manner of consumption is equally important. The implicit goal is for every individual to have at least one of everything. This highly privatistic model of consumption is fostered by business even where the public welfare might be better served by an emphasis on shared facilities. Ivan Illich, a priest and an astute observer of Third World development, used to point out in lectures that every car that Brazil puts on the road denies fifty people good transportation by bus. Each merchandised refrigerator reduces the chance of producing a community freezer. While General Motors can build buses as well as automobiles, and General Electric can manufacture commercial freezers as well as home refrigerators, it is potentially more profitable to develop a mass privatistic market.

In a world where the concept of community must be promoted if we are to survive, and especially in poor nations, where the concept of sharing more equitably must dominate if there is to be progress for all the people and not just for the few, the corporate vision of privatistic consumption at ever higher levels must be combatted, not embraced.

2. The Problem of Distribution

Of course, that private investment does not readily lend itself to equitable sharing of the benefits should not surprise us. By intent as well as by nature, a corporation is non-egalitarian. This is so because the enterprise seeks to maximize profits. Since profit is what goes to investors, the basic principle of corporate enterprise is to minimize the distribution of economic benefits to its associates—suppliers, workers, and consumers—so that maximum returns may be attained by capital owners.

It would be foolish to think that corporations, either global or national, want or need vast numbers of poverty-stricken people. Quite the contrary. In the ideal situation, everyone would have an income large enough to engage in conspicuous consumption. Since that is not possible, however, survival of the system requires that wealth not be so widely distributed as to preclude the existence of a market for industrially produced consumer goods. Thus big business has a structural bias toward the inequitable distribution of income and cannot be counted upon to promote economic democracy in the Third World—or anywhere else, for that matter.

C. The Political Impact

The basic decisions about a nation's economy are political in character. Little wonder, then, that less developed countries are almost as concerned about the political impact of foreign companies as they are about their economic and social impacts.

Size itself can be an important factor. When a government official is dealing with a corporation whose global sales exceed the country's gross national product, the local manager is apt to receive roughly the same courteous attention as the ambassador from another nation, especially if the company is thinking about increasing its investments. Some large firms have grown easily accustomed to dealing at the very highest levels.

Not all political influence, however, comes through the power of reasoned conversation. Bribery and illegal political contributions are commonplace. In 1974, in order to receive immunity from prosecution, 175 U.S. firms admitted to paying some $300 million in foreign bribes and illegal "political contributions"—the genteel phrase for bribery of political figures for undisclosed future considerations. Some bribes are culturally required—the axle grease that minimizes bureaucratic friction. Others are not.

Consider, for instance, the case of United Brands in Honduras. Under new management, the old United Fruit Company was cultivating a new image as the prototype of the responsible foreign investor. It not only provided jobs and paid its taxes but also built roads and schools to aid national development. Suddenly the company was caught having paid one and one-quarter million dollars as a bribe to a government official, probably the president. Why? Not to avoid expropriation or harassment, but to escape a tax increase of twenty-five cents on every forty-pound box of bananas exported. That was good business for United Brands, since it saved them $7.5 million in the first year alone, likely far more than the company anticipated spending on roads or schools. Here again, a nation paid for its own underdevelopment.

Honduras is just one country and United Brands only one firm. If this were a mere aberration of the sytem, one might lament the incident and pass on. But even defenders of the corporate system acknowledge that such political influence is so widespread and integral a part of the transnational system that, while they deplore the practice, they see no way of stopping it.

Indeed, political influence in less developed countries is not always exercised directly by the corporations themselves, but is often brokered through general policies of the home-country government—in our case, the U.S. Embassy. The relation between public and private interests grows more and more ill-defined when one leaves the United States: aid policies have functioned as subsidies to U.S. business interests, the commercial section of the Embassy serves as a mediator between corporate investment interests and opportunities in the host country, and the political section helps to keep track of events that might prove harmful or helpful to our corporations. There is the implicit assumption that what is good for the Fortune 500 is good for America—whether or not it is good for the rest of the world.

Transnational firms did not create the poverty, class structure, and political corruption characteristic of so many Third World nations. However, such enterprises have often used these realities to their own advantage and in the process have frequently made social, economic, and political change more difficult.

A more positive role in Third World development will not result from allowing multinational corporations to follow their own internal logic, which consciously or unconsciously seeks to make a world suited to itself. The great technological and financial potential of these global entities will be bent to the fullest human benefit only when they can be made more truly accountable to society as a whole. Creating the mechanisms of such international social accountability constitutes one of the chief economic tasks for the remainder of this century.

Such a task is not only political and economic in character. It is a veritable spiritual quest. Implicit in it is the need to put into the language of law and the structures of international relationships a higher vision of the meaning of human worth and the shape of an economically just world.

III. Values: Social Accountability as a Moral Issue

The issue of the social accountability of economic power, both at home and abroad, has always been a matter of concern to the church, but it has been especially important in the past fifty or sixty years. Without debating further the somewhat questionable details of the Weber-Tawney hypothesis concerning the religious roots of capitalism, it is nevertheless fair to say that Calvin gave a heartier endorsement to the principles of private property and economic accumulation than did other Reformers. He did not, however, share Adam Smith's faith in the invisible hand of the market. Instead, he endorsed clear precepts of moral responsibility in economic life. Church historian Ernst Troeltsch offers this summary of the economic ethic flowing from Reformed thought:

> Profit is the sign of the blessing of God on the faithful exercise of one's calling. But labour and profit were never intended for purely personal interest. The capitalist is always a steward of the Gifts of God, whose duty it is to increase his capital and utilize it for the good of society as a whole, retaining for himself only that amount which is necessary to provide for his own needs. . . . All surplus wealth should be used for work of public utility.[9]

A. *Individual Responsibility*

The principle is clear: individual piety must motivate social responsibility. This has generally been accepted by the church as the first line of defense against the abuse of economic power.

The principle was translated into a yet more personal theology by John D. Rockefeller, the founder of the world's largest corporation: "I believe the power to make money is a gift from God . . . to be developed for the good of mankind. Having been endowed with the gift I possess, I believe it is my duty to make money and still more money and to use the money I make for the good of my fellow men *according to the dictates of my own conscience*"[10] (emphasis added).

Nothing could express more clearly the atomistic conception of society that lies at the heart of the market sytem. There is a fallacious assumption that a social decision is a mere collating of individual preferences. Economic responsibility is seen as being coterminous with individual philanthropy, and social responsibility a voluntary act defined by the individual conscience.

Rockefeller did not object to the principle that economic power has an ultimate social responsibility before God. What he staunchly defended was the right of each individual to determine the nature of that responsibility by a process of internal reflection alone. He believed that no other individual, organization, or social institution is competent to interpret what conscience requires in a given historical circumstance.

Biblical faith, of course, has never embraced such hyperindividualism. The gospel of grace was never the disavowal of the role of law in social relations. The voice of the prophet regularly challenged the self-serving actions of even the most powerful or well-intentioned individuals. The concept of "the people of God" created the social framework whereby the individual was to find highest fulfillment in community, not in endless private accumulation.

The fact that such principles have always lain at the heart of Christian faith means that we have never placed much hope in the voluntary restraint of economic power as the key to social responsibility.

B. Managerial Intervention

Any lingering hopes that such an approach might be sufficient was shattered by the advent of the modern corporation. Where ownership is highly diffused or changes significantly from one day to the next, as is the case with publicly held corporations, or where it may be hidden in a legal labyrinth, it becomes almost impossible to appeal to the moral sensitivities of those who technically have the ability to correct the abuses of corporate power.

John Kenneth Galbraith has fostered the notion that in the modern corporation the key actor is not the stockholder but the manager, who determines the function of business structures in modern society through control over day-to-day operations. The annual meeting of shareholders serves as little more than the perfunctory approval of all but gross mismanagement. In corporations so large that even 1 percent of the shares may amount to millions of dollars, most individual "owners" exercise no control beyond deciding whether to buy or sell shares. Managers represent the basic force of continuity. The theory is that the owners elect the board of directors, and the board appoints the management. The reality is that the management effectively appoints the board members, and the owners are never heard from except when they mail in their proxy cards.

Even before Galbraith popularized this view, churches had already realized that if individual social responsibility was to have significance in the modern business structure, it would have to be through managerial intervention rather than through the initiative of owners. Thirty years ago there was a large volume of literature in both commerce and church journals about business ethics. Generally it dealt either with the question of how the morally sensitive individual was to handle the ethically questionable demand made by the enterprise, or with the question of how moral integrity might be profitably institutionalized in the organization.

The strategy closely paralleled that of achieving social transformation through evangelism. The underlying assumption was that corporations performed poorly in the social sphere because of a lack of moral fiber or social conscience in individual managers. Convince enough decision-makers to put ethical principles first, and the social impact of the enterprise would change under the weight of their influence. Thus the key to corporate social responsibility was thought to lie in morally sound and socially sensitive individuals impressing their value system upon their corporation.

Revelations about corporate bribery, illegal contributions, political tinkering, and tax evasion seem only to confirm that seeking corporate responsibility based on this model has produced marginal results at best. Its failure is due to three false premises.

First, it assumes that there are actually large numbers of people in upper management who want to change the present system. In a sense, Galbraith is responsible for this misconception. His notion that there is a broad gap between the profit-maximizing interests of stockholders and the career interests of managers is a vast oversimplification. In the modern corporation, the total income of senior managers may depend more on stock options than on paychecks, more on dividends and capital gains than on salary figures. Without achieving multimillionaire status or anything resembling controlling interest in a major corporation, managers nevertheless find their personal interests so closely tied to the short-run profit-maximizing expectation of ownership that they are little motivated to undertake the costs and risks of channeling corporate energies increasingly toward social benefits.

While Christian faith always calls us to self-sacrifice as a principle of responsibility in the achievement of social justice, there is little reason to believe that it will be more effective in the structures of modern enterprise than it has been in the past two hundred years of social history.

The second false premise of the individualistic approach to corporate responsibility is the notion that managers who intervene unilaterally to address social concerns will long survive the attempt. As Richard Barnet so aptly put it, "Corporation presidents who run their corporations like foundations are likely to end up in one—if they are lucky."[11] Both the corporate responsibility literature and the counseling sessions of pastors are filled with stories of managers who opted for new jobs rather than make ethical compromises, or who were pushed out of their organizational structure when they persisted in attempting to make corporate activity fit the mold of their personal morality.

A particularly poignant example is the case of Eli Black, who headed the United Fruit Company, discussed earlier in this chapter. In 1970 he took control of this firm, long recognized as among the worst examples of international exploitation and corruption. Black dedicated himself to changing that image. He personally negotiated the first settlement by a major lettuce producer with Cesar Chavez's United Farm Workers. In Honduras and elsewhere the company began supplying free housing and electricity for its employees and paid up to five times the wages of other companies. Within two years, a major newspaper was able to declare that United Brands "may be the most socially conscious American company in the hemisphere."[12]

It seemed a triumph of human concern over corporate indifference. It was a short-lived triumph, however, made possible only by good economic performance. Within two years, a Honduran hurricane destroyed much of a bumper crop of bananas. This, coupled with the deepening impact of a worldwide recession, brought the company to financial crisis. In order to improve the firm's economic picture, Eli Black did what must have been against every personal moral precept of a lifetime. He engineered the payment of a substantial bribe—one and one-quarter million dollars—to a Honduran official to avoid a large tax increase. A few months later, when the worst of the financial crisis seemed over, Eli Black threw his briefcase through the window of his forty-fourth-floor office and jumped to his death.

Eli Black was a rabbi before he became a businessman, and in the best biblical tradition, he regarded his powerful position as president of a large corporation as a social trust. To quote the *Wall Street Journal,*

> Deep down, he was always measuring himself on a different scorecard from the other fellow. . . . He felt deeply his responsibilities to his shareholders, but he also believed that business was a human operation.
>
> Eli Black's death not only raises questions about the man himself but also touches on several important questions about the business world. Can a sensitive man, a man with high moral standards, survive in an uncompromising financial world that demands steadily increasing earnings? Do the very characteristics that investors and shareholders expect from their chief executive officers lead to those officers' self-deterioration?[13]

Tellingly, it is only the question of whether individual moral sensitivity can survive in the modern profit system that the *Wall Street Journal* raises. It dismisses by silence the possibility that such an individual might be able to transform that structure permanently.

The presumed power of managerial status is ephemeral indeed. The senior manager is highly paid not to place the imprint of personal conscience upon the enterprise but to do what is necessary to maintain a steady, high rate of return. Faltering in that charge means being replaced. In such a structure, corporate social responsibility becomes an act of heroism. While moral courage is certainly to be urged upon the faithful, it is not to be counted as a reliable tool—let alone the primary one—in achieving an economically just society.

The third false premise of corporate responsibility through moral persuasion is that it is only the blindness or stubbornness of managers that stands in the way. We can accept as an axiom that corporate responsibility imposes an economic cost; otherwise, it would not be contested. If a strong manager succeeds in leading one company to social consciousness, the likely result is that the firm will be placed at a competitive disadvantage vis-à-vis other firms that do not choose to undertake works of social benefit. On the other hand, if the dominant firms in a given field agree to undertake jointly a socially conscious action, it normally is with the tacit understanding that prices will be adjusted accordingly. This can hardly be termed social responsibility. It merely means that a noncompetitive market structure allows them the privilege of cost-plus pricing, effectively permitting them to levy a tax on the consumer in order to accomplish a particular social activity. In such a scenario, corporations appropriate for themselves a quasi-governmental function while retaining the sole right to decide which social activities to undertake. The public pays for the activities but is excluded from the process of establishing priorities.

Such a system of corporate responsibility fits well in the conceptual framework of modern capitalism, but it has dangerous social implications. It assumes that people in the business sector know what is best for society, that they can be counted upon to identify needs accurately and establish proper priorities and deal with them benevolently. Theodore Levitt, one of the hard-liners of the Harvard Business School tradition, warns about looking to corporations for social guidance. He writes, "Actually, business has a notoriously bad record in gauging what society wants and believes is good. . . . Organized business has been chronically hostile to every humane and popular reform in the history of Amerian capitalism."[14]

This ought not to surprise us. The corporation is, after all, designed to serve the interests of a particular group of people—its investors. Even when well intentioned, it will view social responsibility through the prism of profit and quite naturally try to shape and serve society in such a way as to advance those interests.

C. Direct-Action Strategies

Relying on the moral persuasion of individual owners and managers to instill a sense of public responsibility in their companies has been unsuccessful by almost any measure. Seeing this, churches in recent years have turned to direct-action strategies. Most of these spring from the churches' growing awareness of the power potential of their own wealth.

American religious groups have assets of hundreds of billions of dollars, with perhaps 20 percent available for market investment.

An early goal in managing such funds was to maintain the moral purity of the church and at the same time pronounce a kind of economic anathema by selling holdings in socially offensive corporations. It became painfully obvious, however, that the whole economic structure is tainted, that to handle investment funds in today's world plunges the church into all the moral ambiguity of the market system. To buy bonds, to put the money out at interest, or even to deposit it in a bank only results in passing the moral decision to someone else; it does not maintain purity.

Accepting the reality of this classic example of situation ethics, hundreds of church bodies have determined to use the role of stockholder as a podium of moral and social concern in the corporate structure. Letters of inquiry, requests for information, open hearings, press releases, public condemnations, and stockholder resolutions are among the standard actions. It is a sobering kind of ministry in which questions to the corporation about deep human issues are often dismissed with the coldness of economic calculation or the feigned concern of a public-relations office note. The realization comes hard that there is virtually no possibility of defeating management with a stockholder resolution; garnering 3 or 4 percent of the vote must be considered a moral victory when management controls 90 percent of the votes to begin with. The hope, of course, is that the glare of public exposure will force the corporation to make changes that petitions and attempts at persuasion could not achieve.

The strategy of the corporate responsibility movement is to focus on the specific abuses and antisocial behavior of individual corporations. Will the company stop making weapons that threaten or do indiscriminate damage to civilian populations? Will it cease polluting air or water? Will it refrain from selling control equipment to repressive regimes? Is the corporation inflating its prices to Third World countries? Is it sexist in its advertising or racist in its hiring policies? Is the company exploiting foreign labor or exporting jobs from the United States? Has the firm given bribes or made political contributions here or abroad? This is little more than a random sample of issues raised in recent years with hundreds of companies. Other lists could be made—equally long, equally diverse, and equally important.

One cannot fault this approach to corporate responsibility for its serious intent. Yet while it has proved extremely valuable as a tool in raising public consciousness about the issues, there are grave problems that keep us from placing much hope in such a movement as the solution to the social contradictions of the modern corporation.

First, success depends on finding an issue with a broad enough appeal—enough shock value, enough guilt, enough emotion—to rouse public opinion. But not all issues of social importance are of that sort. Consequently, the tendency is to focus disproportionately on certain "glamour" issues and topical concerns. Moral comment is thus determined by marketing strategies.

Second, there is the problem of obtaining sufficient reliable information from the company. Since requests seldom carry legal weight and normally depend upon voluntary disclosure by the firm, there is the tendency to ask for data that might reasonably be given. This virtually eliminates any access to financial information, which is so crucial in understanding the true social effect of corporate actions, and tends to focus public attention and effort instead on matters of secondary importance.

The third problem in looking to the corporate responsibility movement too hopefully is that most such action requires an extraordinary effort to bring about the smallest change. If a large company decides to be obdurate, it generally has legal and public relations staffs large enough to wear down the most dedicated of volunteer groups.

Finally, even if the movement is successful in causing one firm to correct a specific social abuse, there may be dozens of other firms engaged in the same or worse activities. Indeed, the problems of achieving corporate accountability through voluntary compliance on a case-by-case basis seem almost insurmountable when one recalls that it means dealing with perhaps a thousand corporations about hundreds of issues in scores of countries.

It is little wonder, then, that millionaires are willing to build churches where they will be lectured on the moral responsibilities of wealth—for as long as the laws are left unchanged, their power is not threatened. Little wonder that the managerial class writes so prolifically for business journals about the way the corporation can serve and save society—for as long as their financial records remain closed to the public, their full potential for good and ill remains unknown. Little wonder that corporate officers are generally willing to carry on a running dialogue with church groups on matters of social concern—for as long as battles must be fought issue by issue and corporation by corporation, the structure of enterprise is safe from the rigors of change.

All of this points to the fact that in the context of contemporary society, corporate social responsibility must be seen not merely as a moral dilemma but primarily as an issue of law and public policy. If we are serious in our concern about the impact the global corporation has on the shape of human life and the development of nations, what we desperately need is significant change in the social role assigned to the corporation, so that social responsibility will be a matter of legal duty, not a matter left to the caprice of individual conscience or market mechanisms.

Notes

1. Historical data on merger movements in the United States are from Willard F. Mueller, *Primer on Monopoly and Competition* (New York: Random House, 1970).

2. Mueller, *Primer on Monopoly and Competition,* p. 71.

3. "Do Mega-Mergers Drive up Interest Rates?" *Business Week,* 16 Apr. 1984, p. 176.

4. Richard Barnet and Ronald Muller, *Global Reach: The Power of the Multinational Corporations* (New York: Simon & Schuster, 1974).

5. These figures were computed from Department of Commerce data.

6. United States Department of Commerce, *Survey of Current Business,* Aug. 1984, p. 19.

7. Fromm, "The Psychological Aspect of the Guaranteed Income," in *The Guaranteed Income: The Next Step in Economic Revolution,* ed. Robert Theobald (Garden City, N.Y.: Doubleday, 1966), p. 179.

8. Lucian Pye, "Communication, Institution Building, and the Reach of Authority," in *Communication and Change in the Developing Countries,* ed. Daniel Lerner and Wilbur Schramm (Honolulu: East-West Center Press, 1967), p. 42.

9. Troeltsch, *The Social Teaching of the Christian Churches,* 2 vols. (1931; New York: Macmillan, 1950), 2: 109.

10. Rockefeller, quoted in the *New York Times Book Review,* 28 Mar. 1976, p. 2.

11. Barnet, *The Crisis of the Corporation* (New York: American Management Association, 1975), p. 25.

12. "Was Eli Black's Suicide Caused by the Tensions of Conflicting Worlds?" *Wall Street Journal,* 14 Feb. 1975, p. 15.

13. "Was Eli Black's Suicide Caused by the Tensions of Conflicting Worlds?" *Wall Street Journal,* 14 Feb. 1975, p. 1.

14. Levitt, "Capitalism and the Corporation Consciousness" (paper delivered at executive seminar, Chicago, 22 Apr. 1959, Social Responsibility of Business series), p. 6.

Chapter Five

The Old-New Economics and the New-Old Economics

I. Concepts: Changing Ideas about Economics

On October 24, 1929, the world of Adam Smith cracked. In February 1933 it came to an end. The stock market collapse of 1929 and the depression that followed obliterated once-sure landmarks. The old economics (that is, the Smithian idealized world of perfect competition among small firms guided only by the invisible hand of the market) passed away in all but the rhetoric of shopkeepers and ideologues. There arose in theory and in practice a new way of thinking about economic life and of shaping it.

A. ". . . and great was the fall . . ."

The economic expansion of America went hand in hand with the rise of big business. The new large corporations proved highly successful in bringing capital and labor together in imaginative ways to exploit the nation's resources, to produce an unprecedented flow of goods, and to develop vast markets for these products. Some worried about the dangers of monopoly, and laws were passed to give at least the impression of controlling the problem, but most people were content to see the economy grow through relatively unfettered corporate activity. Calvin Coolidge captured the spirit of the age when he said, "The chief business of the American people is business." In the halcyon years of the 1920s, even the poor dared to dream of becoming rich. In that decade, corporations tripled their output and their profits. Vast fortunes were made as stock prices were bid up in anticipation of more and more growth and ever higher dividends.

And then came the Crash. There had been panics before, with rapid sell-offs and sharp drops in investment values, but never anything like this. The magnitude of the economic collapse was captured three years later in a *Saturday Evening Post* article:

> The quoted value of all stocks listed on the New York Stock Ex-

> change was, on September 1, 1929, $89,668,276,854. By July 1, 1932, the quoted value of all stocks had fallen to $15,633,479,577.
>
> Stockholders had lost $74,000,000,000. The figure is so large that not many minds can grasp it. It is $616 for every one of us in America. It is, roughly, three times what we spent fighting the World War. . . . In the bursting of the New York Stock Exchange bubble, the value of all stocks fell to 17 percent of their September 1, 1929 price. . . . Never before, in this country or anywhere else, has there been such a general loss in "security" values.[1]

The loss of investment values staggered the economy. By 1933 the nation's production was less than half what it had been in 1929. Unemployment rose to 25 percent of the labor force—with no unemployment compensation and with private charity as the primary tool in meeting pressing human need. Wages plummeted, so that those who did have jobs sometimes seemed little better off. Labor Department figures tell of wages of less than five cents an hour in textile mills, six cents in brick-making firms, and seven-and-a-half cents for construction laborers. Tens of thousands of businesses went bankrupt. Mines closed. Hundreds of banks failed, and millions lost their life savings in whole or in large part. In the end, what collapsed was not the stock market but the economy itelf.

Of course, that statement is misleading, because before the onset of the Depression there was little awareness that there was "an economy" in the sense of a consciously integrated system. People in general and economists as well, if they thought of "the economy" at all, tended to conceive of it as merely the sum of innumerable individual business transactions. Economic theory consisted almost entirely of what we today call *microeconomics,* the decisions of individual firms and households and how they interact through supply and demand to determine resource utilization, wages, prices, and the quantities of goods and services available.

B. Business Cycles

Long before the Crash of 1929, the up-and-down character of the economy had been observed. These movements have never been regular enough for exact prediction, but the pattern has been clear enough for economists to speak knowingly of the *business cycle,* in which a period of business activity or prosperity is followed by decline and then by recovery.

The business cycle does *not* refer to the predictable short-term fluctuations of the economy due to increased retail sales at Christmas or increased automobile sales in the spring or lower cash-register totals for a particularly frigid week in winter. Business cycles last longer than these short blips. How much longer depends on how cycles are defined. A study of business cycles before World War II identified seventeen major ones between 1807 and 1937, each one lasting an average of eight years. Within each were documented two minor cycles that lasted about three-and-a-half years each.[2] Thus it is common to use as a thumbnail rule the idea that expansion and recession periods last about eighteen months each, on the average. Other economists place normal business cycles into a longer time frame of fifteen to twenty-five years. Some even feel that they can identify "very long waves," with about fifty years between peaks.

Knowing that there are cycles and having some idea about their duration does not, however, tell us why they exist or how to deal with them, which are very important issues in economics. It has been suggested that there are three primary factors contributing to a boom or expansion in the economy:

1. *Growth in demand*—which can be caused by population growth, such as an 1890s-style wave of immigration or a postwar baby boom, or by increased spending without an increase in population;
2. *Introduction of new productive resources*—such as previously unused land, or a new energy supply;
3. *Change in technology*—such as silicon chips, which spilled over from computer use into other consumer applications.[3]

It is important to note that the first of these three factors begins with increased demand or consumption. The other two represent changes on the production or output or investment side of the economy. The significance of this distinction is that the economic effect of investment plays out very differently than a straight increase in consumption because of the *acceleration principle*. This important principle can be illustrated in the following way.

Suppose a widget manufacturing firm has ten machines of different ages, each worth $1 million. Each machine produces a proportionate amount of the widgets (one tenth). Suppose further that one machine wears out each year and is replaced. Thus gross capital investment each year is $1 million (the price of one machine), but net investment is zero, because the investment is offset by the worn-out machine. Now suppose that demand for widgets increases by 50 percent one year. To meet the new demand, the company must purchase not the usual one replacement machine, but five more machines (because demand is half again what it was). Now gross capital investment is $6 million—600 percent over the previous year. The 50 percent increase in consumption has been *accelerated* to a 600 percent increase in investment. If demand persists at the new level, investment in capital goods will remain at the new level. The effect on the total economy can be seen by imagining that all 100 widget producers in the country experience a similar rise in demand, and thereby require more machines. As this occurs, more goods are produced, more wages paid, more people employed, and even more goods demanded. All is well as long as growth continues.

But the acceleration principle works in reverse, too. Suppose that after five straight years, for whatever reason, growth stopped. Individuals would consume at the same rate as before but would not increase their consumption. Net investment would drop to zero. Only one machine would be purchased each year. Thus a zero percent fall in consumption would cause a 90 percent drop in gross investment. At the level of the whole economy, production would be dramatically cut, profits and wages would fall, and unemployment would increase. With less income, demand for goods would decrease, making the recession even worse, causing investment to fall even faster, so that it would be several years before any new equipment would be needed.

Of course, things are much more complicated in the real world, but the implications of this simple model are clear. The accelerated effect of investment spending tends to cause wild swings in the economy, making it unstable and leading to the rises and falls of the business cycle. Growth is the necessary ingredient for the success of the market economy. Without growth, the system in itself has no way of avoiding wild gyrations that result in periodic depression. Paul Samuelson summed it up this way:

> Additions to the stock of capital or what we customarily call *net* investment, will take place only when income is growing. As a result, a prosperity period may come to an end, not simply because sales have *leveled* off at a high level (or have continued to grow, but at a lower rate than previously). . . . The minute the system stops its fast growth, the accelerator dictates the end of high investment supporting the boom. Like an airplane that falls once it loses its motion, the economic system plummets downward.[4]

C. The Old-New Economics

Such was the downward spiral of the economy following 1929. As the Depression wore on year after year, the old economics, the classical constructs of Adam Smith and his disciples, did not seem to work anymore. The system was not correcting itself, as all the old-schoolers thought it should. They had admitted that there might be temporary malfunctions, but if left alone, the economy would straighten itself out. That was a comforting dictum for those who wanted to get on with business. By 1933, however, the vital signs of the economy and of the nation had been in a four-year decline. No correction was in sight, and optimism had vanished.

1. The New Economics in Practice

The theory and practice of economics had to be recast. The change in practice came first. When Franklin Roosevelt arrived in the White House in 1933, there was a moral and political as well as an economic disaster to face. Millions of people were suffering, and most of the nation recognized that it would be immoral to do nothing about the human tragedy. Politically the situation was explosive. Roosevelt himself had come to office on a great wave of anti-business sentiment. There had already been marches and strikes, and it could not be denied that many were attracted to Marxism. Some regarded Roosevelt as the last chance to save capitalism. The system, however, seemed bankrupt of ideas. The standard wisdom knew only one kind of advice to give to government in good times or bad: cut spending, increase taxes, and balance the budget.

Almost intuitively, public officials knew that this time the old formulas would not work. Roosevelt understood, and jettisoned traditional wisdom in favor of new, untried methods. In the first hundred days of his administration, fifteen major legislative programs were conceived, written, and passed into law. These programs radically changed the nature of government in the United States and its relation to people and to the economy. That was not the goal, but it was the result.

The immediate goal was to do something about human suffering so deep and widespread that it robbed individuals of their humanity and plunged the nation into a social stupor. The hope of recovery was all but lost. Direct relief programs were expanded, but that ran against the grain of the nation's work ethic as a long-term solution. Work projects were a more congenial way of putting money into people's hands. Simple jobs like cleaning parks and sweeping streets soon gave way to more productive efforts of repairing roads and sewers. Soon the government found that it could benefit the nation's economic infrastructure by using the labor in larger construction and renewal projects—building post offices, dams, and highways and undertaking reforestation. The federal government had suddenly become the nation's largest investor. At the same time, it also became the largest borrower, because taxes had been dramatically reduced by the drop in national income, and it could not otherwise pay for its projects. The government as investor and borrower was alien to the traditionalist economic mind-set.

Roosevelt's audacious experiment was not a total success. Though the economy stopped sinking and floated upward, it did not break free of the Depression undertow. People no longer starved, and economic activity increased over the next five years, but unemployment scarcely fell below 15 percent. It remained for the wartime buildup to put an end to the darkest decade of America's economic history.

One reason that full recovery was not achieved sooner is that bold concepts were coupled with what we now recognize as a timidity of spirit. Most economists continued to urge restraint, the business community fervently attacked the socialist tendencies of government, and Roosevelt himself believed in the need for a balanced budget almost as if it were religious dogma. Not until 1936 did federal spending rise 50 percent above the 1930 level. Even when the hastily devised programs produced positive results, they were expanded only cautiously and were seldom fully embraced intellectually. In retrospect this hesitancy seems puzzling, but the leaders are not to be too greatly faulted. For one thing, even when economists and bureaucrats saw a positive change, they could not be certain that it resulted from something they had done. They faced the problem of the lag time between decisions and results. Making the situation even more complicated was the fact that so many concepts and programs were being introduced simultaneously that no one was quite sure which benefit resulted from which actions. The New Deal was not like a controlled laboratory experiment. It was more like the efforts of a frantic medical team trying to save the life of a patient in cardiac arrest—only no one had seen it done before, and there was not even a theory to guide them.

2. The New Economics in Theory

The requisite theories were already taking shape in the mind of British economist John Maynard Keynes. In 1936 he published *The General Theory of Employment, Interest, and Money,* which stands alongside Adam Smith's *Wealth of Nations* and Karl Marx's *Das Kapital* as books that reshaped the economic ideas of an age. So dominant has Keynes's work been over the past fifty years that his concepts have come to be known as "the new economics," or simply "Keynesianism." He put into orderly theory what the New Deal had begun to do out of desperation. Whereas the old *microeconomics* focused on the interrelated decisions of households and firms, Keynes focused on the aggregate impact of all firms and all consumers on the national economy as a whole—savings, investment, employment, monetary policy, taxation, and the role of government spending. Thus he effectively created the discipline that we today call *macroeconomics*.

The new economics grew out of Keynes's concern to understand and correct the malfunctioning economy that had collapsed into depression. Classical theory argued that high consumption reduces savings. With few loan funds available, interest rates rise so high that business cannot borrow for investment. With a slowdown in investment, the business cycle enters the recessionary phase. But, the argument continued, there is no cause for alarm because when income declines, consumption decreases, savings grow, and interest rates ultimately fall to a point where business is ready to borrow for expansion. Then recovery begins.

What Keynes realized and what the prolonged depression proved was that the supposed automatic corrective of the market was not working. According to pre-Keynes theory, the economy would return to equilibrium; Keynes's insight was to realize that a market economy could sink to the bottom and stay there unless something were done. He agreed that increased investment was the key, but he noticed that investors would not invest when the prospect for profit was extremely dim. Investors surveyed the current economic landscape and saw low interest rates, but they also saw that from 1929 to 1933 the national income had dropped by almost 40 percent. That had the same effect on business as if over a third of the population had died—there simply were not enough consumers to make investment worthwhile.

And while business called for wage cuts to drive down production costs and interest rates in order to revive investment, Keynes saw that the crucial need was to increase *aggregate demand* (i.e., the nation's total demand for products and services) by putting money into people's hands so that they could buy things. Only then would business be lured into investment. To bring this about, Keynes defined a new and larger role for government in the economy. Its duty was to use its spending power and its power as an investor and employer to stimulate the economy, to increase demand, and to end unemployment. The goal for government was not to dominate the economy but to provide the impetus necessary to get it moving upward so that private investment opportunities would revive and normal business functions would resume.

3. Institutionalizing the New Economics

Can there be another depression like that of the 1930s? Most economists do not think so. We have learned much since that time about managing aggregate demand, and we probably can prevent a recession from spiraling into a depression. Several structural changes have also occurred that make a repetition of the years from 1929 to 1933 unlikely.

Among these changes is wider income distribution. In the boom years of the 1920s, income was so heavily concentrated—the richest 5 percent received 33.5 percent of the income in 1929—that when the Crash came, large numbers of lower-income people went from just getting by to penury almost overnight. As a result, aggregate demand plummeted. Since then, income concentration has been reduced: by 1971 the richest 5 percent received only 14 percent of the income. Because income is better distributed, if a deep recession were to hit today, many more people would be able to avoid destitution, and aggregate demand would not drop so drastically.

Other changes have to do with the financial institutions of our society. The investment laws were reformed and the Securities and Exchange Commission was created to eliminate the wild speculation that led to the crash of the stock market in 1929. Even more important to the small saver was the establishment of the Federal Deposit Insurance Corporation (FDIC), by which the government guarantees deposits of up to $100,000 in case of bank failure. This increases the confidence in the banking system and reduces the likelihood of a run on small banks, which could precipitate a collapse of the whole system.

The key to a more stable economy, however, are the so-called *automatic stabilizers*. Economic problems, when they appear, do not stop and wait for government to figure out what is going on, debate the various solutions, and implement the correct policy. The problems just keep getting worse. Automatic stabilizers do not wait for legislative or administrative action—they take effect automatically to counter early signs of instability. In the 1930s, for example, the individual who lost his or her job suffered an immediate and complete loss of income, a blow occasionally softened by private charity (of which there was never enough). Today, unemployment compensation supports the income of those who lose their jobs for up to one year. Other income-strengthening government programs exist for those who fall on hard times and are unable to pay full market rates. While such programs are praiseworthy on humanitarian grounds alone (discounting some measure of abuse), their importance to the economy as a whole is often overlooked. They do not just provide food for the hungry and some measure of personal safety for the unemployed and the underemployed. They also protect the society against a sudden drop in general consumption that could push a weakened economy into depression.

Paul Samuelson sums up well the standard wisdom about the ability of the new economics to forestall another major depression:

> Although nothing is impossible in an inexact science like economics, the probability of a great depression—a prolonged, cumulative, and chronic slump like that of the 1930s, the 1890s, or the 1870s—has been reduced to a negligible figure. . . . Economic science *knows how* to use monetary and fiscal policy to keep any recessions that break out from snowballing into *lasting* chronic slumps. . . . We have eaten of the Fruit of the Tree of knowledge and, for better or worse, there is no returning to laissez faire capitalism.[5] (Emphasis added)

In assessing these optimistic words, we would be wise to recall that Keynesianism clearly establishes the principles for dealing with a depression in the *national* economy. But Keynesianism does not tell us how to deal with an unstable *global* economy. Any future depression will not be "like that of the 1930s." It will have as much to do with resource cartels, the policies of transnational corporations, and the default of Third World debtor nations as it will have to do with managing aggregate demand in our own country.

D. Limits to Economic Policy-making

Keynesian economics does not have built-in answers for all present and future economic dilemmas. What it has done is to change economics from a passive discipline to an active one that offers other options than merely accepting whatever an unsuspecting society is dealt by the invisible hand. Government is no longer conceived of as a mere spectator of the economic drama but rather perceived as an actor in it. Its *fiscal policies* (i.e., taxing, spending, and borrowing) and *monetary policies* (i.e., its ability to control the supply of money in the economy and thus the interest rates) are to be used as mechanisms to steer the economy and thus to avoid the destabilizing gyrations of the business cycle. These are known as *countercyclical policies,* because they counteract the oscillatory tendencies of the business cycle. For a number of years the more enthusiastic later disciples of Keynes spoke of the possibility of "fine-tuning" the economy, of eliminating not only the extreme swings of the business cycle but virtually all fluctuations, thereby producing an economy with regular growth and full employment.

As is so often the case, hopes and expectations have exceeded performance. To begin with, there are data problems. Economists find out how the economy is doing only after the economy has started doing it. Because most diagnoses are based on quarterly statistics, known as *lead-*

ing economic indicators (e.g., orders for new plants and equipment, housing starts, sales, inventories), economists are always three months behind the times.

What's more, once the problem is correctly identified, it may take several months to implement the necessary corrective steps and several months more before their effects are felt. The result is that economists and policymakers must treat today's problems on the basis of how they assume the world will be twelve to fifteen months from now. In the meantime, things may change. Thus, if economists misdiagnose or guess wrong as to how the economy will react to some stimulus that was identified in data three to six months old, actions taken today could make the problem worse or create an altogether different problem. For instance, suppose the government instituted a large spending program on the assumption that the economy was headed for recession and unemployment. If by the time the contracts were let and payment was actually begun the recession had bottomed out and a recovery had started, the added stimulation of government spending could push the economy into a high rate of inflation.

A deeper problem, of course, is that today's economic world is very different from the one of 1936. Most of the specific remedies Keynes advanced may have outlived their time. Nowhere is this more evident than in the inability of economists to deal with the modern phenomenon of *stagflation*—the simultaneous occurrence of stagnation and high rates of inflation. Despite these difficulties, Keynesian concepts seem to be here to stay, rich rhetoric about laissez-faire notwithstanding. In the words of former president Richard Nixon, "We're all Keynesians now."

II. Realities: The New-Old Economics

Some will object—and rightly so—to the use of the phrase "the new economics" to describe a perspective that has dominated the economic scene for almost fifty years. It is really "the old-new economics" mentioned in the title of this chapter. In recent years, more specifically since Ronald Reagan came to the White House in 1981, there has been much talk of another kind of economics—"supply-side economics." It has been billed as a revolutionary approach to economic policy. In practice it seems more an attempt to repeal the economic programs of the past fifty years than an attempt to cast new solutions. It rejects a large and activist role of government and seeks an economy at peace with Adam Smith. In that sense, supply-side economics is really "the new-old economics."

A. Supply-Side Economics—What Is It?

Supply-side economics begins with two basic concerns. First is that the Keynesian formulas that have long dominated national economics grew out of the Depression experience and tended to focus on consumption needs, the demand side of the economic equation. Supply-siders argue that present realities require policies that focus on how to attract investment for production. The second concern is that government spending, and thus taxation, has become so large a part of the economy that incentives to work, save, innovate, and invest are being stifled.

Economist Arthur Laffer sought to address both these concerns by policy recommendations that are elaborations upon a simple diagram bearing his name. He and his followers maintain that the Laffer Curve (Figure 5.1, below) contains both the analysis of and the prescription for our economic dilemmas.[6]

Implicit in the diagram is the assumption that government revenues depend upon there being production in society that can be taxed. The Laffer Curve says that if there is a zero tax rate, if people are free to keep all that they produce, there will be a massive output but no government revenues. Effectively this means anarchy. On the other hand, if the tax rate is 100 percent—that is, if the government confiscates all that people in society produce—there will also be no revenues because people will stop producing for sale, and society will return to a barter economy with no taxable cash exchanges. At point B, people give up some of what they produce, but the services provided by government with the tax revenues actually cause them to produce more. At point D, higher tax rates induce still greater production and increased government revenues. But at some point—E in the diagram but not necessarily 50 percent—government programs will have done as much as they can do. If taxes are raised beyond that level, as they are at point C, some people become discouraged and produce less. With less output to tax, higher rates still produce lower

Figure 5.1—The Laffer Curve

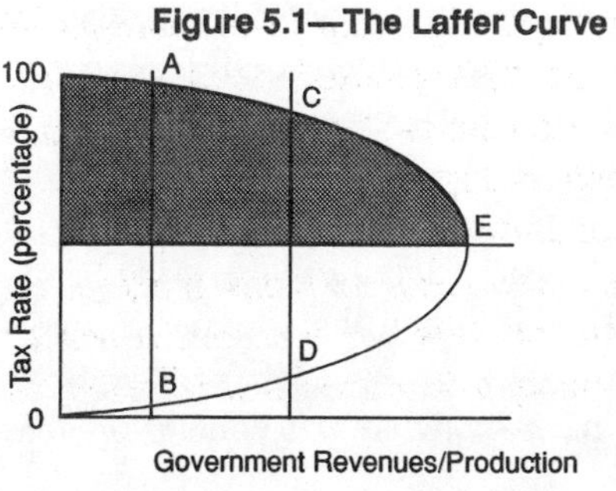

government revenues. And if, at point A, taxes are raised still more to try to cover the lost revenues, even less will be produced, and revenues will diminish further. This shaded area is what Laffer calls "the prohibitive range for government."

Laffer argues that the United States economy has already entered the prohibitive range of government involvement, where tax rates designed to put money in public programs are becoming an increasing drag on the nation's ability and willingness to produce.

To solve this problem, supply-siders prescribe drastically lower tax rates that will give people incentives to work, save, invest, and produce more. The theory says this can be done because we can reduce tax rates and increase production simultaneously (start at C on the graph and move right and down along the curve). Seen this way, the Laffer Curve is the Midas touch of the invisible hand.

But, as our grandmothers taught us, "If something seems too good to be true, it probably is."

Empirical support for the Laffer Curve is weak if not altogether lacking. No one has ever established what the optimal tax rate is (the one corresponding to E). Supply-side aficionados usually advance historical arguments to bolster their case. One example is the policies of Presidents Harding and Coolidge. Following World War I the excess-profits tax on industry was repealed, and over the course of several years (by 1925) the 77 percent tax rate on the highest income bracket was reduced to only 25 percent. "As a result," one economist concludes, "the period 1921-29 was one of phenomenal economic expansion."[7] This argument ignores the fact that such actions increasing the concentration of income were among the important causes of the Depression. Supply-siders are also fond of pointing to the Kennedy tax cut of 1964 and the resulting economic rebound as proof of the soundness of their case. However, Walter Heller, who designed the Kennedy program, points out that supply-siders misuse the data in that argument. The increased investment of that period resulted not from a general tax reduction but from focused measures such as the investment tax credit, liberalized depreciation allowances, actions to reduce interest rates, and wage-price guidelines. The general tax cut of 1964 was simply a Keynesian measure to stimulate demand.[8] And while Laffer claims to have achieved significant correlations in his own statistical analyses, attempts by others (Evans Econometrics, Otto Eckstein's Data Resources, Inc., and the efforts of Princeton economist Don Fullerton) have turned up only negative results.[9]

In the end it is hard to avoid the conclusion that supply-side economics is not so much motivated by either theory or observation as it is by ideology: it seeks to restore Adam Smith to economic dominance, notwithstanding the experience of the 1930s. As David Stockman, President Reagan's former Director of the Office of Management and Budget, once acknowledged in a moment of candor, supply-side economics is just the old trickle-down economics in new dress. That is, it rests on the hope that if income is allowed to concentrate in the hands of the few, some portion of it will ultimately trickle down to the many. But as an oft-quoted but unnamed sage once said, "Giving horses more oats cannot be the best way to feed the birds."

B. Reaganomics: Supply-Side Meets the Real World

Supply-side economics would probably have remained an issue more elaborated on paper napkins in cocktail lounges than in economic journals and government offices had it not been for Ronald Reagan. It provided a congenial, if shaky, theoretical justification for his own preference—a world closer to that of Adam Smith and Harding-Coolidge than to that of Keynes and Kennedy-Johnson, a world of striving individualism, not government interventionism. The economic centerpiece of what might now be called supply-side Reaganomics was the 1981 proposal of a 10 percent cut in personal income tax each year for three consecutive years and a reduction in the top rate of income from investments from 70 percent to 50 percent. Did that produce the promised torrent of work, savings, and investment? There is strong evidence it did not, even though in economics a strict cause-and-effect relationship can seldom be proved or disproved.

The tax cut was billed as an across-the-board reduction. That phrase gives the impression of proportionality in benefits that did not exist in fact. The majority of the incentives went to those in the highest tax bracket. For them each new investment dollar was now worth fifty cents instead of the previous thirty cents. In addition, they benefited from the 10 percent cut in the personal income tax rate. The individual reporting a taxable income of $50,000 who would normally have been taxed at 50 percent, or $25,000, saved 10 percent of that, or $2,500 in taxes not paid.

By contrast, the individual reporting $10,000 in taxable income whose normal tax might have been $1000 would have saved $100. Or, as one analyst put it, "A taxpayer whose rate was cut from 30% to 27% has increased the take-home pay on each additional dollar from 70 cents to only 73 cents. Because he is already in a low-tax bracket, a 10% tax cut does not significantly increase his incentive to earn taxable dollars."[10] It is not surprising that three more dollars a week did not generate a tidal wave of industriousness in the work force—especially where few firms worked overtime and where most people were lucky to have one job, let alone two.

Of course, equity was never the intention of the supply-side formula. Generating investments was the goal, and the tax cut put tens of millions of dollars into the hands of those deemed most apt to invest: the already well-to-do. Unlike the Kennedy tax cut of 1964, the Reagan tax cut offered no special incentives or directives to invest in the productive economy. Instead, the underlying ideology insisted that the individual investor had to be free to use the tax-cut windfall however he or she chose. A sharp increase in the number and price of Mercedes Benz automobiles is only one testimony to the fact that many chose a more ostentatious life-style over against the risks of investment. Another more significant result is that net investment shrank from 3.1 percent of the gross national product in 1981 to 2 percent in 1982 and finally to 1.5 percent in 1983. Fewer new factories were built in the latter year than in any other in the post–World War II period.[11]

Despite such drawbacks, society at least had the assurance of supply-side theory that the experiment would not diminish the public till. Tax revenues were to increase and counterbalance the tax rate cut. But did it happen? Making the comparison between the way the world is and the way it might have been is so complex that we may never know for sure, but there is some unsettling evidence that it did not. According to one analysis, average taxes paid by people earning over $50,000 a year declined by almost 5 percent from 1981 to 1982 after the first year of the tax cut.[12] Seemingly the rich got more from the government and returned less than usual. That runs counter to the experience following other major tax cuts in the 1920s and in 1964: in those instances higher-income groups increased their average tax as well as their share of total taxes.

The results of the bipartisan Tax Reform Act of 1986 are still unclear. It dramatically lowered tax rates, supposedly in exchange for simplified tax formulas and the closing of many tax loopholes that favored wealthier individuals and corporations. It may well be, however, that the changes will have the net effect of simply continuing the income concentration desired by supply-siders. Indeed, part of the political price of getting a bipartisan bill was the commitment that the reform would be both income-neutral and revenue-neutral. That is, assurances had to be made that the changes of law would not shift income from one group to another and would not increase the proportion of the national income going to the federal government.

Since supply-side economics failed on almost all counts in its limited test, it is not surprising that the term is more sparingly and more modestly used than in the early days of the Reagan administration. But the tax cuts survived, and so did the conviction that government was too large.

C. Reaganomics and Redefining the Role of Government

It may very well be that the real purpose of the tax cuts was less to stimulate investment than to discourage government by defunding it. The homey aphorism that "the government that governs least governs best" is a fitting summary of the political attitude that accompanied the interest in supply-side economics. The Reagan administration spoke freely of "getting the government off the backs of the American people" and "off the back of business." Implementation of the concept meant wholesale slashes in budgets for human services. Consider the following examples:

- The length of time for receiving unemployment benefits was reduced from 39 to 26 weeks.
- The food-stamp program was cut by $2 billion, 80 percent of that sum being deducted from food-stamp support for families below the poverty line.
- Aid to Families with Dependent Children cut benefits by $1.7 billion.
- The budget for school lunch programs was reduced by 30 percent.
- Medicaid funds dropped by almost $1 billion.

Clearly the message was that people should gird themselves and be prepared to stand more alone in the economic environment.

A new message was also being sent to business: less regulation by government and more freedom in the market. The pro-business philosophy was not just a matter of rhetoric; it took concrete form, as the following examples demonstrate:

- The Occupational Safety and Health Administration made 17 percent fewer workplace inspections in the first two years of the Reagan program, and fines assessed against violators dropped by 78 percent.
- Huge tracts of land and the continental shelf were leased to energy companies for exploration despite environmental risks and in the face of a petroleum and natural-gas glut.
- The Antitrust Division of the Justice Department adopted a passive stance regarding market structure, and that set off what may prove to be the greatest merger movement in U.S. history.

Is government too large? There are two quite different ways of answering that question. One is to compare U.S. government with that of other industrialized countries. The ideological image that is perpetuated is that the United States is the most governmentally top-heavy society in the Western world. In fact, just the opposite is the case. The supposedly crushing American tax burden is actually far less than the tax burdens of our friendly rivals. In 1984 taxes were equal to 27 percent of the national income in the United States, versus 38 percent in Great Britain and West Germany, 39 percent in France, and 46 percent in the Netherlands. Of all industrialized nations, only Japan collects a smaller portion of its national income in taxes than does government in the United States.[13]

Nor is there a bloated federal bureaucracy. The civilian work-force of the federal government fell from 5 percent of all workers in 1952 to only 3.2 percent in 1980,[14] a statistic not mentioned in President Reagan's speeches! It is apparent that the size of government was being reduced well before supply-side enthusiasts came to the fore. Since the public sector does not have the natural corrective of competition, periodic campaigns against unwarranted growth are both healthy and necessary. Present attacks, however, go well beyond the question of efficiency and seem to stem from ideology.

The second way of determining whether government is too large is to focus on its purpose. If government's only task is to punish crime and prevent invasion, it will be a government of a very limited size and function. Our constitution, however, has committed us to a government that "provides for the general welfare." The definition of that phrase may shift, but in no way can it be interpreted to mean that government should play a passive, minimalist role in society. The function of government under such a definition is not merely protection or even regulation. The definition assumes a government that meets necessities and creates possibilities. When the philosophy of government is changed, when expectations of it are enlarged, so too will be its size. Tasks that are so implicitly moral and economic presuppose a government that is large enough, active enough, and interventionist enough to implement those tasks.

The determination to reduce the size of government as a matter of ideological preference not only has humanitarian impact as social welfare programs are cut dramatically; it also represents a threat to the viability of the economic system as a whole. Perhaps the most dangerous expression of this determination is the pressure to adopt a constitutional amendment that would require a balanced budget. Such a requirement would greatly increase the danger of depression. As Keynes made clear, the government's ability to spend, even to deficit-spend, to create aggregate demand in the face of a slowing economy is crucial to escaping a downward spiral. A similar limiting of the countercyclical policies of government may occur through the massive shift of programs from the federal level to state and municipal levels, since states and municipalities would not be able to infuse enough funds into the society fast enough to stem a major downturn.

The great danger of the minimalist philosophy of government, if it were to prevail, is that it might well create a situation in which the only available response to an economic downturn would be to increase military spending dramatically. For that, there already seems an almost unlimited tolerance.

III. Values: The Ethical-Economic Implications of the Military Buildup

In the post–World War II years, military spending has constituted a major economic activity of the federal government. Quite apart from the moral uneasiness many people have about the whole issue of war, there is legitimate cause for alarm about the ethical, social, and economic implications of the present military buildup.

In his oft-quoted farewell address to the nation in 1961, President Dwight Eisenhower said,

> No matter how much we spend on arms, there is not safety in arms alone. Our security is the total product of our economic, intellectual, moral and military strengths. . . . There is no way in which a country can satisfy the craving for absolute security, but it easily can bankrupt itself, morally and economically, in attempting to reach that illusory goal through arms alone. The military establishment, not productive of itself, must necessarily feed on the energy, [the] productivity, and the brainpower of the country, and if it takes too much, our strength declines.

The bottom line, of course, is how much is too much?

A. Facing Economic Bankruptcy

From 1946 through 1980, the United States military spent just over $2,000 billion. Between 1982 and 1987, the Reagan administration spent almost $1,800 billion. (Such expenditures account only for a peacetime buildup of "defense" capability. A war of even modest proportions would have pushed the budgetary figures still higher.) In 1987, 36 percent of the federal budget went to the military.

These high levels of military spending are dangerous to our viability as an economic society. When Wassily Leontief was asked about the economic implications of huge increases in defense spending, the Nobel prize-winning economist replied,

> If handled improperly, these huge jumps in military spending will mean high inflation, a worsening balance-of-payments gap, a drain on productive investment, soaring interest rates, increasing taxes, a debased currency, and, in the long-term, more unemployment. Reagan proposes to leap across—rather than bridge—the nation's economic gap. What worries me is that if you jump even five inches short, you face economic calamity. It is a very great gamble.[15]

The economic consequences of this massive military buildup are unnerving, even though they may be temporarily masked by other economic factors.

First, military expenditures tend to be inflationary. Such spending injects money into the economy in the form of wages, salaries, and profits, but it does not create new products that people can buy. (Very few people want a tank in their driveway or a missile site in their backyard.) As a result, consumers as a group have more money to spend on the same stock of goods that existed before the military spending. Thus there tends to be too much money chasing too few consumer goods. Classic inflation.

President Johnson's "guns and butter" policy of 1968 illustrates the problem. Most economists trace the inflationary pressures of the 1970s to the huge military expenditures of the Vietnam war that were not offset by a tax increase. We tried to live well and fight an expensive war at the same time—on borrowed money. The fact that we have thus far escaped an inflationary spiral in the Reagan era is due to a massive inflow of cheaper foreign goods and of foreign investment funds to cover the cost of financing our massive government deficits.

A second consequence of military spending is that it diverts capital from the domestic economy. In the years after the Vietnam war and before Ronald Reagan became president, military procurement drifted downward. The major defense contractors remained healthy, but many of the smaller subcontractors went under or switched over to market-oriented production. A sustained military buildup requires massive borrowing for companies to retool. As scarce capital is diverted to the military-industrial complex, other industrial enterprises and the construction industry may be shortchanged. Not only may the "reindustrialization of America" be postponed, but the dream of building a home may become the impossible dream for most American families.

Capital is not the only resource that weapons spending bids away from civilian industry. The military establishment also absorbs the time, energy, and creativity of half a million scientists and engineers. This diversion of research and development funds and personnel helps keep the United States economically behind other countries like Japan and West Germany, which invest virtually their entire research and development capacity in the civilian sector.

Advocates of high levels of defense spending are fond of arguing that the defense industry provides a huge number of jobs. The "more jobs" fallacy goes back almost fifty years, when the buildup for World War II finally brought an end to the depression of the 1930s. What is neglected in the argument is the fact that equivalent government spending on most anything would have had the same effect. The 1940s represent a vindication of Keynesian theory, not of the employment advantages of massive military budgets. Moreover, recent studies show that military spending creates fewer jobs than equivalent investment in other sectors of the economy. Estimates indicate that 24,000 more jobs would be created for every $1 billion shifted by the federal government from military spending to the support of much-needed employees in service occupations such as teachers, police, construction workers, and environmental employees.[16]

There are clear economic reasons why the United States should reject its growing commitment to military spending and turn its energies toward peace conversion. Quoting Marion Anderson's study entitled *The Empty Pork Barrel* is enlightening:

> If every person directly affected by a $10 billion military procurement cut were laid off for one year, it would be possible to pay each individual 90% of his/her salary up to $25,000, continue all job-related benefits, and provide each person with $1500 to go back to school, at a total cost of under $3 billion, or only 30¢ on every procurement dollar spent.
>
> More jobs would open up for seven out of the eight major occupational categories. There would be a net employment gain for professional and technical workers, managers and proprietors, sales workers, clerical workers, factory workers, service workers and laborers. Ninety-one percent of the craft and kindred workers would find new jobs in the conversion industries within their own trade![17]

Conversion has thus become an economic as well as a theological concept.

The present weapons buildup is committing us to another course entirely. What is really at stake in the huge increases in the military budget is a redefinition of the priorities of American society and its basic commitments. It represents a massive shift from attempts to improve the ability to deliver a better life to attempts to improve the ability to deliver death more efficiently.

B. Facing Moral Bankruptcy

The moral issue at stake in the present militarization is not just its size and cost but who bears the burden of it. When Murray Weidenbaum resigned as President Reagan's Chief Economic Advisor, he said, "We've shifted priorities. . . . We've cut nondefense spending substantially. But have we on balance cut the budget? . . . No. It's a wash."

One result of Reaganomics has been to make the economically crippled of our society pay the bill for the huge military buildup. In 1983 nondefense spending was cut by $46 billion, and defense spending rose by almost $45 billion. In human terms, there were some very specific trade-offs.

- $35 million was added to the military budget for missile silo batteries for generating electric power *after* a nuclear attack. $40 million was cut from feeding programs for women, infants, and children.
- $2,000 million was added to keep the B-1 bomber program alive, and $2,400 million was cut from the food-stamp program.
- $475 million was added to the military budget as a first installment on a nuclear aircraft carrier. $1,000 million was cut from Medicaid.
- Similar shifts were made in foreign expenditures. $450 million was added in military aid to Pakistan; meanwhile, $7.5 million was cut from the Peace Corps budget, and the nation's contributions to UNICEF were reduced by $15.5 million.[18]

This is moral bankruptcy. The weakest elements of our society, those least able to defend themselves politically, have been sacrificed to a militaristic mind-set.

Military spending is already the largest form of government expenditure except for Social Security. That too is under attack by budget-cutters who are trying to prop up an economy that is top-heavy with arms while they are also trying to continue cutting taxes. In the process the government has run up the largest deficits ever in its non-wartime history. Those anxious to defend the administration point to the progress made in reducing both inflation rates and unemployment. With no basic changes in the structure of the United States economy, however, the problems of the recent past loom larger in the near future. Inflation was controlled by creating the deepest and most humanly damaging recession in forty years. Having hit bottom, the economy began a recovery encouraged by government spending. Thus supply-siders appear to be taking credit for the results of a perverse Keynesianism.

There is little evidence that the overall role of government in society and in the economy has been reduced. There is only evidence that the goal of its intervention is more than ever to seek military might above all. Those of biblical faith would be hard-pressed to call that progress.

Notes

1. Quoted by Robert L. Heilbroner and Aaron Singer in *The Economic Transformation of America* (New York: Harcourt Brace Jovanovich, 1977), p. 172.

2. Alvin H. Hansen, *Fiscal Policy and Business Cycles* (New York: W. W. Norton, 1941), pp. 16-27.

3. The categories are suggested by Hansen, *Fiscal Policy and Business Cycles*, chaps. 1 and 2, but the illustrations within those categories are my own.

4. Samuelson, *Economics*, 8th ed. (New York: McGraw-Hill, 1970), p. 247.

5. Samuelson, *Economics*, p. 250.

6. Legend has it that Laffer first drew his now-famous curve on a cocktail napkin while trying to explain his ideas to a government aide at an airport lounge. The economics trade has moved far from the stuffy surroundings of ivy-covered towers!

7. Jude Wanniski, *The Way the World Works: How Economies Fail and Succeed* (New York: Basic Books, 1978), p. 64.

8. Heller, in a statement before the Senate Appropriations Committee, 28 Jan. 1981, p. 3.

9. John Judis, "The Way the World Doesn't Work," *World Papers*, May-June 1981, p. 53.

10. "The Reagan Tax Cuts: Were the Supply Siders Right?" *Business Week*, 28 May 1984, p. 68.

11. "The Sudden Rush to Spend on America's Factories," *Business Week*, 30 Jan. 1984, p. 83.

12. "Reagan's Good-Times Budget," *Business Week*, 30 Jan. 1984, p. 72.

13. *Government Finance Statistics Yearbook* (Washington: International Monetary Fund, 1986), p. 86.

14. *U.S.: A Statistical Portrait*, ed. Andrew Hacker (New York: Viking Press, 1983), p. 196.

15. "Big Boosts in Defense Risk 'Economic Calamity,'" interview with Wassily Leontief, *U.S. News and World Report*, 16 Mar. 1981, p. 26.

16. Marion Anderson, *The Empty Pork Barrel: Unemployment and the Pentagon Budget* (Lansing, Mich.: Employment Research Associates, n.d.), p. 4.

17. Anderson, *The Empty Pork Barrel*, p. 3.

18. Marion Anderson, *Converting the Work Force* (Lansing, Mich.: Employment Research Associates, n.d.), p. 8.

Chapter Six

Sharing in Economic Society: The Problem of Distribution

I. Concepts: The Theory and Practice of Distribution

The distribution of wealth and income would never be an issue if there were enough of everything for everyone. Indeed, there would be no need at all for the discipline of economics, since it is essentially the management of scarcity. But we do not live in such a world of unlimited abundance, and predictably the matter of sharing what is available is a key issue for most people. It was not, however, a topic of great concern to early theorists.

A. Distribution and the Market

When Adam Smith stood in the last quarter of the eighteenth century looking back on the moribund feudal epoch, he saw that the chronic economic problem had been the inability of society to provide enough goods to meet the needs of its people. He conceived of economics as primarily a matter of how to increase production. The distribution of economic benefits was a side effect of the automatic, internal workings of the economic system—a "black box" where the invisible hand performed its miracle.

Thus, from the beginning, capitalism has had no philosophy of distribution. The market mechanism, lacking the concept of need, responds only to *effective demand* (i.e., need or desire plus money). How much an individual can have is determined by how much he or she can buy. The transfer of resources on any other basis—need, justice, or charity—is outside the economic model. Capitalism does not struggle with the question of who ought to receive how much. Economists normally insist that is a moral and not an economic question. Nevertheless, there is implicit in the market concept a very specific mechanism of distribution, which was more fully elaborated by English economist David Ricardo (1772-1823) than by Adam Smith.

According to Ricardo, income was generated by each of the three factors of production. Land could be rented out; labor paid wages; capital paid interest if loaned to others or profits if invested directly. That much was uncontroversial. But of the economic value created, how much should go to the laborer, how much to the landlord, and how much to the capital owner and entrepreneur (the person who takes the responsibility of bringing the factors of production together in a productive relationship)? In theory, each factor should be compensated in proportion to its contribution in creating something of economic value; however, in reality, Ricardo observed, things were quite different. Throughout history, landholders had gotten a disproportionate share of income. Why? Ricardo believed the reason was that the population grew faster than the food supply. In order to meet the growing demand for sustenance, it was necessary to bring land that was less fertile into production. This depended upon putting more workers into clearing and preparing the fields, thus increasing costs to the landowner and the rents charged for it. According to theory, income generated by wages was also determined by mechanisms of supply and demand. The problem was that in David Ricardo's world, there was such an abundance of labor that wages were almost a fixed cost for the employer. They were set at a level equal to a subsistence standard as defined locally.

Since wages could not be allowed to fall below subsistence level—then there would be no workers—and since land rents were constantly rising, Ricardo believed that, in the end, capital received less than it merited for its contribution to production.

Later economists rejected Ricardo's analysis, but by then doubt had been introduced into the heart of the economic system. Whereas Adam Smith had seen competition as leading ultimately and always to greater production and therefore to greater social good, Ricardo saw that competition also led to conflict about the distribution of the benefits of production. Landowners, wage earners, investors, and entrepreneurs could not be counted on to reach accord on who should receive how much. In effect, Ricardo opened a crack in the black box of classical economics, and its implicit class struggle was glimpsed.

B. Distribution: Distinctions and Definitions

In considering the distribution of society's economic resources, the basic question for most people is, "Who gets how much?" This query is not so easy to answer as it might seem. First, we must distinguish between income and wealth. While they are related concepts, they are not the same. *Income* is the *flow* of money or goods that an individual (or group or nation) receives, wages paid to labor, and interest or profits received on capital invested. Income may also include gifts received from others.

The image of income to bear in mind is that of a stream of money—or goods that can be exchanged for money—flowing in to the individual. *Wealth,* by contrast, is a *stock* of assets that have *economic value.* That is, they can be sold for money or traded for other goods, but they do not themselves produce income. While the mental image for income is one of a stream of money, the image for wealth is one of the lake or reservoir where money has collected in the form of income that has not been spent.

Of course, in discussing economic distribution, the focus is not upon the income level or the wealth holdings of one person or family but upon an aggregate comparison. The most common comparisons involve references to the *gross national product.* The GNP represents the total money value of all the final goods and services produced in a country during a specific period of time (usually one year), plus gains or losses from foreign trade. The phrase "final goods and services" is important because it means that all potential double counting has been removed. For instance, there are dozens of large and small firms that make hundreds of millions of dollars in sales of components to automobile manufacturers. But these intermediate sales are not included in the GNP because they are reflected in the final price of the new car.

One more set of definitions may be helpful in dealing with data on economic distribution. In making such comparisons, it is common to speak in terms of averages. One way to calculate such a figure is simply to add up the total amount of money involved and then divide by the number of people involved. Such an arithmetic *mean* is useful in that it tells us what things would look like if there were absolutely equal sharing. The problem in using such an average is that it may mask extreme inequalities. Imagine, for instance, a community of 1,000 families in a mining town where 950 families earned $10,000 a year, and families of the 50 company executives received $1 million each. The mean (average) income would be $59,500, giving the impression that most people are nearly six times as well off as they actually are. Generally speaking, a more helpful approach in thinking about averages is to focus on the *median,* the figure at which half the group is above and half is below. In the case of our imagined community of 1,000 families, the median income would be $10,000. That figure also represents a distortion, but it reflects more accurately the reality of most families.

Comparing the mean and the median figures is a way of getting some feeling for the amount of inequality that exists behind the average. The nearer the mean and the median figures are to being the same, the less likely they are to hide extreme inequalities. There are statistical tools that express these relationships with great precision, even in a single figure. However, such calculations are seldom available, and even if they were, the degree of abstraction involved would obscure from most of us the situation of the people hidden inside the calculations. For our purposes, comparisons will be made using groups of people and families within certain ranges.

II. Realities: Income and Wealth in America

A. Income Distribution—Who Gets How Much?

At the heart of the American historical experiment has been something of a populist if not an egalitarian spirit. It is embedded in the Declaration of Independence in this famous sentence: "We hold these truths to be self-evident, that all men are created equal, that they are endowed by their Creator with certain unalienable Rights, that among these are Life, Liberty and the pursuit of Happiness." The final phrase was something of a hedge, since it is a recasting of the social trinity of John Locke—"life, liberty and property." It was perhaps a bit too revolutionary for the founding fathers to declare that property was a divine right of all people. Despite the vision, equality has never been the reality of this nation. Nevertheless, there has arisen—at least in this century—the conviction that in a country so wealthy, no one need be poor.

The growth in *real income* (i.e., income that is discounted for inflation) *per capita* in the United States has been steady and strong for a very long time, as Table 6.1 below shows. From 1865 to 1929, average real income rose by almost 400 percent. By 1971 it had almost doubled again, and within another dozen years the average person added another 22 percent to real income. In a little more than a century, per capita income in the United States increased almost tenfold.

Table 6.1

Real Income per Capita

(in 1865 dollars)

1865	$ 278
1929	1101
1971	2147
1983	2614

Data from 1865-1971 cited by Robert Heilbroner and Aaron Singer in *The Economic Transformation of America* (New York: Harcourt Brace Jovanovich, 1977), p. 213. Figures for 1983 calculated by the author from data in U.S. Bureau of the Census, *Statistical Abstract of the United States, 1985,* (Washington: U.S. Department of Commerce, 1985), p. 433.

Of course, a rapidly growing income says nothing about how it is shared. Part of the popular economic optimism of the United States has been the belief that as the economy grew larger and richer, the distribution of wealth and income would become automatically more equal. For more than half a century, a significant measure of economic leveling has occurred, but it has not necessarily been associated with economic growth.

The decade of the 1920s was a boom period for the U.S. economy. It was also a time when the richest segments of the population dramatically increased their share of the national income. As Table 6.2 below shows, the top 1 percent of income receivers moved from a 12.2 percent share in 1919 to a 19.1 percent share in 1929, more than half again as much. Similarly, the top 5 percent showed a gain of almost 25 percent in their share.

There is the tendency to diminish the significance of increasing inequality during boom times by saying, "Everyone did well; some just did better." But income concentration is not quite that benign even in good times. A study by the Brookings Institution, one of the oldest privately funded social research "think tanks," indicates that in 1929, a $2,000 annual income would provide the basic necessities for a four-person family. But the study also showed that in 1929 nearly 60 percent of American families received less than $2,000.[1] Clearly the benefits of the boom concentrated in the hands of the few at the top, and very little trickled down to the majority of the population.

However, the stock market collapse, a decade of depression, and the economic impact of World War II brought major changes in the income patterns of the nation. As Table 6.2 shows, by 1941 both the top 1 percent and the top 5 percent of income receivers had seen their share of the national income fall back to levels below those of 1919, and those levels declined even further during World War II.

Table 6.2

Percentage of National Income Received by Top 1% and Top 5% of the U.S. Population, 1919-1986

Group	1919	1923	1929	1941	1946	1986
Top 1%	12.2%	13.1%	19.1%	9.9%	7.7%	NA
Top 5%	24.3	27.1	30.0	24.0	21.3	17.0%

Compiled from U.S. Bureau of the Census, *Historical Statistics: Colonial Times to 1973* (Washington: U.S. Government Printing Office, 1974), G 135, 105 (for 1929, 1941, 1946) and combined with data reported in a Joint Economic Committee of Congress for 1986, and data reported in *The Economic Transformation of America,* by Robert Heilbroner and Aaron Singer (New York: Harcourt Brace Jovanovich, 1977), p. 177.

Table 6.3

Distribution of U.S. Family Income by Population Segment, 1950-1986

Population	1950	1960	1970	1980	1986
Poorest 20%	4.5%	4.8%	5.4%	5.1%	4.6%
Second 20%	11.9	12.2	12.2	11.6	10.8
Third 20%	17.4	17.8	17.6	17.5	16.8
Fourth 20%	23.4	24.0	23.8	24.3	24.0
Richest 20%	42.8	41.3	40.9	41.6	43.7
(Richest 5%)	(17.3)	(15.9)	(15.7)	(16.0)	(17.0)
Median Real Income (in 1986 dollars)		$22,125	$27,862	$27,974	$29,458

Source: U.S. Bureau of the Census, *Current Population Reports,* P-60 series (Washington: U.S. Government Printing Office, various years)

The income-leveling effect of the Depression tends to confirm Ricardo's observations that with wages set somewhere near subsistence level, economic losses will be borne mainly by capital. In other words, if the poor are just barely hanging on for survival anyway, bad times cannot take much more from them, and those better off will have to lose proportionately more. However, the fact that the Depression closed the income percentage gap somewhat between the rich and the poor was hardly consolation to those at the bottom. After all, a larger share of a much smaller pie still left them hungry. It was surely cold comfort that the rich also were a little less well off.

The period since World War II has been particularly important in the study of income distribution because during much of that time sustained economic growth was combined with slow but steady progress toward income equality.

The statistical story picks up in 1950. The economy had largely recovered from its wartime footing. Moreover, the Depression-era programs shifted more income into the hands of those who otherwise would have been poorer. By 1950 the richest 5 percent of families held 17.3 percent of the national income, down from the 1929 high of 30 percent. Still, in 1950 the poorest fifth of U.S. families received only 4.5 percent of the national income. That rose to a high of 5.4 percent in 1970 with the help of the so-called war against poverty in the early and mid-1960s. Indeed, without federal government income-transfer programs (Social Security, unemployment compensation, and welfare), the poorest fifth would receive only half as much as they do.[2] Although the shift in income shares was modest, eight out of ten American families received a larger proportion of the nation's income in 1970 than they had in 1950.

Only the richest 20 percent of families got less, with their share falling from 42.8 percent in 1950 to 40.9 percent in 1970.

The proportion lost by the upper class (the top 20 percent) was not great: only an additional 2 percent of the national income slipped from its control. There was no great outcry from this group, largely because of the phenomenal economic growth that accompanied the proportional redistribution. They were doing so much better that they could hardly complain if the less well-to-do were doing better at a slightly faster rate.

Likewise, the small increase in the share received by the poorest fifth of the population (less than 1 percent) was magnified by a booming economy. Economically the 1960s seemed the best of all possible worlds. The satisfaction of greater equality was being achieved painlessly, paid for primarily with the proceeds of unprecedented economic growth. Time and a growing economy would make almost all things possible, it seemed.

A second glance at Table 6.3, however, makes us realize how short were the golden years and how timid and temporary the commitment to economic redistribution. Beginning early in the 1970s, the economy stagnated. During that decade the median real income of the family remained virtually unchanged. By 1980 the income shares of the lower 60 percent of families had decreased, while that of the top two groups had increased. By 1982, U.S. income distribution was more unequal than it had been in 1950, with the top 20 percent of families receiving over nine times what the bottom 20 percent received. The richest fifth of American families received 43.7 percent of the 1986 national income—the highest percentage ever recorded. Meanwhile, the poorest fifth received 4.6 percent—the lowest percentage ever recorded.

Speaking in fractions of a percent can be deceptive. The difference between 5.4 percent of the national income and 4.6 percent may not seem great when viewed on a chart, but it becomes very large in a family budget. If the poorest fifth of the population had been able to maintain the percentage of the national income that they received in 1970, the average family in that group would have had over six hundred dollars added to its 1986 income. An extra fifty dollars a month is no small matter to those struggling not just to get by but to avoid destitution.

Who are the poor in the United States, and what does it mean to be poor? Since poverty is not an exact concept, it is likely that there will never be complete accord on the answers to such questions. Nevertheless, the Census Bureau each year computes a series of poverty thresholds. People who do not receive income above those levels are defined

Table 6.4

U.S. Poverty Thresholds, 1986

Size of Family Unit	Cash Income, 1986
One person*	$ 5,574
Two persons	7,133
Three persons	8,738
Four persons	11,200
Five persons	13,257
Six persons	14,979
Seven persons	16,976
Eight persons	18,868
Nine persons or more	22,508

**Unrelated individual*

Source: U.S. Bureau of the Census, *Current Population Reports,* P-60 series (Washington: U.S. Government Printing Office, 1987).

as poor and may be eligible to participate in government aid programs. The poverty thresholds for 1986 are shown in Table 6.4 (above).

By these standards, 13.6 percent of all American families were poor in 1986—more than 32 million people! And this does not tell the whole story, for the burden of poverty falls much more heavily on some groups than on others. For example, of families headed by women, 34.6 percent are in poverty, and over one-fifth of all children under age fifteen live in families with incomes that fall below government poverty thresholds.

For one to get the full impact of such figures, they should be written in colors, because poverty in America has a racial bias. Over two-thirds of poor people are white, but blacks, who make up just 12 percent of the national population, constitute 31 percent of the nation's poor. While the proportion of those in poverty has increased for both groups, one out of every three blacks was poor in 1986, compared with only one in nine whites. Perhaps even more significant is the age distribution. Of all black children under fifteen years of age, 43 percent are poor, whereas of all white children under fifteen, only 16 percent are poor. And among those under three years of age, almost half of all black children—46 percent—live in poverty, while just 17 percent of all white children do. This last category is particularly important, since dietary restrictions at that age may have lifelong consequences for health and intellectual capacity.[3] Thus many in the new generation start with handicaps that will make it difficult for them to keep up, much less catch up.

It is not just that a few blacks are poor. Table 6.5 shows that as a whole their income has traditionally been much lower than that of

Table 6.5

Median Family Income in the United States, 1960-1986, by Race

(in current dollars not discounted for inflation)

Year	Black	White	B/W Ratio
1960	$ 3230	$ 5835	.55
1970	6297	10236	.61
1975	8779	14268	.62
1980	12674	21904	.58
1982	13598	24603	.55
1986	17604	30809	.57

Source: U.S. Bureau of the Census, *Current Population Reports*, P-60 Series (Washington: U.S. Government Printing Office, 1986).

whites. In 1960 employed blacks earned just 55 percent of what their white counterparts made. By 1970 black income jumped to 61 percent of that of whites, and it reached a peak of 62 percent in 1975. That represented a leveling upward of 13 percent for blacks in a decade and a half. It was not the kingdom of God, but it was significant progress. What accounted for such a change? An important factor was that a booming national economy increased the income across the board. "A rising tide lifts all boats," but it lifts them only by the same amount. Something else had to account for the shift of relative shares of income. The so-called war against poverty and the "Great Society" program of the period were of particular help to minorities because minorities are disproportionately poor. When legislation aims at helping the poor in general, it helps minorities especially.

With the slowing of the economy, the slackening of concern about civil rights, and the return of a laissez-faire philosophy in the Reagan administration, the relative progress of blacks was eliminated. By 1982 they received the same percentage of white income as they did in 1960. Figures for 1986 show only a slight improvement. In terms of absolute numbers of dollars, that is still an advance because the economic pie is larger. But the sense that there has been a basic shift in the economic structures of the nation that moves black Americans closer to equality has been lost. The disillusionment was captured by one writer in these words: "The bald truth is that not only has movement toward narrowing the socio-economic gap that separates black and white Americans come to a dead halt, retrenchment has set in and blacks are actually retrogressing."[4]

Minorities are not the only groups among whom there is a disproportionate number of poor. Poverty in America is also increasingly feminine. Of the elderly poor, two out of three are women. Households headed by women are three times more apt to be poor than other families. Sixty-nine percent of families receiving food stamps are headed by women, and of the three million people receiving the minimum monthly government allotment, 86 percent are women.[5]

Economic maldistribution and the poverty that it produces do not exist in splendid social isolation. They are entwined with other social dilemmas to create a compound crisis. No combination of governmental programs will be able to deal in an effective and lasting way with the dilemmas of the elderly, of women, of minorities, or of poverty without focusing also upon the structural maldistribution of income in our society that underlies them all.

Perhaps most disturbing of all is that structural changes in the U.S. economy are tending to sharpen the income inequalities that already exist. Paramount among these is the so-called postindustrial shift of the economy from manufacturing (e.g., automobiles, appliances, steel) to the service sector (e.g., insurance, financial activities, advertising).

Jobs in manufacturing industries were the mainstay of the income leveling that occurred during and after World War II. Recently, however, traditional heavy industry has been the slowest-growing sector of the economy, and whole segments are in decline. In many industries large companies are failing because of erroneous business decisions made years ago, because of changes in technology, and because of foreign competition. As companies have failed, the jobs they once provided have not been replaced. Millions of workers have been displaced and forced to look for new work. Many have been unable to find it—some because they have no other marketable skill, others because they can't sell a house or walk away from family responsibilities in order to go where the jobs are said to be.

Even for those lucky enough to find new work, the outlook is not rosy. The major problem is the difference in wages between the manufacturing sector and the service sector. Wages in the manufacturing jobs now average about $310 a week plus significant benefits hard won by unions, such as health insurance and retirement plans. The fast-growing service industries, generally not unionized, provide about 20 percent of all jobs but pay an average of just $210 per week, often with no additional benefits.[6] People who previously enjoyed relatively well-paid positions and a measure of financial security to provide for illness and old age are suddenly faced with much lower wages and no way to cope with the uncertainties of life or the certainty of old age. Of course, some of the service-sector jobs are high-paying professional and technical positions like those of lawyers, accountants, and stockbrokers. But these are vastly outnumbered by low-skill, low-income occupations like hamburger flipper at McDonald's. Between 1979 and 1984, 58 percent of all newly created jobs paid $7,000 a year or less (in 1984 dollars).

The message of this trend is plain: if left unchecked, it will further concentrate income in the hands of the more well-to-do, create a more rigid class structure than has been characteristic of this country, and condemn sizeable segments of the population—minorities, the aged, single mothers—to the unrelieved poverty of a permanent underclass. This would be a human tragedy of unacceptable proportions.

B. Wealth Distribution: Who Keeps How Much in the American Economy?

A highly unequal income distribution not only leads to higher consumption and greater security for some than for others; it also creates huge differences of wealth in the society. *Wealth*—the market value of all accumulated goods—is far more highly concentrated than is income in the United States. The top 10 percent of the population owns 70 percent of all assets held by private citizens. Throughout this century, in good times and in bad, the top 1 percent of the population has consistently owned over one-fourth of all private national wealth, and recent years have seen a marked increase in that ratio. In 1963 the richest half percent of the population owned 25 percent of all assets. By 1983 they owned 35 percent.[7]

It is interesting to see what that means for everyone else. One way of dealing with the question of wealth is to focus on an individual's *net worth*. That is the amount a person would realize in cash if he/she sold everything—house, stocks, bonds, car, appliances, clothing, and finally the calculator used to keep track of it all—and then paid all outstanding debts. A 1983 study for the Joint Economic Committee of Congress shows that only 10 percent of all American families have a net worth of over $42,000, and most of that is in the hands of just one-half of 1 percent of the families whose average wealth is almost $7 million. Meanwhile, one-quarter of American families have a net worth of less than $3,300. And 13 percent of families—including almost one adult in four—are worth nothing at all in a financial sense.[8]

There is a great mythology in our culture about how wealth is acquired. The Horatio Alger formula goes something like this: work hard, spend little, save much, invest prudently, and reinvest the profits. Repeat the cycle often, and bit by bit, modest income will be transformed into self-generating wealth. Myths persist because there is a measure of truth in them. In this case, however, the measure may be small. MIT economist

Lester Thurow points out that most fortunes are inherited, not made, and that, failing a legacy in one's own family, the next surest way to become rich is to marry wealth. For others, achievement of wealth is more like a lottery than it is a test of hard work and frugality. It is largely a matter of having the luck to stumble upon some technology, product, or market at the right time. That is not to say that those who become wealthy do not show more talent, intelligence, or drive than average people in the society. But they seldom show more of these qualities than many, many others who do not become wealthy. Thurow points out that the biographies of millionaires seldom show signs of their having made two financial leaps forward. Instead, when some combination of skill and luck granted them a fortune, they tended to generate increased wealth at about the average rate of return for the investment market as a whole. If genius or drive were the determinative factor, one would expect repeated performances, not just one.[9]

Income and wealth are not unrelated, however. One of the surest routes to fortune is to rise to a high managerial position in a large corporation. In 1983 the twenty-five highest-paid corporate executives received an average salary and bonus package of $856,520. But that was only the beginning. In addition, each received "long-term compensation," mostly in the form of stock options and other tax-avoidance devices. That amounted to an additional $3.1 million on the average. Thus their average compensation totaled almost $4 million for the year. The top individual among them received $13.2 million.

These figures are high, but they are not anomalies in corporate America. Two hundred sixty-nine companies reported paying salaries and bonuses that averaged $604,190 to their 515 top executives. Only about half the firms reported on the additional long-term compensation; that averaged another $507,570. If that was typical for the entire group, the total amount received from the companies by each of these 515 management superstars was over $1.1 million.[10]

Now, a million dollars is not what it used to be, but it still puts the person who has it in a very different class of society than most. The average pay received by one of these corporate managers for one year is more than a worker who earned the 1983 average family income would receive for an entire working life beginning at age eighteen until retirement at age sixty-five. Little wonder that 76 percent of the American public does not believe that top corporate executives are worth what they get![11]

Of course, high salaries are only the first brick in the wall of income and wealth differentials. While the ordinary worker must spend virtually all income for family maintenance, the $1-million-a-year earners can comfortably invest several tens or even hundreds of thousands of dollars each year. The yield on such investments often greatly exceeds the already large salaries, making it easy for the rich to continue to get richer. In 1979 people with incomes of over $1 million received less than 25 percent of the total from wages and salaries, professional fees, royalties, and business profits. The rest came from amounts generated by accumulated wealth.[12]

Once in place, such wealth assumes tremendous power in shaping the goals of society and in settling the rules by which the position and fortune of the few will be protected.

C. Inequality and Incentive

In the capitalist system, inequalities of wealth and income are maintained and defended not so much out of perversity as out of the conviction that they are necessary to the proper functioning of the system. The hope of greater gain is the carrot that lures the ambitious and the talented to ever higher performance, and the fear of not having enough is the goad to make the complacent produce at minimally acceptable levels. Looked at from either side, inequality is perceived as a necessary incentive.

The logic is summed up well in these words of economist Arthur Okun:

> I would perfer more equality of income to less and would like complete equality of income best of all. . . . [But] in pursuing such a goal, society would forego any opportunity to use material rewards as incentives to production. And that would lead to the inefficiencies that would be harmful to the welfare of the majority. Any insistence on carving the pie into equal slices could shrink the size of the pie. That fact poses the trade-off between economic equality and economic efficiency. Insofar as inequality does serve to promote efficiency . . . I can accept some measure of it as a practicality.[13]

The policy issue, of course, is how much inequality is required for the functioning of the system? Is it enough that the top incomes be three or five times those at the bottom, or must they be ten or fifty or five hundred times larger?

To ask such a question is to move beyond the realm of economics and into that of psychology. For ultimately the question being asked is, what does it take to motivate a person? There are no hard-and-fast answers, but there is evidence to be cited. The American income ratio of nine to one between the top 20 percent and the bottom 20 percent of the population is defended as necessary. Yet West Germany functions well with 36 percent less income inequality, and Japan somehow gets by quite efficiently with 50 percent less. These are the very countries whose productivity we would most like to emulate. Indeed, of all major industrial-market countries, only France has a more unequal income distribution than does the United States.

Turning to our own recent history, we see that increased inequality does not guarantee better economic performance. Those inequalities are greater now than they were during the 1950s and 1960s, yet it is hard to imagine a measure by which it can be claimed that our present situation is more sound or satisfying.

It is clear that every economy has its system of incentives, and a significant element must be appropriate financial reward. It is equally clear, however, that beyond a certain point disparities in financial rewards become counterproductive. Those at the top come to require such large increments for only marginal increases in productivity that all economic rationale is lost, and those at the bottom are demoralized beyond cooperation when their relatively modest demands are rebuffed on the grounds that wages in this country are forcing production overseas.

Part of the poverty of our system is that it knows only one way to show the value of an individual—how much money he or she has or makes. Until additional incentives are found, there is little hope of narrowing the large and growing gaps of wealth and income in our society.

D. Myths of the Tax System

No discussion of the distribution of income and wealth would be complete without at least a mention of the tax system. Two myths deserve special attention.

The first of these is that the tax system in this country is truly progressive—that is, that those who earn more money are taxed more heavily than those earning less. Such an assumption certainly fits well with the public's general notion of fairness. But proving or disproving such an assumption is more difficult than it might seem. Neither the Internal Revenue Service nor the Census Bureau nor most state and local governments do the sort of calculations that would provide the necessary data; neither do they allow outsiders to have access to their records. However, Joseph Pechman of the Brookings Institution has devised a computer model that reveals the outlines quite clearly. It takes into account all major forms of taxation: individual and corporate income taxes, property, sales, and payroll taxes, and levies on personal property and motor vehicles—at federal, state, and local levels.[14]

Table 6.6

Total Taxes as a Percentage of Income for Groups of the U.S. Population, 1966 and 1985

Income Group of U.S. Population	*% Paid in Taxes with* Most Progressive Assumptions		Least Progressive Assumptions	
	1966	**1985**	**1966**	**1985**
Lowest 10%	16.8%	21.9%	27.5%	28.2%
2nd 10%	18.9	21.3	24.8	25.6
3rd 10%	21.7	21.4	26.0	24.6
4th 10%	22.6	22.5	25.9	25.2
5th 10%	22.8	23.1	25.8	25.3
6th 10%	22.7	23.1	25.6	25.6
7th 10%	22.7	23.7	25.5	25.4
8th 10%	23.1	24.6	25.5	26.3
9th 10%	23.3	25.1	25.1	26.1
Richest 10%	30.1	25.3	25.9	23.3

Source: Brookings Institution MERGE files from various federal, state, and local tax records as reported in Joseph A. Pechman, *Who Paid the Taxes, 1966-85?* (Washington: Brookings Institution, 1985), pp. 77, 80.

In the first column of Table 6.6 (above), Pechman projects the rate of taxation for various groups based on the most progressive assumptions—that is, that those who have more carry a heavier tax burden. The second column projects the effect of the least progressive assumptions. It is clear that even in the most liberal scenario, the percentage of income actually paid in taxes differs very little from group to group. At most, the richest people in the population pay not quite 3.5 percentage points more in taxes than the poorest group. If less generous assumptions are made about how the taxes are levied, the poor may actually pay 5 percentage points more of their income than do the rich!

The second startling fact in Table 6.6 is that regardless of the assumptions made, the top 10 percent of the population are paying a smaller percentage in taxes now than they were twenty years ago, while the poorest 10 percent are paying a larger portion of their income.

Whatever the positive values in our various forms of taxation, it is hard to make the case that the system as a whole is truly progressive. And without progressivity, it is difficult to craft a definition of fairness that could apply to the tax code.

Indeed, the policies of government sometimes seem designed to widen the gaps in our society. The combined effects of tax and budget cuts in 1982 are a good example. A Congressional Budget Office study shows that between 1983 and 1985, individuals with incomes of over $80,000 per year (just 1.5 percent of the country's population) increased their after-tax income by $24,000. By contrast, those with an income below $10,000 per year (almost one-quarter of the population) lost $1,100 from the same policies.[15]

The second myth of our tax system is that corporations pay too much in this age of big government. Just how much is too much is, of course, a matter of public debate. But we can at least note in Table 6.7 (below) that the share of federal income tax paid by corporations has been falling steadily for over thirty years. By 1983 the corporate burden was less than one-fourth what it had been in 1950.

No one knows how the new tax reform law of 1986 will play out over the next several years. It is for this reason that an extended discussion of the American tax system here would be almost fruitless. What those of biblical faith must do is scrutinize the new law, keeping in mind the myths just exposed, and decide from the perspective of human dignity whether it fairly allocates the burdens and benefits of society. That is what an exemplary tax system should do. If the new program repeats the perverse results of the 1982 tax cut and causes the poor to continue bearing a proportionately equal burden with the rich, the law deserves to be challenged and changed.

III. Values: The Christian Struggle with Class

A. Class: An American Definition

In the political culture of this country, it has been acceptable to express concern about the problems of poverty as long as poverty is regarded as an accident of history or the result of the personal failings of the impoverished. Great sympathy for the poor may be expressed. Far-reaching programs of government to alleviate hardship may be debated and even enacted into law. What has not been acceptable is any attempt to deal with poverty and wealth as interrelated realities. That smacks too much of class analysis.

Table 6.7

Federal Income Tax Shares of Corporations and Individuals, 1950-1983

% of Federal Income Taxes Paid by:	1950s	1960s	1970s	1983
Corporations	27.6%	21.3%	15.0%	6.2%
Individuals	54.8	63.1	73.5	82.9

Sources: Joint Committee on Taxation, Tax Policy and Capital Formation, the 1983 Economic Report of the President, and data from the U.S. Department of the Treasury.

Generally speaking, when people think of class at all, what comes to mind is a three-tiered income structure of upper, middle, and lower groups. However, the phrase "lower class" has such a derogatory, judgmental ring to it that, in the name of an egalitarian spirit, it is usually replaced by the word "poor." To speak of "the upper class" sounds either accusatory or arrogant, depending on whether one is in or out of it, so this phrase too is seldom used. That leaves "middle class" as the only truly palatable term. Not surprisingly, almost everyone thinks of himself or herself as being middle class. When Congress tried to limit some of the supply-side tax cuts going to those with a $50,000 income, the Reagan administration charged that such interference was an attack on America's great middle class, even though anyone making above $50,000 was in the top 10 percent of the population. Years ago, when running for president, even Nelson Rockefeller felt compelled to describe himself as part of the middle class. Nothing could be a surer sign of the utter bankruptcy of a popular concept.

The main reason that Americans have such difficulty in speaking meaningfully about class is that it is perceived as part of the Marxist vocabulary. For Marxists, class is a technical concept that divides the population by the way in which income is derived rather than by the amount of income received. Capital owners (the bourgeoisie) live by the power and income their investments produce, and these are constantly regenerated and enlarged. Laborers (the proletariat) live by the incremental sale of their time, bodies, and minds; these resources are constantly depleted. Workers have no control over the process of the product and have no share in whatever profit is made. Thus the two classes[16] are perceived as being hostile camps engaged in an unending economic struggle.

Do such class realities exist in today's world, or is this merely the inflammatory vocabulary of dissidents who long for economic benefits they do not deserve and political power they cannot obtain? It is clear that the class relationships Karl Marx described in England over a hundred years ago have little direct applicability in the United States today. That does not mean, however, that the concept of class is meaningless. Over 98 percent of the population earns under $80,000 a year. Yet in 1979 there were 3,542 families that filed income tax returns indicating an adjusted gross income of over $1 million. (In fact, they averaged $2.2 million.) More than three-fourths of their income was "unearned"—that is, derived from such sources as dividends, interest, royalties, and the sale of assets. Wages and salaries played only a small part in their income stream.[17] People who live on their investments are in a very different economic world than those who live on the wages and salaries that their employment can produce. Of course, an income gap is not the same as a *class struggle*. That is what does *not* exist in the United States. A class struggle is a *conscious* attempt by dispossessed segments of society to reshape society along new lines that will focus on the universal meeting of need rather than on the unfettered right to seek profits. Such a struggle does exist in many Third World countries. There, capitalist economic structures are often closer to the naked nineteenth-century forms criticized by Marx than are the structures in this country that have served 80 percent of the people in the United States well enough to prevent the raising of a class consciousness.

It is only natural, then, that churches in the Third World have begun to incorporate class struggle into a new theological framework. But that is running ahead of our discussion. First we must consider the church's more traditional attitudes toward class issues.

B. Church Thought on Class Issues

The biblical tradition has been cumbersome economic baggage for the church since the advent of capitalism. It is not just that the Old Testament features prophetic tirades against injustice, or that Jesus' parables and teaching so often touch upon economic responsibility. There is running through much of the biblical literature an underlying assumption of equality and of God's commitment to the well-being of the whole people and of the whole world, not just of Israel. This sense of universal equality is captured in Paul's words in Galatians 3:28: "There is neither Jew nor Greek, there is neither slave nor free, there is neither male nor female; for you are all one in Christ Jesus."

Such radical equality did not fit well with an emerging economic order that counted upon the aggressive seeking of personal gain not only as the motive force but also as the reward structure and the system of checks on abuses of power. Equality came to be equality of spirit and equality before God—not necessarily equality in social or economic condition.

Relieved of the burden of seeking equality on earth, Calvin and his followers led the way in formulating concepts more congenial to capitalism. The theological purpose of the doctrine of predestination was to testify to the absolute sovereignty of God and to demonstrate the wonder of God's grace. In the hands and hearts of the businessmen who dominated church life in Calvin's Geneva, however, the doctrine was twisted in form and became a justification for indifference to the plight of the poor. Thus the elements of a firm class system were established on the grounds of doctrine.

Both rich and poor had interrelated roles in glorifying God. As Calvin himself put it in his commentary on Deuteronomy 16:11, "When the rich have the wherewithal to do good and the poor thank God for having something to eat, they all glorify God." Calvin always stressed what his followers often forgot—if wealth is a blessing of God, it carries the responsibility of doing good. Even so, while acts of charity were duties of faith, they were nevertheless voluntary. The exhortation to help the poor has always been tolerable to the privileged because it leaves to the individual the matter of how much is to be given and how it is to be done. That leaves the essential relationship between wealth and poverty intact.

C. Class and Liberation Theology

It is precisely the unwillingness to see the gospel reduced to mere individualistic pious actions that lies at the heart of what has come to be known as liberation theology. The fact that the movement emerged first from the Roman Catholic traditions of Latin America is significant. There, perhaps more than anywhere else in Western Christendom, the church had become the willing accomplice of the rich in domesticating the poor. Poverty was idealized. "Blessed are the poor" became not only consolation but a subtle mechanism for maintaining the status quo. Because Jesus was with them in their poverty and their powerlessness, no change of circumstance was needed to bring greater blessing. Wretchedness was sacralized, and the right of the rich and powerful to rule was confirmed theologically.

The liberation movement in the church also begins with the conviction that God stands on the side of the poor to console but also to intervene on their behalf and work against the rich and the powerful who administer an unjust system. God takes sides. The Exodus deliverance is the paradigm. The problem is not the failure of individuals but a social-economic-political system that dehumanizes people by holding them in bondage. God calls his people to free themselves from that system, to speak and act against it. Through them God is acting in history for the liberation of the poor as a class and the liberation of the world as a whole.

Liberation theology has been attacked on the grounds that it fosters a Marxist concept of class struggle. The charge is usually twofold: that to acknowledge class reality undermines the Christian message of unity, and that the concept of class struggle controverts the gospel of love.

To answer the first charge, liberation theologians point out that class conflict is a fundamental fact of the struggle for justice, not something invented by Karl Marx. To quote Gustavo Gutiérrez, a Peruvian and one of the first expositors of liberation theology,

> Paradoxically, what the groups in power call "advocating" class struggle is really an expression of a will to abolish its causes, to abolish them, not cover them over, to eliminate the appropriation by a few of the wealth created by the work of the many and not to make lyrical calls to social harmony. . . . To "advocate" class struggle, therefore, is to reject a situation in which there are oppressed and oppressors. . . . To build a just society today necessarily implies the active and conscious participation in the class struggle that is occurring before our eyes.[18]

The second common charge is that to advocate class struggle violates precepts of Christian love. To state that God adopts a preferential option for the poor in the struggle with the rich seems to mean that God loves the rich less. To this objection liberation theologians answer that God loves the rich not less but differently. Both rich and poor, both exploiters and exploited are caught at different points in the web of economic injustice. It is a situation in which both are dehumanized, a situation from which both must be liberated simultaneously. God shows love for the poor by seeking to change the system that deprives them of truly human dignity. God shows love for the rich by seeking to change a system that diminishes their humanity by making privilege dependent on the oppression of others.

How is such a system to be changed? Goodwill and reason are seldom enough. There are few historical examples of the voluntary abandonment of power and privilege by classes or nations or even individuals. Pressure from below has usually been required. This raises the spectre of violence. Does not class struggle ultimately end in violent revolution? And how can authentic Christians condone the use of violence? These are difficult questions. Regarding the answer to the first question, there is virtual unanimity among liberation theologians: the choice is not between violence and nonviolence. The present class system exists by countless daily acts of violence. A Mercedes Benz purchased in Bogotá is financed by the surplus profits generated by having an unfairly low minimum wage. Malnutrition rises in Brazil because a few foreign companies and a few hundred large landowners decided that more money can be made by growing soybeans for export than by growing black beans for the local diet. Millions of Mexico's poor consume less when imports are slashed to comply with an International Monetary Fund austerity program designed to pay interest to foreign banks. Tens of thousands of peasants seeking land are terrorized by Salvadoran death squads at the service of the rich.

All this is violence, but the world does not hear the cries. The poor suffer quietly, and they die quietly. In the strange morality of church and society, violence is generally called by name only when someone dies suddenly from a bomb burst or a gunshot used to protest or resist an established, unjust system.

Revolutionary change need not be violent. There can be peaceful change if it is allowed to occur. The level of violence is determined primarily by the manner in which and the ferocity with which the entrenched classes defend their privilege.

Liberation theologians are divided on the second question of whether Christians should support armed struggle. Some reluctantly support it, arguing that in many Third World countries all other options have been exhausted. Others, like Dom Helder Camara, the retired Brazilian bishop, reject it on tactical grounds. They argue that the forces opposed to change are so strong that they cannot be overthrown or that the cost of doing it in terms of human misery would be unacceptably high. Still others maintain that the only Christian course is nonviolence, following the example of Jesus.

José Míguez Bonino, an Argentinian Methodist theologian, agrees that Jesus certainly rejected the role of messianic leader of an armed rebellion against Rome. He did not become a Zealot, but he left no doubt that he sided with the poor against the powerful: "When the crucial moment arrived, he was judged and executed as a subversive. If a Christian wants to follow in his steps and make his option for non-violence credible, he will have to make sure that he has so clearly made his choices that he will unequivocally be convicted for the subversion of the oppressive order! One may doubt that this is the case in much that poses as *Christian* rejection of violence."[19]

Table 6.8

Income Distribution in the United States and in Less Developed Countries

Income Group	**% of National Household Income**	
	U.S.	**LDCs**
Wealthiest 20%	41.6%	51.4%
4th 20%	24.3	20.7
3rd 20%	17.5	13.4
2nd 20%	11.6	8.7
Poorest 20%	5.1	5.8

Sources: U.S. Census data cited in *U.S.: A Statistical Portrait*, ed. Andrew Hacker (New York: Viking Press, 1983), p. 144. LDC data cited in *U.S. Foreign Policy and the Third World: Agenda 1983*, ed. John P. Lewis and Valeriana Kallab (New York: Praeger, 1983), p. 228.

D. Seeking Justice—The American Context

Even for North Americans of moderate perspectives, the bald realities of class in Latin America justify a radical stand for the church there. However, many such sympathetic people find it hard to see any connection between that situation and reality as they know it in this country.

However, the size and wealth of the American economy as a whole tend to mask similar realities in the distribution of income and power in this country. A look at one last table—Table 6.8 (on p. 122)—may help make that clearer.

Income distribution is unquestionably more equitable in the United States than in less developed countries, but it is not dramatically better. Predictably, the wealthiest American families have less of a stranglehold on the economy, receiving 10 percentage points less than their LDC counterparts. The middle groups in the U.S. get a larger share, as might be expected. The surprising factor is that the poorest fifth of the U.S. population gets somewhat less of the national income than the corresponding group in the economically less developed countries. (It is important to stress, however, that the life circumstances of these two groups are not comparable. The American poor are far better off.)

What the figures really tell us is that similar patterns of income sharing are softened in the United States by the overall wealth of the country. Thus 5.1 percent of a three-trillion-dollar national economy doesn't hurt as much as 5.8 percent of a desperately poor national economy. Nevertheless, the United States has depended on long-term economic growth to make a very unequal income distribution palatable. Such wealth has allowed this country to escape the kind of social turmoil and overt class conflict that we see in so many other countries.

Yet we cannot afford complacency. For what would happen if economic growth slowed or stopped? To what lengths would the upper classes go to maintain their privileges? To what lengths would the poor be pushed to survive? Perhaps we can only speculate on the answers to these questions, but our speculations may determine how we try to prevent the problem, or how we would respond if it arises.

Even apart from apocalyptic prognostications, we may not escape the issue of income distribution. The usual assumption is that as long as abject poverty is avoided, relative income shares do not much matter. But income gaps may be more important than we have thought.

Between 1946 and 1970, the American Institute of Public Opinion made ten surveys on the correlation between income and happiness in the United States.[20] Predictably, the rich had a higher proportion of people describing themselves as happy than did the poor. But by 1970 the average income of the people at the bottom of the scale was higher than that of those in the middle brackets in 1946. Simple logic would lead us to expect a larger proportion of people to describe themselves as happy. But it was not so. The percentage of people describing themselves as unhappy remained about the same.

Why? Mainly because definitions of rich and poor are relative, not absolute. It is what social scientists sometimes call "the reference group phenomenon." Whether one "feels" poor is as much a matter of what other families possess as it is a matter of absolute level of income. Such a realization could go far in helping us understand the present malaise in the nation. While we no longer hold the title of the richest people on earth, the United States still ranks high on the list, and when various factors are taken into account, we still have one of the highest standards of living. Nevertheless, there is a sense of unease and unfulfillment that a few more dollars in the per capita gross national product will not likely cure. Perhaps we are beginning to feel, if not yet to understand, that a greater measure of equality may be crucial to our future well-being as a people.

If it is the right of all people to have property sufficient to meet their needs, there will have to be a more equitable distribution of resources to make it happen. But what do we mean by equality? Ours is a culture where the general concept of equality is much admired, but when pressed, most people limit it to the idea of equality of opportunity. That accords well with the notion that society, especially in its economic relationships, is a competitive struggle. There is the sense of fairness that says that even in the most fiercely competitive struggle, all the participants should at least start from the same point. However, what that would mean for blacks, Hispanics, women, and poorly educated children of the traditional underclass is far from clear. Indeed, "equality of opportunity" seems more a phrase to mask indifference than a term to express a serious conviction about the way society should work.

The equality sought by biblical faith is different. It must be an equality defined in human terms, not in terms of shares of this or that good, talent, or opportunity. As ethicist George Thomas put it two decades ago, "Christians must supplement the individualistic ideal of equality of opportunity with the more humane ideal of *equality of consideration*. This is the principle that everyone should be genuinely taken into account in the distribution of social benefit and should be helped by the state to develop his capacities and fulfill his needs as far as possible."[21]

As we consider Thomas's prescription, we must understand that the struggle is a hard one, for it is a struggle to change basic attitudes, to win hearts and minds. Harvard philosopher Christopher Jencks perhaps expressed it best: "A successful compaign for reducing economic inequality probably requires two things. First, those with low incomes must cease to accept their condition as inevitable and just. . . . Second, some of those with high incomes, and especially the children of those with high incomes, must begin to feel ashamed of economic inequality."[22]

There will be no voluntary relinquishment of power and privilege by most of those at the top. The impetus for change must come mainly from below, from those who suffer the most. However, they must be joined by what Jürgen Moltmann calls "class betrayers," those who sense a higher loyalty than the shared interests of the privileged.[23] The church has such people in its midst. Let our call be to a commitment that is beyond class in the search for a more just distribution of economic resources both in our own country and in a global setting.

Notes

1. Cited by Robert L. Heilbroner and Aaron Singer in *The Economic Transformation of America* (New York: Harcourt Brace Jovanovich, 1977), p. 177.

2. *Survey of Economic Opportunity* and *Current Population Survey* (Washington: Department of Commerce, 1979).

3. *The State of Black America, 1984,* vol. 8, ed. James D. Williams (New Brunswick, N.J.: Transaction Books, 1984), p. i.

4. *The State of Black America, 1984,* vol. 8, p. i.

5. Data cited in *Probe,* May-June 1982, p. 1.

6. Data cited in "Slimmer Middle, Bigger Bottom," *Dollars and Sense,* Apr. 1984, p. 5.

7. These figures were documented in studies cited by John A. Brittain in *Inheritance and the Inequality of Material Wealth* (Washington: Brookings Institution, 1978), and in a study of the Survey Research Center of the University of Michigan for the Federal Reserve and other federal agencies. The latter was reported in the *Washington Post,* 26 July 1986.

8. Statistics from a study by Professor James Smith of the University of Michigan as cited in *The Polarization of America* (New York: Industrial Union Department [AFL-CIO], 1986), p. 49.

9. Thurow, *The Zero-Sum Society: Distribution and the Possibilities for Economic Change* (New York: Basic Books, 1980), pp. 175-77.

10. Figures calculated from a data report in *Business Week,* 7 May 1984, pp. 96-110.

11. "Top Executive Pay Peeves the Public," *Business Week,* 25 June 1984, p. 15.

12. *U.S.: A Statistical Portrait,* ed. Andrew Hacker (New York: Viking Press, 1983).

13. Okun, *Equality and Efficiency: The Big Trade-off* (Washington: Brookings Institution, 1975).

14. Pechman, *Who Paid the Taxes, 1966-85?* (Washington: Brookings Institution, 1985), pp. 77, 80.

15. Congressional Budget Office, *The Combined Effect of Major Changes in Federal Taxes and Spending Programs since 1981* (Washington: U.S. Government Printing Office, 1984), p. 10, table 5.

16. Marx did acknowledge the existence of something of a middle group, the petite bourgeoisie, made up of artisans, producers, and merchants who had small investments in their own businesses in which they both worked and hired a few others. He maintained, however, that large enterprises would ultimately force this group into the laboring class.

17. *U.S.: A Statistical Portrait,* p. 172.

18. Gutiérrez, *A Theology of Liberation,* trans. Inda Caridad, Sr., and John Eagleson (Maryknoll, N.Y.: Orbis Books, 1973), p. 274.

19. Míguez Bonino, *Doing Theology in a Revolutionary Situation,* ed. William Lazareth (Philadelphia: Fortress Press, 1975), p. 123.

20. R. A. Easterlin, "Does Economic Growth Improve the Human Lot?" in *Nations and Households in Economic Growth: Essays in Honor of Moses Abramovitz,* ed. P. A. David and M. W. Reder (New York: Academic Press, 1974), p. 109.

21. Thomas, *Christian Ethics and Moral Philosophy* (New York: Scribner's, 1955), pp. 317-18.

22. "Egalitarianism: Threat to a Free Market," *Business Week,* 1 Dec. 1975, p. 64.

23. Moltmann, "The Liberation of Oppressors," *Journal of the I.T.C.*, n.d., p. 81.

Chapter Seven

The Trading Game: The Economy Goes Global

I. Concepts about Trade

In a sense, an economic system is little more than a highly elaborated series of observations about life as a trading game. It describes the circumstances under which people will part with some of what they have in order to get something else. Adam Smith did not invent the process. Trade is older than history, probably as old as humankind. Of course, it cannot exist unless there is a surplus. As long as the family of the farmer or hunter, the clothing or food maker uses all that can be produced, there is nothing to exchange. But the moment there is something beyond necessity, it can be traded for someone else's surplus that will meet other needs or bring greater pleasure.

The early classical economists argued that what individuals do by nature is equally logical for nations. But international exchanges raise myriad questions. If bananas can be grown in Florida, why does the United States import them from Guatemala? The U.S. has both iron ore and coal; how can it be that we are importing steel from Japan, which has neither? Would it be better for all countries to produce locally as much as possible of everything they consume? Can all countries benefit at the same time from global trade, or must some always be sacrificed to the good of others?

We can begin to get at answering these questions by looking first at the theory and then at the practice of international trade.

A. Comparative Advantage: The Theory of Practice

David Ricardo in the early nineteenth century first elaborated what still serves as basic trade theory. The law of *comparative* advantage (or of "comparative costs," as it is sometimes called) sets out to explain why international specialization and trade occurred and why it persists even when it is not absolutely necessary. It is not just a matter of each nation specializing in something that it does more efficiently than anyone else.

Ricardo explains why trade is profitable for both countries even when one does everything better than the other.

That is not as strange as it sounds if we put the concept into a real-life situation. When I was in high school, a good friend of mine won the annual award as best typist. He was able to type well over a hundred words a minute (in the days before electric typewriters!) with a very high degree of accuracy. He was also very bright and went on to graduate from Harvard College and Harvard Law School before becoming head of a petroleum distribution company. My guess is that he still types faster than his secretaries but seldom bothers to prove it. His time is more profitably spent on the intricacies of managing a complex business than on the mechanics of producing neat letters and reports. Although he holds an absolute advantage over his secretaries in both management skills and typing speed, it is still better for him to leave the typing to others—even when they may not do it as efficiently.

Ricardo's analysis of international trade is essentially the same as my analysis of my friend's situation—just a bit more complex. As economists are wont to do, Ricardo created a simplified model to make his point. Suppose there were just two countries, England and Portugal, and that they each produced just two products, cloth and wine. Obviously, if there is no interference, trade will occur if one country produces cloth more efficiently; the other, wine. But Ricardo showed that trade would occur even if Portugal was more efficient than England on both counts. He used the following data to illustrate:

Labor hours per unit of output

Country	Wine	Cloth
England	120	100
Portugal	80	90

In this case, although Portugal can produce both wine and cloth more efficiently than England, both countries would be served by an exchange of Portuguese wine for English cloth. The Portuguese, by trading the 80 labor hours used to produce a unit of wine, produce instead a unit of cloth that would have required 90 hours of labor had they done it themselves. Likewise, the English receive a quantity of wine that would have demanded 120 labor hours to make; by trading they use only 100 hours. The result is that by specializing and trading, there will be 20 percent more cloth and 12.5 percent more wine produced by the same amount of labor. How that is actually shared between the two countries is a matter of bargaining on the exchange rate of wine for cloth. Clearly, however, both countries can benefit.

The model is simple, but the implications are profound. Theoretically at least, what is true of two countries and two products is true of all. Specialization and trade can serve the interests of all nations and the consumers within them. Real wages in all countries rise because workers are able to consume more from the same amount of labor expended. (Portuguese winemakers get cloth worth 90 hours to them for only 80 hours' work, and English clothmakers get wine worth 120 hours to them for just 100 hours' work.)

Indeed, implicit in the theory of comparative advantage is the demise of national economies and the seed of a single global economy. Under the logic of comparative advantage, economies should be reorganized along the lines of absolute specialization. According to the model, the greatest gains are achieved when one nation produces *only* wine and the other produces *only* cloth. Any attempt at *autarky*—that is, national economic self-sufficiency—will only reduce overall productivity and thus the total supply of goods to be shared.

As with most economic models, the theory of comparative advantage makes some assumptions that must be carefully noted in trying to apply it to the real world. First, it does not include any transportation costs. That is a small matter, however, since they may simply be calculated into the cost of the goods to be traded. Second, the model also assumes constant availability of products. In other words, it assumes that it is perfectly safe for a nation to specialize in one product or a few products and trust that other needs will always be supplied by trading partners at the appropriate times and in the necessary amounts. "Neither sleet, nor snow, nor gloom of night" (nor crop failure, nor ill will, nor war) will keep the trading ships "from their appointed rounds." Third, and most important, the model assumes *free* trade. This means that there must be no *tariffs*—taxes placed on imported goods, usually with the intent of protecting local producers and workers from foreign competition.

A tariff can be *prohibitive*—that is, it can be so high that it keeps out all imports of a certain product by making its price higher than that of all local producers. Or a tariff can be *partial*—high enough to protect some local producers, but low enough to leave the less efficient exposed to foreign competition. In either case, the effect is to raise the price of goods to the local consumer. It is not just the price of imports that rises. The price of *all goods* of that type will rise, whether produced domestically or abroad. Why? Because a tariff serves to reduce the available supply of a product. By the laws of the market, when supply is reduced and demand remains high, the price of the products will float up to a new equilibrium point (see Chapter One).

Import quotas have the same effect as a tariff. Domestic producers are protected by limits placed on how much of a good may be imported. For example, federal statute limits the amount of European cheese that is allowed into the United States, while diplomatic pressure puts a lid on the importation of Japanese steel and automobiles. Whatever the mechanism, the result is that the price of the good to the consumer rises. The only real difference between a tariff and a quota is that a tariff produces revenues to the government while a quota does not.

There are few things that unite economists of all stripes more than their opposition to tariffs and quotas. There is one situation, however, in which economists are divided on trade barriers. It involves the so-called *infant industry* argument. Classical economists acknowledge that a newly established industry cannot be fully competitive until it reaches a large enough size to be able to take advantage of economies of scale. A new plant faced by a flood of cheaper foreign imports before it reaches optimal size might never have a chance to prove how efficient it can be. This problem is especially acute in the developing country, whose industries are all "infant industries." The danger is that capital, confronted by such a bleak outlook, will tend to seek other investment opportunities, thus leaving the country in a permanent state of underdevelopment. In such a situation, even many diehard free-marketers agree that protection may be necessary. While some favor a temporary tariff, others would argue for government's directly subsidizing the investment to accelerate growth to optimal scale.

The usefulness of the comparative advantage model is limited because it makes some other assumptions that do not fit well with the real world. It assumes, for instance, that the same people will benefit from the increased flow of traded goods as benefited from the goods when they were produced locally. That is certainly not always the case. A few years ago, it made perfectly good economic sense for Brazil to stop planting large tracts of black beans in order to exercise its comparative advantage in growing soybeans for export. The economic logic, however, failed to calculate the increased hunger of peasants who had counted upon the black beans as part of a subsistence-level diet. A few foreign corporations and a few hundred large landowners made fortunes, and poor consumers suffered. The logic of trade assumes that it is economically better to sell a high-value crop like soybeans and, if necessary, import a lower-value crop like black beans. Perhaps, but unless there is a guarantee that the poor who depended on the locally produced beans receive the imported beans at the same price, the suffering may cancel out the macro-economic gains.

Another assumption of the model is that there is complete mobility of labor—that workers displaced from one area of production will always find work waiting for them in a more productive sector. In short, the comparative advantage model assumes away the problem of unemployment. If only it were so easy. In reality, the handling of displaced workers in a global trading environment is one of the issues of contemporary economics that most bedevils economists and policymakers in both industrially advanced and less developed countries.

Despite its huge assumptions and blind spots that bring it into conflict with the real world, the comparative advantage model elaborated by David Ricardo created a powerful tool for economic analysis. Despite all its limitations, it provides a glimpse of the promise held out by a global economy of rational and just interdependence. To acknowledge the possibility, however, is not to ignore the problems that must be addressed.

B. Trade: The Practice of Theory

For two hundred years the theory of comparative advantage has served well as a principle to guide international exchange. The call to free trade is still regularly invoked in college texts and congressional debates. But in economics, as in most fields, principle and practice ought never to be confused. Even in Ricardo's time, the Ricardian world of trade did not exist. It was always more aspiration than explanation. Much less does that world exist today.

The world is not made up of four-and-a-half billion individuals, but of four-and-a-half billion people living in 175 countries. International trade is not a transaction between individuals or even between companies, but between nations. Even in Ricardo's simplified model, the exchange was not between winemakers and clothmakers but between Portugal and England. Despite free-trade rhetoric, governments have taken a more active role in promoting the trade of their country's industries. Public agencies are increasingly involved in facilitating, negotiating, and administering international trade transactions. Canada has its Wheat Board, Colombia has its Coffee Federation, Gabon has the Cocoa Bureau, Japan has MITI, West Germany has unending trade delegations, and the United States, bastion of free enterprise, has the Export-Import Bank, the Departments of Defense and Agriculture, which hawk products abroad, and a commercial section in every fair-sized embassy to push sales of all sorts.

The main reason for all this official trade activity is that economic exchange across international borders creates problems vastly more complex than exchanges within the same country. Ricardo noted this fact in commenting on his simplified model: "The labour of 100 Englishmen cannot be given for that of 80 Englishmen, but the produce of the labour of 100 may be given for the produce of the labour of 80 Portuguese, 60 Russians, or 120 East Indians. The difference between a single country and many is easily accounted for, by considering the difficulty with which capital [is] moved from one country to another, to seek more profitable employment."[1]

Of particular concern to many nations today is their *balance of payments* position—that is, the relationship between the money value of goods exported and that of goods imported. Countries seeking to develop an industrial base typically borrow capital from abroad. Interest on these loans must be paid, and eventually the principal must be returned. At the same time, the country may import a variety of goods for its people, ranging from machine tools for industry, to luxury automobiles for elite groups, to grain to supplement the inadequate diet of the poor. The only means a country has to pay for such goods is to export products, capital, or services in return. If it is unable to sell enough abroad to pay for its imports and for past debt, its future is effectively mortgaged to finance its present consumption. Neither national politics nor international bankers will allow that to continue indefinitely. Thus there is constant pressure on developing countries to increase exports to match imports. Governments often stand or fall on their ability to do that, or at least to convince creditors that the goal is in sight.

The need to manage trade relationships in order to achieve other macro-economic goals has led to significant changes in business behavior and in the way both policymakers and theorists think about international exchange. Consider the revival of barter arrangements in the global economy. In a world dominated by international finance, the Ricardian model of wine exchanged for cloth seems overly simplistic. But in a world of petroleum cartels and hard currency shortages, barter has its benefits. Mexico has arranged a long-term trade of petroleum for French technology in an agreement that avoids the dilemmas of drastic changes in price or currency values. People in Hungary like Levi's blue jeans, but the government can't afford to import them. So Levi-Strauss agreed to sell them production equipment and technical expertise—not for dollars, but for a portion of the plant's annual output. McDonnell-Douglas has traded passenger jets to Yugoslavia for such things as crystal glassware, cutting tools, leather goods, and canned hams.[2] It involves only one more short step for international trade agencies of governments to undertake such nonmarket transactions directly instead of involving corporate intermediaries.

The purpose here is not to predict that this will happen or that it should. Rather, the purpose is simply to note that new realities are giving rise to new practices that do not accord well with traditional theories about free trade. International exchange has become too crucial to national life for it to remain outside the realm of public policy, as followers of Adam Smith might prefer. Given the seriousness of the problems that lie before us as the world gropes its way toward a truly global economy, government involvement in international trade is bound to increase. As happened with the Keynesian correction in the 1930s, theory will simply have to adjust to reality. It is likely that the coming years will see significant additions to trade theory that both build upon and depart from the law of comparative advantage.

II. Realities: Real-World Trade—Open Doors and Barricades

A. First World Trade: The Problem of Protectionism

Everyone is in favor of free trade—in good times, when producers can sell all they can make, and when everyone who wants to work has a job. But when the economy goes sour, when sales go soft and unemployment lines grow long, protectionist pressures build for a nation to keep what it has and to get more if it can whether or not it has a comparative advantage. The results can be disastrous.

A case in point is the Smoot-Hawley Tariff Act of 1929. For several years before the stock-market collapse of that year, American agriculture had already been in a depression. Since farmers were part of the backbone of the Republican Party, it is not surprising that in the 1928 presidential campaign Herbert Hoover ran on a platform that promised to help farmers by raising tariffs on agricultural products. Once in office, Hoover did just that. But what started as an attempt to help distressed farmers soon grew into a bill that fostered across-the-board protectionism. As economists had warned with almost a single voice, other countries retaliated with their own versions of the Smoot-Hawley Act. International trade plummeted. In just three years, overall U.S. exports fell by more than two-thirds. Auto exports dropped by 85 percent and wheat exports by over 95 percent. Ironically, the farmers that the protectionist legislation was designed to help may have suffered most from the deepening depression.

After World War II, remembering the disaster of the Smoot-Hawley Act, world leaders awoke to the need for a more open international economic environment. Through the Marshall Plan, the Bretton Woods agreement, and a European and Japanese recovery based on international trade, the world economy became interdependent as never before. The result was that for over a quarter of a century the industrialized nations showed steady progress in reducing barriers to trade. By the 1970s, however, protectionist sentiments began to revive. In the 1980s the world teeters on the brink of a new trade war that has the potential to plunge us into another global depression. How has this happened, and why?

One reason, ironically, is the successful economic recovery of Japan and Europe. For over two decades following World War II, the U.S. was the unchallenged leader of the global market system, and ran a steady trade surplus with both countries. Neither Japan nor Europe could contest U.S. trade supremacy because both were occupied primarily with rebuilding war-ravaged economies. Indeed, there was so much rebuilding to be done that all industrial economies could run perpetually in high gear without raising the cry for protectionism. But by the mid-1970s both Europe and Japan had recovered fully from the war and had resumed full competition with the U.S. in the international arena. Within a decade the American trade balance turned negative: America was importing far more than it was exporting. National industries began to feel the pinch of competition from foreign firms with up-to-the-minute technology. The clamor for protectionism increased.

A second reason for the new spirit of protectionism is the rise of transnational corporations. In response to saturated markets and increased foreign and domestic competition, large corporations began to move abroad, first to other industrialized countries and then to less developed areas. There had always been a few such companies, but the 1960s saw a flood of them, mostly American, but later European and Japanese as well. Many firms set up shop in developing nations because local governments wanted (and required) local production, not imports. Other firms responded to the lure of a highly protected, monopolistic market with cheap labor. They were able to preserve for themselves the small local market free of international competition and use the host country as a base for exports. As a result, foreign investment became a substitute for foreign trade. An increase in international sales that previously might have meant more jobs in Pennsylvania or Illinois now meant more plants and work in Europe or Asia. Labor economists estimate that the $227 billion in U.S. investments abroad created 4.2 million jobs in other countries rather than in the U.S. Naturally, organized labor in the U.S. has become a vociferous supporter of efforts to extend controls over the functioning of transnational corporations.

A third reason for the concern over protectionism has been the development of so-called export platforms—industries in Third World countries producing exclusively for export to markets in rich countries. These platforms have threatened workers and some manufacturers in the U.S. and other industrialized nations. Workers are worried because these industries have shifted hundreds of thousands of jobs to South Korea, Taiwan, Hong Kong, Singapore, and Mexico along the U.S. border. In these countries wages are low, and unions are weak or nonexistent. Some domestic manufacturers are worried because their competitors operating from export platforms are able to produce goods at a substantially lower cost. It is worth noting that export platforms owe their development in large measure to U.S. laws permitting American companies to send components abroad for assembly and to re-import the final product with import taxes paid only on the value added—essentially labor costs. Unions argued that this was really a tax subsidy to keep consumer prices low and business profits up at the expense of jobs for American workers. At first, business supported the tax because it was a cheap method of assembling final products. But now the export platforms have moved beyond contract assembly work for foreign firms to making their own products. Business has therefore joined labor in seeking protection from these operations.

A fourth reason for the recrudescence of protectionist sentiment, at least in the U.S., is the labor productivity crisis. Average growth in worker output was just 1.1 percent from 1973 to 1978, compared with 3.2 percent from 1948 to 1965. Worse still, during the two-year period from 1978 to 1980, growth was actually negative—that is, worker productivity declined. Management has been quick to blame American workers for this, charging poor work habits and extravagant wage demands (which, properly speaking, are not directly related to labor productivity). A major reason for this decline, however, lies in the decision that management made fifteen to twenty years ago not to invest heavily in the new technologies of basic industries such as steel and automobiles. Today these same managers join labor in pleading for a temporary reprieve from the pressures of more technologically advanced foreign firms, whose goods claim a larger and larger share of the American market. Their argument, in a sense, is akin to the "infant industry" argument previously discussed: give us time to retool, through quotas or tariffs, and we will regain a competitive position in the international market.

A fifth and final reason for the new protectionist sentiment has been the rise of the dollar against other world currencies. There was a time when all of the world's currencies were pegged to the dollar, which in turn was pegged to gold. The value of the dollar was known—thirty-five of them could always get you one troy ounce of gold. But the U.S. went off the gold standard in 1971, and since then the dollar has floated in international currency markets just like any other currencies, responding to the demand of investors, speculators, and consumers and to the supply of money created by commercial banks and the U.S. Federal Reserve. The rising dollar created a double problem for the U.S.: American consumers bought more imports because their price, relative to that of goods produced in the U.S., had dropped, and foreign consumers bought fewer U.S. goods because their price, relative to that of domestically produced goods, had risen.

This factor has also contributed to the trade imbalance that has been in the news so much in recent years. Since 1986, the U.S. government has attempted to address this problem by allowing the value of the dollar to drop sharply relative to the value of other currencies, in the hope that U.S. goods would become cheaper and thereby raise the demand both in this country and abroad. This decline of the dollar against other currencies was caused in part by the growing U.S. deficit and trade imbalances that diminished international confidence in the American economy. But devaluation of the dollar is also a policy designed to recapture foreign markets for American goods and to protect the jobs of American workers.

Trade and protectionism are complex issues that tie countries together. The United States' attempts to defend its economy by allowing the value of the dollar to slide have sparked other countries to consider similar measures. The protectionist spirit could set off a trade war that would be disastrous to our highly integrated world economy. Tariffs and quotas, for example, might protect a beleaguered American steel industry, but at the same time hurt Mexico and Brazil, both of which depend heavily on steel exports to generate foreign exchange to meet payments on international loans held by American banks. A default by either of these countries could lead to bank failures in the U.S. and possibly bring on a collapse of the international financial structure.

So why not abandon all protectionism and go with Adam Smith's idea of totally free trade? In theory it would make a lot of sense. In practice, however, it will not happen—at least not in the near future. Comparative advantage is not permanent. It shifts from one country to another and from one product to another. And it oftentimes does so faster than labor and capital can adjust to the changes. The problem of displaced workers remains long after an industry has died. The long-term solution is to manage these changes, soften the blow to individuals and communities, and realize that there might have to be sacrifices in one part of the world to prevent misery in another. This is a tall order, but without such global thinking we shall never escape the spectre of protectionism and its consequences.

B. The Double Dilemma of Third World Trade

It is true that industrialized countries have trade problems. But their trade problems pale by comparison with those of less developed countries, which have always been regarded as "the hewers of wood and drawers of water" in international economic relationships. The problem goes back centuries to the European "discovery" of the rest of the world. The new lands were regarded as treasure troves of precious metals, raw materials, agricultural products, and cheap labor.

It was not just a matter of comparative advantage. The colonial powers systematically restructured traditional economies to provide goods for European consumption and to ensure a market for European exports. Needs of the local population were secondary. An instructive example is the development of plantation agriculture. Land was shifted from the production of the traditional combination of foodstuffs to the production of specialized export crops—sugar, tobacco, coffee—and later to bananas, soybeans, coconuts, and cattle. Vast tracts of land could be dedicated to such crops only if basic grains and other food necessities were shipped in. Thus, from a very early date many countries were made dependent on imports for the necessities of life and were integrated into an international trading system over which they had little control.

1. How Fair the Trade?

This history lies at the heart of the first trade dilemma of Third World countries—that they are still basically the providers of *primary products* (i.e., unprocessed minerals and agricultural goods) for the world market and the purchasers of manufactured items. The declining value of these primary products lies at the root of the problem of economic development. Julius Nyerere, former president of Tanzania, captured the dilemma in his description of the country's changing trade situation: "In 1965 I could buy a tractor by selling 17.25 tons of sisal. The price of the same model in 1972 needed 42 tons of sisal. Even during the much talked of commodity boom of 1974, I still needed 57% more sisal to get the same tractor than I did nine years before. And now the sisal price has fallen again, but the tractor price has gone up further."[3]

This, of course, is not just the problem of sisal from Tanzania. It is the story of dozens of other commodities affecting the lives and opportunities of scores of nations and hundreds of millions of people. World Bank data show that an index of thirty-four commodities, representing about 60 percent of Third World exports other than petroleum, purchased 40 percent fewer industrial goods in 1972 than in 1954. The situation has deteriorated further since then. In 1982 the International Monetary Fund reported that the gap in purchasing power between primary products and manufactured goods was the greatest it had been in twenty-five years. And at the 1987 meeting of the United Nations Conference on Trade and Development, it was noted that commodity prices have remained at a level even lower than those witnessed during the Depression years of the thirties.[4]

Why is this happening? Partly because of market factors. In some cases, artificial substitutes have cut deeply into the demand for natural products—for example, synthetic rubber is being used instead of natural rubber, polyester instead of cotton, wool, and silk. In other cases, alternative sources of supply have sprung up, creating a surplus that has driven the world price down. For example, African coffee now competes with that of Brazil and Colombia. Such surpluses do not always result from blind market forces, however. Corporate buyers and processors in the more developed countries have often encouraged new areas of production in order to assure supplies, drive down prices, and increase profit margins.

A more sinister reason for the devaluation of primary products vis-à-vis manufactured products is that industrialized countries manipulate the values of goods to their own advantage. To quote former Tanzanian president Julius Nyerere again,

> The tractor price is fixed according to two criteria: first, those costs of its production which will enable its producers to enjoy a high standard of living; and second, what the market will bear—which is determined by competition among the rich. And Tanzania will either buy at the price set, or go without. Conversely, we shall either sell our sisal at prices fixed by competition among the rich countries, or we shall earn no foreign exchange from it at all. . . .
>
> In a so-called free market economy, economic power depends on wealth. The wealthy can determine what will be produced because only they have power to invest. They can determine the price levels of the goods produced in their own countries and elsewhere because they have the power to buy, or to withhold sale. The poor buy and sell at whatever price suits the wealthy.[5]

If the trading game is to be more helpful in the development of Third World countries, *the price of primary products must rise* in comparison with that of manufactured goods. The only long-term success story in this regard has been the Organization of Petroleum Exporting Countries (OPEC), which caused an economic revolution in the 1970s by forcing an elevenfold increase in the price of oil. Despite this success, however, cartels probably are not the long-term answer to the trade problems of developing countries. Other producer cartels aimed at raising prices and regulating the output of a variety of primary products—from bauxite and copper to bananas and coffee—sprang up after OPEC. For the most part they have failed because the industrialized world is dependent on no other product as it is on petroleum. The more likely route for developing countries to attain more favorable terms of trade is negotiated agreements with the industrialized countries. Numerous commodity agreements already exist, and in many cases they have helped to stabilize production and prices. But they have not been designed to change the basic price relationship between primary and manufactured goods.

This can happen only if the prices of Third World exports are permanently pegged to the prices of industrial goods that less developed countries need in order to develop. Such price *indexation* would be similar to escalator clauses found in union labor contracts and would serve the same purpose of keeping poor countries from falling further behind economically. The primary prerequisite to indexation is for the U.S., Japan, and Western Europe to realize that their own long-term interests are tied to dramatically improving the economies of developing countries.

Even such dramatic changes as these in the terms of trade of primary commodities would still represent only an interim measure. Ultimately, economic improvement for less developed countries rests upon their having something more than food products and raw materials to trade. Therein lies the second dilemma for Third World nations.

2. How Free the Trade?

The world trade picture for less developed countries is a "good news–bad news" story. The good news is that the Third World share of total global exports rose from 22 percent in 1960 to 28 percent in 1981. The bad news is that if you discount the very special situation of petroleum, the non-OPEC exporting countries had their share fall from 14.8 percent in 1960 to 13.7 percent in 1981. The good news is that from 1970 to 1980, less developed countries increased their share of world manufacturing exports by 40 percent. The bad news is that they still have only 9 percent of the total. More bad news is that they garner only about 4.5 percent of the global export of technologically advanced items such as chemicals, machinery, and transportation equipment.[6] That means that the bulk of Third World manufacturing exports are in less complex consumer goods such as shoes and clothing and in first-level producer goods such as basic steel products—plates, rods, and wire, for example.

Worse news still is the fact that just four countries—South Korea, Taiwan, Hong Kong, and Singapore—account for 60 percent of the manufacturing exports of the Third World. If Brazil, Mexico, and Argentina are included, the total rises to 75 percent. Thus the situation of most poor countries is not significantly different than it was a quarter of a century ago. They rely heavily on the export of one or two primary products and are only at the beginning stages of trying to establish an industrial structure that will allow them to diversify their exports.

Success in that effort depends upon their access to major markets like the United States and Western Europe. Yet, when less developed countries try to export manufactured goods, they run headlong into protectionist tariffs and other barriers. In the U.S., for instance, tariffs have been lowest for raw materials (e.g., raw cotton), higher for semi-processed goods (e.g., bolts of cotton cloth), and highest for finished products (e.g., a cotton shirt packaged for sale). Or take Brazil, for instance. The U.S. is willing to let Brazil export virtually unlimited amounts of coffee beans to our markets. However, the government threatened not to renew the International Coffee Agreement and to withdraw foreign aid if Brazil persisted in an attempt to enlarge its position in the processed coffee market. Not surprisingly, Brazil backed off from its effort to become a major exporter of instant coffee.

The United States and other industrialized countries have shown some willingness to open their markets to certain goods from selected developing countries through programs such as the Generalized System of Preferences and the Caribbean Basin Initiative. The language of such legislation, however, is always carefully hedged. The Trade Reform Act of 1974, which at this writing still represents this country's major trade policy, is a good example of the problem. Under title V of the Act, "the President *may* provide duty-free treatment for any eligible article from any beneficiary developing country" (emphasis mine). The hedge is contained in a paragraph instructing the president on what factors to consider in granting duty-free treatment: "The President shall have due regard for . . . the extent to which other major developed countries are undertaking a comparable effort to assist developing countries by granting generalized preferences."[7]

In other words, the United States will cease a poverty-causing trade relationship with Third World countries only if all other rich countries do the same. Since it is highly unlikely that all will agree on the details of such a major joint effort, improvement in the terms of trade for poor countries is left to the caprice of foreign policymakers and the pressure of special interest groups—which has always been the case.

Finally, it should be observed that the economic progress of countries producing industrialized goods for export may be constrained by the inability of wealthier countries to absorb all the goods produced. Hard though it may be to believe, there is probably a limit to the number of TVs and cars that Western nations can absorb. Part of the solution for the poor countries, then, must be to raise gradually the economic level of their own population, in the hope of one day integrating them into the industrialized world economy. For a time this may mean that some part of these countries' resources will have to be devoted to meeting the basic needs of a depressed population rather than to the constant striving to satisfy the needs and tastes of rich consumers far away. And advanced nations may have to help this process along, easing the pain of reduced foreign-exchange earnings by granting better terms of trade to less developed countries.

Such statements are not in keeping with the theories and vision of classical economics and its law of comparative advantage, but they are in keeping with the social and political realities of our time.

III. Values: In Search of Justice

From the preceding discussion it should be evident that the continued underdevelopment of many Third World nations may be attributed to the unfairly low prices they receive for the goods they export, and to the unjustly high prices they must pay for the products of industrial economies. This raises the question of just what constitutes a "fair" price—not only in the international economy but in the domestic economy as well. For instance, is it fair that some basketball players can command six-figure salaries when teachers and social workers get by on a pittance? Is it fair that medical care should be so expensive? Is it fair for automakers to raise the price of their cars by $1,500 from one year to the next just because they added a few extra doodads? It seldom occurs to us to ask such questions. The culture of capitalism dictates that the practical value of a good is the price at which it sells in the market. This idea is so deeply ingrained that any other form of pricing can seem illogical or even immoral. It was not always so. Through most of its history, the biblical faith community has dealt uneasily with price, whether as a proper measure of worth or as a fair means of distribution.

A. The Doctrine of the Just Price: Guarantor of Order

For over five hundred years before Adam Smith, what concerned the church was not the market price but the *just price*. Classical capitalism accepts the principle that an item has different values for different people, but its price is objectively determined by the opposite interests and the bidding of buyers and sellers. Medieval Scholastics, however, thought of goods as having an *intrinsic value* that must be expressed in their price. Modern economists strive to be scientific, to eliminate normative issues from their discipline. They are primarily absorbed with the mechanisms of exchange. Medieval Scholastics were more concerned with the relationship of people than with the relationship of commodities. Their goal was to see that the price of goods properly expressed the relationship of human lives. The doctrine of the just price was intended to be the evidence of justice in the arena of commerce. Justice was not relegated to the confines of the confessional. It was an ideal that was to be made manifest in the most common exchanges of ordinary living. Economic exchange was to be the expression of life lived by the precepts of faith.

A lofty principle indeed, but how was the just price to be determined? For a thousand years before Aquinas, that was a question the church fathers hardly had to ask. The one clear rule of canon law was that it was wrong to "buy cheap and sell dear"—a tactic later presumed to be the key to commercial success. If there was to be exchange, it was to be exchange of two equal values. This concept was not difficult to enforce in the early Middle Ages, what we commonly call the Dark Ages. Trade was minimal, markets were local, and money transactions were few. In such a sluggish economic environment, prices changed little if at all, and they were more often determined by the lord of the land or by fiat of the sovereign than by anything resembling market mechanisms. Traditional prices were easily accepted as just prices.

By the eleventh and twelfth centuries, however, economic life began to revive. Trade increased, and a nascent merchant capitalism began to challenge rigid medieval structures. Buyers and sellers were no longer necessarily from the same village, trade was increasingly for gain rather than for convenience, and payment was based on currency, not barter. A whole class of middlemen emerged whose livelihood depended upon the fractional differences they could extract by selling for more than they had paid. Under such circumstances, developing clear moral guidelines about the fairness of the pricing mechanism became a crucial theological issue. Bringing Christian doctrine and tradition to bear upon that question was a major task taken up in the thirteenth century by Thomas Aquinas.

His chief purpose was ethical rather than economic, but in order for him to judge what was morally acceptable, he had to reflect upon how prices were determined. Scholastic analysis recognized two cost factors—labor and materials, the latter of which really represented previously invested labor time. In laying the stress of just price upon the cost of labor, Aquinas was something of a precursor of David Ricardo and Karl Marx in their development of the labor theory of value—the belief that all value was ultimately a measure of the human time and effort embedded in the product.

For the Scholastics, a just price was intimately tied to the concept of a just wage. No price, however low, however favorable to the consumer, was morally acceptable that did not fairly pay workers involved in making the product. It should be stressed that "fairly" did not mean "equally." Even thirteenth-century theologians held to the medieval social hierarchy in which people were born to a class and to a trade as a part of the natural order. It was asssumed that they should be paid what was necessary to maintain their status, but not more. The just wage reinforced the existing social order; it did not encourage upward mobility. Justice served order, not change. By the same token, it was not morally acceptable for a seller simply to charge whatever consumers could or would pay. The price was in principle determined by the sum of expenses plus labor. Throughout the Middle Ages, the church opposed the concept of profit, deeming it immoral and against the laws of God to sell a good for more than was paid for it.

Nonetheless, in the more active economic environment of the thirteenth century, Aquinas recognized the need to legitimate the increasingly important role of merchants in meeting the needs of society. He did so by expanding the concept that Augustine and earlier Scholastics had applied to artisans and craftsmen. Since the products that artisans sold—wood, canvas, paints, stone—had been improved by their skills, they were entitled to raise the price of those goods in resale. Similarly, Aquinas maintained, merchants were justified in obtaining a measure of profit. This he defined not as a return on capital invested but as a "labor stipend." Profit became legitimate insofar as it represented compensation for the merchant's time and effort.

In principle, this maintained continuity with the church's traditional teachings that prohibited *usury*—that is, making money on money rather than by labor. In practice, however, the newly justified role of merchant's profit marked the point at which the church stopped defending the medieval economic order and opened the door, ever so slightly, to emerging capitalism.

In his *Summa Theologica,* Aquinas gives an example of how far the church had departed from the concept of just price by the thirteenth century. The problem was one first raised centuries before by Cicero. It involved a merchant taking grain for sale to an area beset by famine. The merchant knew that others were also coming with grain to sell. The question Cicero asked was whether the merchant was morally bound to tell the buyers that more supplies were on their way, which would lower the price of his goods, or was he free to remain silent and increase his profits? Cicero offered various solutions, including that of the Stoic philosopher who held that the merchant had the duty to tell the truth and lower his price. Aquinas disagreed. He reasoned that since the arrival of other sellers was unsure, the merchant was not required to mention them, and thus he was morally free to charge the higher price his grain could command that day. It would be a virtuous act to share the good news of greater supplies and settle for a lower profit, but justice did not require it.[8] By such logic, the just price becomes the market price.

By the sixteenth century, Roman Catholic theology was still tied to the *doctrine* of just price, but it no longer discussed profits as a moral issue. With profit allowed, the just price was no longer an objective factor that could be calculated from labor costs. It became instead a subjective factor measured by a sliding scale that in effect equaled the prevailing current price of the good in the marketplace.

B. Liberation Theology: The Challenge to Established Order

Not until well past the midpoint of the twentieth century did a major theological movement emerge that challenged the firm alliance of Christian theology with market economics. It is significant that it emerged from the experience of Latin Americans and is now spreading to other Third World areas that share similar realities of poverty, powerlessness, dependency, and domination.

This theological perspective is so rich and varied that any in-depth description or comment is impossible here. There are a few observations, however, that bear upon the issue of justice and trade.

1. A Focus on Life and History

Traditionally, theology has been a reflective discipline more akin to philosophy than to the social sciences. The spirit of St. Anselm's classical definition of theology would be recognized even by those who have never seen the Latin words *fides quaerens intellectum* (faith in search of understanding). Liberation theology accepts that as a starting point, but moves quickly beyond it. Juan Luis Segundo, a Jesuit theologian from Uruguay, writes, "By 'theology' I mean *fides quaerens intellectum* in order to give guidance and direction to historical praxis."[9]

Liberation theology begins not with timeless truths but with the life situation of the poor, the powerless, and the oppressed. It concerns itself less with their consolation than with their deliverance. Deliverance is the theme because of the conviction that the continuing tragedy besetting two-thirds of the human race is not accidental. It results from a long history that has seen the earth's resources systematically diverted from the benefit of the many to the benefit of the few. The so-called developed nations and the elite groups within poor countries have combined economic and political power to assure their privilege and have fostered the notion that present structures are unchangeable, or at least changeable only through a long process of social evolution. Liberation theology begins by challenging the absolutist pretensions of the prevailing economic order.

Karl Marx once wrote, "Philosophers have sought to understand the world, but the goal is to change it." This is the perspective of liberation theology. Whereas traditional religion has tended to regard history as a given to which believers must adjust, liberation theology calls believers to the transformation of history. To quote Gustavo Gutiérrez, the Peruvian theologian who first formalized the new currents of this strain of theological thought,

> To conceive of history as a process of the liberation of man is to consider freedom as a historical conquest. . . . The goal is not only better living conditions, a radical change of structures, a social revolution; it is much more: the continuous creation, never ending, of a new way to be a man, a permanent cultural revolution.
>
> In other words, what is at stake above all is a dynamic and historical conception of man, oriented definitively and creatively toward his future, acting in the present for the sake of tomorrow.[10]

2. A Rediscovery of Biblical Theology

The work of the medieval Scholastics has been a powerful force in the thought of the church. It has been said, only half in jest, that until recent decades all Catholic theology was merely an extended commentary on the *Summa Theologica,* that the thought of Aquinas *was* the theology of the church. Western theology since the thirteenth century has been conceived of primarily as the meeting ground of faith and reason. Its main goal has been to make the doctrine of the church understandable and unassailable. Appeals to Scripture were made more to bolster definitions of orthodoxy than to measure the performance of social institutions.

Liberation theology grows out of a different encounter with the Bible and with the attempt to see contemporary reality through the experience of the biblical faith community. The Bible as a whole is seen as the testimony of God's commitment to the deliverance of the poor, the powerless, and the oppressed. God does not seek to show mercy to an unfortunate few; he seeks to transform the social order that has led to their misfortune. Thus the people *as a whole* were liberated from the hand of Pharaoh and brought into a new land. The prophets called for justice to be done by the dominant classes and by Israel and Judah, not just by particular individuals. In Matthew's last judgment (Matt. 25:31-46), it is the nations of the world that will be held responsible for their treatment of the hungry, the naked, and the defenseless. The final vision of Revelation is for a new creation, not just for rescued individuals.

In this biblical account, God is not impartial but rather takes the side of the poor against the oppressive power of the rich. In liberation theology, the sign of faith is believing that God has made such a commitment and joining God in that commitment. Such theology does not and cannot end with dogma but only with transforming action. In 1981 the Ecumenical Association of Third World Theologians met in New Delhi, India. The document they produced contained this declaration: "The starting point for Third World theologies is the struggle of the poor and oppressed against all forms of injustice and domination. The committed involvement of Christians in this struggle provides a new locus for theological reflection. Their participation is faith in action and the manifestation of Christian commitment, which constitute the first act of theology."[11]

Herein lies the difference between traditional and liberation theology. In the ordinary Western mold, theology has been somewhat of an elitist activity; it is usually carried on by professionals in seminaries. Liberation theology, by contrast, is theological populism. The rediscovery of the Bible upon which the movement is based was not a product of seminary scholarship so much as the result of the encounter with Scripture of hundreds of thousands of ordinary Christians in tens of thousands of "basic Christian communities" throughout Latin America. Most groups have from twelve to a hundred members and normally meet "without benefit of clergy." The role of church leaders in this context is to listen rather than to tell, to ask clarifying questions rather than to write dogma, to be present but not to direct. Bible study becomes relevant because it begins with the life circumstance of the people and asks, "What does the divine word say to such a reality as ours? What does justice mean to us in this place?"

In societies where there are vast inequalities and where the masses of people exist at the margins of survival, the main component of justice is economic. And in a capitalist society where price is the determinant of distribution, the terms of exchange become a crucial moral issue. Liberation theology is the modern-day heir of the concerns that produced the "just price" doctrine. The original medieval concept aimed at creating and maintaining the proper relationship between people as buyers, sellers, and workers, not at developing a pricing formula that would neatly express the comparative value of commodities.

The intent of liberation theology is to bring the structures of society, including the economy, into greater conformity with the biblical vision of justice. Because neither the price theory of capitalism nor its performance in Third World settings seems able to accommodate such change, liberationists have looked for other economic models that will.

3. A Socialist Orientation

Many liberation theologians have looked toward socialism. An example is Sergio Méndez Arceo. When he was bishop of Cuernavaca, Mexico, he asserted that "only socialism can enable Latin America to achieve true development. . . . I believe that a socialist system is more in accord with the Christian principles of true brotherhood, justice and peace. . . . I do not know what kind of socialism, but this is the direction Latin America should go [in]."[12] Socialism, of course, takes many forms, from social democracy to worker cooperatives to Soviet-style bureaucratic centralism. And Third World liberationists are certainly not of one mind concerning the final details beyond the desire for greater equality and a sense of social solidarity that transcends the individual interest inculcated by capitalism.

Most liberation theologians acknowledge a debt to Marxism. Their goal is not to adhere slavishly to Marx's ideas. It is, rather, to put Marxism at the service of Christ. Indeed, the Marxist conception of human nature is not so far from theology at its starting point. Marx believed that "man is to be basically and radically understood as a worker, as the being who appropriates, transforms, and humanizes the world through his work and who himself comes to his own identity, becomes man through this same work."[13]

As Christians the liberationists reject the atheism of Marxist theory and the totalitarian practices of the Soviet state. But as Christians they almost universally accept Marx's criticism of capitalism as relevant and valid.

Such a view seems foreign to those of us who have known capitalism only as citizens of a rich and powerful country. It seems especially strange to people whose image of capitalism is the post-Keynesian sort softened by the social effects of the welfare state and who have been taught to believe that Marx is passé. But the reality is that the capitalism of most Third World countries is much closer to that of the nineteenth-century England that Marx criticized than it is to the capitalism of late–twentieth-century America, Germany, Japan, and Sweden.

In the Third World, class structure is not a subject for discussion in Sociology 101; it is an obvious and painful reality of daily life. For liberation theologians to endorse class struggle seems not so distant from the biblical proclamation that God sides with the poor and calls both individuals and nations to righteousness. Such a perspective is often accused of fostering hate rather than love. But liberationists did not invent class struggle. It has existed for a very long time. The rich have struggled to get what they want and to keep what they have with little regard for the poor. To say that the poor must resist and strive for change is not to foster hatred; it is to foster justice. It may also foster revolution.

For most North Americans, revolution means violence. But that is not its essence. Revolution is a dramatic change in the social, economic, and political structures of a society. The level of violence necessary to achieve it is determined primarily by the recalcitrance of the entrenched classes and by the assistance they receive from countries like ours in resisting the growing demands for justice.

4. A Global Perspective

A key factor in the economic outlook of liberation theology is its global perspective. With its roots in biblical theology, this is not surprising. Whatever tendency there was for the Old Testament to work according to a double standard of justice—one for the people of Israel and one for those outside the chosen circle—was done away with by the New Testament. Nowhere is this more clear than in Paul's words in Colossians 3:11: "Here there cannot be Greek and Jew, circumcised and uncircumcised, barbarian, Scythian, slave, free man [and in the Galatians parallel he added "neither male nor female"], but Christ is all, and in all."

But this is not the world that the liberationists see before them. Centuries-old structures have created a world of a few dominant nations that, in the struggle for economic advantage, have effectively determined the nature of economic life in most other countries that are tied to them in dependent relationships. First colonialism and later transnational corporations came into these countries, plundered their natural resources, and extracted the greatest profit possible.

Vast majorities of the populations of these countries—60 to 80 percent—have received little or no benefit. The number of the hungry and the impoverished has swollen, and the gap between rich nations and poor nations has grown ever wider.

Liberation theologians do not see this as an accident of history but as the result of an international trading system that is controlled by a few and manipulated for their benefit with indifference toward the vast majority of humankind. It is this system that transforms the present situation from merely a tragedy to a moral outrage and a theological concern. In such a world, liberation must include freedom not only from domestic ruling classes but also from the dominance of powerful nations over poor nations exerted through the normal mechanisms of international exchange. The struggle for such liberation is not merely a political and economic battle; it is a spiritual quest. A change in the structures of international trade can become a vehicle of God's justice.

Notes

1. Ricardo, "On Foreign Trade," in *Free Market Economics: A Basic Reader*, ed. Bettina B. Greaves (Irvington-on-Hudson, N.Y.: Foundation for Economic Education, 1975), p. 1182.

2. Examples cited in Richard E. Feinberg's *Intemperate Zone: The Third World Challenge to U.S. Foreign Policy* (New York: W. W. Norton, 1983), p. 100.

3. Nyerere, "The Economic Challenge: Dialogue or Confrontation?" *International Development Review*, Jan. 1976, p. 4.

4. The observation was made in a plenary presentation by Dr. Roberto de Abrue Sodre, Minister of External Relations of Brazil, Geneva, Switzerland, 29 July 1987.

5. Nyerere, "The Economic Challenge: Dialogue or Confrontation?" p. 4.

6. *U.S. Foreign Policy and the Third World: Agenda 1983*, ed. John P. Lewis and Valeriana Kallab (New York: Praeger, 1983), p. 249.

7. *The Trade Reform Act of 1974*, Hearings before the Committee on Finance, United States Senate, 93rd Congress (Washington: Government Printing Office, 1974), p. 146.

8. Recounted by John W. Baldwin in "The Medieval Theories of the Just Price," *Transactions of the American Philosophical Society* (Philadelphia: American Philosophical Society, 1959), pp. 5-93.

9. Segundo, quoted by Jorge Lara-Braud in *What Is Liberation Theology?* (Atlanta: General Assembly Mission Board, Presbyterian Church in the United States, 1980), p. 15.

10. Gutiérrez, *A Theology of Liberation,* trans. Inda Caridad, Sr., and John Eagleson (Maryknoll, N.Y.: Orbis Books, 1973), p. 32.

11. Quoted by Gustavo Gutiérrez in "Talking about God," *Sojourners,* 19 Feb. 1983, p. 27.

12. Arceo, quoted by Gutiérrez in *A Theology of Liberation,* p. 111.

13. José Míguez Bonino, *Doing Theology in a Revolutionary Situation,* ed. William Lazareth (Philadelphia: Fortress Press, 1975), p. 108.

Chapter Eight

Banking on Money

I. Concepts: The Meaning, Making, and Managing of Money

A. The Meaning of Money

Most of us probably think of money as *currency:* the bills—fives, tens, and twenties—and the assortment of coins we use in our daily purchases. Yet if we stop and think for a moment, it is obvious that most of us pay out more money by check than we do in cash. We usually write checks to cover the mortgage or rent, the telephone bill, utilities, even clothing and food purchases. Similarly, most people receive more funds by check than in currency. Governments and corporations seldom deal in cash. If money is what a society accepts in payment for goods and services, then certainly checks as well as currency must be counted as money. Thus the narrowest and most common definition of the national *money supply* (referred to as "M one"—M_1—by economists) is the total of all currency plus demand deposits—that is, accounts on which checks can be written.

Technically speaking, funds that we have in savings accounts have not traditionally been regarded as part of the money supply because the bank could legally invoke a clause requiring a period of waiting before money could be withdrawn. Even before laws were changed to allow more immediate access to these accounts, it was clear that such funds had an impact on the amount of money that circulated through the economy. Thus many economists like to count as the money supply figure what they refer to as M_2, which includes M_1 plus the total of savings accounts and other time deposits. Some definitions of the money supply (M_3) also include government bonds and other securities that can be used to settle debts or can be easily turned into cash, as well as credit card charges, one of the newest ways our society has of creating money.

Those who visit the Treasury Department in Washington, D.C., and see the printing presses turning out millions of dollars in new bills are always dazzled. Yet these bills are only a small part of what economists define as money. In 1983, currency accounted for only 27 percent of M_1, 7 percent of M_2, and less than 6 percent of M_3. Obviously, most of our money is created in other ways. Perhaps more startling is the fact that most money is not created by the government at all but by commercial banks through their system of receiving deposits and making loans.

Most of us are not very comfortable walking the streets with our pockets bulging with cash. So we deposit our paychecks in the local bank and take out only the currency we expect to need for a few days—walking-around money. The rest we leave in the account the bank carries under our name. We write checks against the account for the rent, the groceries, and car payments, but even if our uncle is the bank president, we have to put more in than we take out. Of course, when we make deposits, the bank does not put the money into a box with our name on it and simply hold it there until we withdraw it. Instead, the bank does something far more useful and profitable. It takes our unused funds, along with those of all other depositors, and creates a single pool from which it can make loans to individuals, to businesses for investment, or to governments through the purchase of bonds, Treasury bills, or other commercial paper.

Of course, a bank cannot loan out all the money that it holds. As depositors (and withdrawers), we may need it, and the bank has promised that we can have it when we do. If we keep the money in a checking account that earns little or no interest, the bank says we can have it whenever we want. But if we place it in a savings account and agree to give a few days' warning before we withdraw it, we receive a higher interest rate, and if we purchase certificates of deposit for several months or years, we receive a still greater rate of return. Of course, in these days of deregulated banking, the distinction between banks and savings and loan associations and the interest they pay has been blurred.

Experience has shown that if a bank holds 10 to 20 percent of its balances in cash reserve, it can meet the normal demands of depositors who want currency. The remainder of our balances on deposit is what banks lend out at rates greater than they pay us as depositors for keeping funds in that bank. That produces both profits for the bank and new money in the society.

The first result is clear. The second requires a bit more reflection. When a bank makes a $100,000 loan to the Smith family to build a new house, it does not normally turn over to them a packet of a hundred $1,000 bills. Instead, the money is deposited in the Smiths' checking account, and they are authorized to spend it. Technically, the bank agrees to pay cash to anyone who presents a check signed by one of the Smiths. In reality, however, since most people are content simply to trade checks in payment of various obligations, the likelihood is that the bank will never have to pay out in cash the $100,000 but only the 10 to 20 percent that is typical for all their deposits. In effect, therefore, the $100,000 loan has created $80,000 to $90,000 in new money that circulates within the economy.

This, of course, is a highly simplified telling of the story. The main detail left out is the role of the *Federal Reserve banks*. In reality, each commercial bank that is a member of the Federal Reserve system has an account at the nearest of the twelve Federal Reserve banks. If our local bank has a lot more cash on hand than it really needs for normal business, it can reduce the risk of theft by depositing the surplus with the Federal Reserve. In turn, the Federal Reserve helps to stabilize the whole banking system by guaranteeing to supply currency should commercial bank depositors demand amounts greater than are normally kept in vault reserves. (Didn't you always wonder where all those Brinks trucks were going?)

All of the checks cashed from the entire region also go to the district Federal Reserve bank. There each check is deducted from the account of one commercial bank and added to that of another, and each bank is informed daily of its balance on account. Local banks then know precisely what they can lend, minus what the Federal Reserve establishes as a *reserve requirement*—the minimum amount a bank must keep on deposit at the Federal Reserve. This control over the fractional reserves is one factor that determines how much new money will be created through the bank loan process. If the required reserve percentage is raised, the national money supply is reduced; if the reserve requirement is lowered, more loans can be made and thus the money supply increased.

The Federal Reserve also has two other tools by which it can determine the amount of money circulating in the economy. One has to do with its own lending function. The Federal Reserve bank does not loan money to families or firms, but if a commercial bank finds that its loans exceed the legal limit of the reserve requirement, it can borrow the difference from the Federal Reserve at interest. The rate of interest is known as the *discount rate*, since it is normally below the amount of interest the bank will be able to receive when it reloans the money in a commercial transaction. If the discount rate is set low, there will be more loans and thus more money created. If the banks are made to pay more for what they borrow, there will be fewer loans, and the growth in the money supply will thus be reduced.

The third way the Federal Reserve has of determining the money supply is through so-called *open market operations*. If the board members of the Federal Reserve system decide to increase the amount of money in the country, they usually do so by buying government bonds from commercial banks in normal market transactions. The amount of the sale is credited to the Federal Reserve account of the bank involved. Since the Federal Reserve pays from its own reserves without a corresponding debit to another bank, the result is that the total amount of loanable funds in the system is increased. So, for example, if the Federal Reserve purchased $100 million in government bonds, the money supply would be increased initially by $100 million minus the required reserve.

Of course, the story works the same way in reverse. If the Federal Reserve wants to reduce the money supply, it sells government bonds to a commercial bank and debits its account without having to credit another bank's account. The net effect is to reduce the amount of loanable funds available and thus the supply of money in the society.

There is one more noteworthy part of this story of how money is created. If the Federal Reserve acts to increase the loan money available by $100 million—whether by changing the reserve requirement, lowering the discount rate, or making open-market transactions—the total increase in the money supply will be much greater because of what is known as *the multiplier effect.* As the funds work their way through the economy, being spent, deposited, and reloaned several times, the total increase in the money supply, given the 10 percent reserve requirement, will approximate $900 million.

Clearly, then, the amount of money available in our system is determined not by the invisible hand of the market but by specific decisions of the Federal Reserve board—whose chairman is appointed by the president of the United States. The rate of growth in the money supply is a very political decision.

B. Monetarism

But why so much concern about the money supply? Long before there were any formal textbooks in economics, merchants and monarchs had noted that there was a relationship between the amount of money in circulation and the price of goods available. They reasoned that if there is suddenly twice as much money available to purchase the same amount of goods as existed before, the price of goods will double. This crude *quantity theory of money* was the early forerunner of today's monetarist school of economics.

All modern economists are deeply conscious of the importance of the money supply in the national economy. It is a crucial factor in determining interest rates and, therefore, investment and ultimately employment levels. Where Milton Friedman and other contemporary monetarists differ from mainstream economists is in their conviction that all national-level economic adjustments not only can be but must be accomplished primarily if not exclusively through the control of the money supply. Nothing else matters nearly as much. *Monetarism* goes beyond merely advocating the quantity theory of money and holds that the money supply cannot be entrusted to the analysis or whims of the Federal Reserve. Friedman, a longtime spokesman for the monetarist view, is convinced that even with the best of intentions, economic policymakers actually make problems worse rather than better. He argues that there are so many variables in the economy that no one can be absolutely sure what action is best. In addition, there is the matter of timing. It takes several weeks, perhaps months, for policies to take effect, and by that time the original situation may have changed. Consequently, the Federal Reserve may end up stimulating the economy at a time when a reduced money supply would be in order.

Friedman argues that these problems could be avoided if the money supply was not determined by the Federal Reserve board but was allowed to grow at a fixed rate equal to the normal historical growth of the country's output of goods and services, about 4.5 percent per year. Then all other matters could be left to market mechanisms without the need for intervention by government. There would be no inflation because the right amount of new money would be available to counterbalance new production. There would be no prolonged recessions because when production fell below its historic rate of growth, more money would automatically come into the system to reduce interest rates and stimulate investment.

The great conviction of monetarism is that in the long run an unattended market will be self-correcting. That is an enticing hope, but monetarism has an Achilles' heel. It assumes that the future will or should look like the past. Because the U.S. economy has had, for the past century or so, an average growth rate of 4 to 5 percent, the assumption is that this rate can be used in current calculations. But is this the appropriate rate for the present and for the next century as well? Our growth rate over the last several years has not exceeded 3 percent. In a period of more rapid technological change, might not greater economic growth be both possible and desirable? Or, conversely, in an era of limited resources, might not growth have to be held somewhere below its traditional norms?

There is a kind of Procrustean logic in monetarism that does not correspond well with the modern conviction that life need not be a mere repetition of past experiences nor left wholly to chance. In the post-Keynesian epoch, the limits of economic intervention are clearly appreciated, but the notion that economics should retreat to a policy of passivity that relies more on luck than on human rationality seems unlikely if not absurd.

C. *Inflation: The Evaporation of Money*

Monetarism is a total economic worldview. Its deep, abiding preoccupation is inflation. In that regard, monetarism assumed mainstream status during the 1970s, when inflation became the cause célèbre of the global economic community.

Monetarists are convinced that inflation has just one cause—government policy. For political reasons, government often tries to force growth by introducing money into the economy at a rate far in excess of increases in the output of goods and services. This is the classic illustration of *demand-pull* inflation, which holds that when people have money to buy more than is available, the price of what is available will rise. In the end, people have no more than they had before, but the price of everything is higher, and those whose wages and other income have not risen fast enough lose out. For a very long time, this scenario of "too much money chasing too few goods" virtually defined the meaning as well as the cause of inflation.

It is clear, however, that there is a *cost-push* side to inflation as well. Of course, it is nothing new that increased production costs contribute to an inflationary spiral. If raw materials and wages cost a manufacturer more, the price of the product will normally have to rise. However, major changes in the nature of the American economy have made cost-push inflation more significant than ever before.

The most commonly recognized change is the rise of *labor unions*, which emerged as a major economic force only in the 1930s and probably hit their peak of power in the United States during the 1960s. Before that time, theory assumed that general wage levels could not rise as long as any worker remained unemployed. Each individual simply had to take what management was compelled by the market to pay in order to have the kind of workers needed. With unions, however, higher wages could be extracted—not on the basis of individual performance but under the threat of slowdowns, walkouts, and strikes that could severely affect the ability of a given firm to engage in business. The settlement with one firm became the model for an industry, and that industry the example for others. The importance of union power lay in its ability not only to help workers keep up with general price increases but to shift a larger measure of the nation's economic resources into the hands of the working class.

The impact of unions on inflation has certainly been matched by the growth of very large corporations and the consequent development of a *less than competitive business environment*. Classical economic theory had always assumed that firms would be numerous, competitive, and too small to have any unilateral impact on the markets they served. The great reality of the twentieth century is that a few firms have dominated sales in a great many product lines and industries. Companies learned that cut-throat price competition hurts all producers, and by the heyday of the 1950s and 1960s, most of the huge corporations had adopted a live-and-let-live approach. It was far less damaging to profits to give a modest wage increase to workers than to endure a long strike—especially since competitors would also pay the increase, and all producers would simply pass the cost along to the consumer. The classic example of this system of pass-through pricing was the automobile industry. Each contract year, negotiations were held with one firm, and after usually token resistance, a pattern contract was signed that the other three companies adopted with little struggle and few changes. The price of next year's model was increased to cover the cost plus the firm's additional profit margin.

The third major change in the economy of the past fifty years that underlies the tendency to inflation is the growing role of the federal government. In 1929, federal expenditures were only 2.8 percent of the U.S. gross national product. By 1983 the total was 25 percent—very nearly a tenfold increase. It is not that politicians and government bureaucrats are more profligate now than before but rather that new and larger roles have been assigned to government in today's society. Its direct purchases to maintain the military, the highway system, and the necessary bureaucracy to deliver a vast array of services are a major element in the economy. Because most of what government does is not subject to massive productivity increases through technology, its spending tends to increase inflationary pressures.

The federal government has also tended to feed inflation indirectly through a variety of laws and programs. Corporations complain that their production costs are forced up by environmental protection legislation. Agricultural subsidies quite clearly increase the price of food, cotton, and tobacco. Protectionist trade laws keep out lower-priced industrial goods from foreign countries. Unemployment compensation is said to be one of the factors that keeps unions from coming to wage terms more quickly and that keeps people who are between jobs from simply taking the first thing that comes along. And, of course, the federal government is the major force that determines the money supply, interest rates, investment levels, and ultimately employment, all of which have an impact on the rate of inflation.

If the great enemy of the economy is inflation, then the government is an accomplice, but so too are most unions and large corporations. The role of government in the economy has increased mostly because deflation (recession or depression) is feared even more than inflation.

D. Dollars, Debt, and Deficit

Government intervention, of course, means government spending. And when that increased spending is not matched by offsetting tax revenues, the result is a budgetary deficit leading to a larger federal debt, and normally to inflation and higher interest rates.

President Johnson's decision to fight the Vietnam war by borrowing money rather than by raising taxes has been justly criticized for kicking off the inflationary spiral of the 1970s. The same kind of irresponsible Keynesianism has been exhibited by President Reagan in his insisting on a large increase in military spending (which is only partially offset by reductions in other federal programs), while simultaneously engaging in a major tax-cut program. The result has been the largest peacetime deficit and the greatest debt load in the nation's history.

By the mid-1980s, annual deficits were in the $200 billion range, adding to the public debt that by 1982 reached $1,142 billion and is projected to be $3 trillion by the end of the decade—$11,000 for every man, woman, and child in the country.[1] We are the world's biggest debtor nation. The need for the government to finance these very large deficits has had a great impact on the federal budget. Interest on the debt, which had averaged 10.6 percent of federal expenditures from 1971 to 1980, jumped to 14.5 percent in 1981 and is projected to be 22 percent in President Reagan's 1988 budget. Obviously, what must be collected in taxes to pay federal debts cannot be invested by business in productive equipment. Likewise, what the government must pay in interest cannot be spent on programs of human welfare. A growing debt takes a double toll on national life.

II. Realities: The Global Debt and Banking Crisis

Traditionally, banking has been different from other kinds of business. It was intentionally conservative, even dull—a characteristic that even bank architecture proclaimed with massive granite structures, ornate pilasters, and an air of calm confidence and stability. Risk-taking was kept to a minimum. Government insurance kept people's money safe, and government supervision and regulation, established in the wake of massive bank failures during the Great Depression, prevented the kind of competition that led managers in other lines of business to run greater risks in hope of greater profits.

In recent years bank managers have chafed under the restrictions and have lobbied for the deregulation of the banking system so that they might be free to compete more energetically with other financial institutions in the effort to increase profits.

All of that sounds wholesome enough and in the best tradition of free market economics. But the desire of banks to become business highflyers has introduced a level of risk-taking that threatens not only depositors' savings and individual institutions but the entire global financial structure. Bank failures in the United States are occurring at a rate greater than at any other time since the Depression. Between 1982 and 1984, 153 banks failed, and more than 750 others were on the federal government's problem list—which means they are perilously close to bankruptcy. Among them are some of the nation's largest and most prestigious financial institutions. One of them, the Continental Illinois Bank, was rescued only by a $7,500 million federal government loan and a guarantee of 100 percent of all deposits.[2] Effectively, the government had to buy a major bank to keep it from collapsing for fear that its failure would precipitate a general panic that would threaten the whole banking system.

A. The Third World Debt Dilemma

The transition of banking from a cautious, conservative business to a fast-money business was facilitated—some would say demanded—by the rapid rise in petroleum prices over a decade ago. In October 1973 the average price for Saudi Arabian crude stood at $2.10 per barrel. By November 1974 the price had increased almost fivefold to $10.24, and before the end of the decade, the price tripled again and stood above $30 per barrel. A world that was hooked on oil and had few other immediate energy options had little choice but to pay the bill. This resulted in a massive shift of income to petroleum producers, particularly the Organization of Petroleum Exporting Countries (OPEC). Most of these nations were able to use only their own portion of their petroleum revenues for economic development. Being fiscal conservatives and lacking experience in the technical skills of global investment banking, the OPEC countries chose to place a large portion of their funds on short-term deposit with scores of banks around the world.

The financial community suddenly faced the need to recycle some $200 billion a year in "petrodollars," as the OPEC deposits were called. There were grim jokes in the mid-1970s about how to deal with the problem. One suggested that the OPEC nations should save for three years until they had accumulated $600 billion. With that they could buy all of the firms listed on the New York Stock Exchange, and the United States could then simply nationalize the industries!

Bankers had other plans. The sudden glut of funds created the opportunity for new, more adventurous, more profitable—although risky—investments: loans to less developed countries (LDCs).

There was a legitimate need. Most Third World nations import petroleum. When the price of oil jumped fivefold in just a year, these countries had no alternative but to borrow heavily to maintain their energy supply. In 1975 alone, they required $38 billion collectively to cover oil-related deficits. That amount of money was available only from commercial banks in industrialized countries. It is a major error, however, to assume that the present debt crisis of Third World countries is the creation of OPEC. Some of the largest debtors—Mexico and Venezuela, for example—are themselves petroleum exporters that required vast amounts of new capital to expand their production.

A major cause of the debt crisis is the development model adopted by Third World leaders and promoted by international banks itching to do something with the huge glut of petrodollars. This model called on LDCs to borrow heavily in the hope that the economy would grow fast enough to generate the funds with which to repay loans as they came due. Bankers encouraged the vision and multiplied their loans to businesses and governments with increasingly shaky economies. The symbol of the new breed of international financiers was Walter Wriston, chairman of Citibank, who has been described by a critic as "a glorified vacuum cleaner salesman, a small-town smooth-talker whose only goal in life was to make a buck."[3]

Profit potential, not Third World need, attracted the attention of the banks. In most years from 1978 through 1983, for example, non–oil-producing LDCs paid from 1 to 1.5 percentage points *more* for loans from private banks than the average market rate.[4] The ten largest banks receive an average of 45 percent of their profits from international operations, and for a giant like Citibank, the figure rises to almost 70 percent.

Under the pressure of competition, and with the lure of hundreds of millions of dollars in profits, conservative banking practices of the past were cast to the wind. In less developed countries, the ratios of debt to gross national product and exports rose dramatically, as did the average amount of debt per citizen.

Just how serious the problem is can be seen in Table 8.1. By 1985, foreign loans constituted an average of 45 percent of the gross domestic product of all less developed countries, compared with only 28 percent in 1980. And in the case of Latin American and African countries, international debt equaled 62 percent and 80 percent respectively of the value of all the goods and services produced annually.

Foreign debts differ from those within a country because the former must be paid in dollars or some other hard currency that can be gained only through exports or borrowing. Since international banks do not permit LDCs to pay their debts in weak local currencies, trade earnings create the base for all imports. Dollars paid out to foreign banks in interest cannot also be used to import capital goods needed for development programs, basic grains to supplement the diet of the poor, or luxury products to keep middle and upper classes content. The debt / exports ratio, then, becomes a very crucial economic factor.

As can also be seen in Table 8.1 (below), all Third World borrowers had debts in 1980 that equaled 134 percent of their total export earnings. By 1985 that had risen to 194 percent. The situation of Latin American and low-income African countries was and is much worse. Latin American countries would have to use their entire export earnings for over three years to pay their debt, and for the African nations it would take over four years.[5] Why then don't such countries just bite the bullet and stop importing for three or four years, wipe the slate clean, and start over again? Because it would create such economic and political chaos that many governments would not survive. With no imports, factories would close, industrialization would virtually cease, dams, roads, and port facilities would not be built, emergency food for hungry populations would not be available, and the lack of investment opportunities and con-

Table 8.1

Developing Country Debt Ratios (%)

Area	**Debt/Exports**		**Debt/GDP***	
	1980	*1985*	*1980*	*1985*
All countries	*134%*	*194%*	*28%*	*45%*
Latin America, Caribbean	*193*	*311*	*35*	*62*
Low-income Africa	*218*	*425*	*47*	*80*

**Gross Domestic Product*

Source: World Bank, *World Debt Tables,* 1986-87 edition, Supplement no. 1 (Washington, 1987).

sumer products would cause the wealthy to send even more of their money out of the country. There are very few governments that could survive such strains. Consequently, any thought of devoting all export earnings to debt repayment is effectively foreclosed.

Most countries, far from retiring their debt, are hard-pressed to pay even the interest they owe. In 1987 all less developed countries together owed foreign banks and governments over $1 trillion and paid over $100 billion to service that debt. Even so, many are behind in their payments and are unlikely ever to pay in full. Perhaps a score of nations are in such straits that they would be declared bankrupt under any common definition.

There is an old saying that goes something like this: "If you owe the bank a thousand dollars and you can't pay, you're in trouble. But if you owe the bank a million dollars and you can't pay, the bank is in trouble." Now there is a new addition to the logic: "If a handful of countries owe the bank a trillion dollars and they can't pay, the whole world is in trouble." The "trouble," of course, is that if even one of the large debtor nations should default, it would likely take some of the major banks down with it. The whole structure of modern finance rests upon a very fragile sense of confidence. If that confidence is shaken by the failure of one major bank, there could be a run on them all that could not be stopped. What concerns both bankers and bureaucrats about the present situation is not just whether the profitability of a given loan will be realized, but whether the whole international financial structure can be maintained as a viable system.

To prevent nations on the edge of the financial abyss from actually defaulting, financiers have devised the three R's of international banking: rollover, refinancing, and rescheduling. A nation in trouble can be granted a *rollover* of its loan by the creditor bank. In such an arrangement, a new loan is created for the same amount and under the same terms as the old, which is then regarded as having been paid. Or shaky loans can be *refinanced.* That is, new loans are extended to allow the country to consolidate and pay off several old loans. Under particularly severe circumstances, banks may also allow the *rescheduling* of an existing loan so that the debtor nation suspends payments for a period, with the agreement to continue them at a later time.

If all this seems more like magicians using mirrors than responsible leaders working with sound principles, that is only because it is so. The goal is to create the illusion that all is well and that the loans in question are actually being paid off, or at least are being dealt with responsibly. The reality is that hundreds of billions of dollars of loans have been made on very questionable business and political assumptions. Bank profits have been enormous, but no one knows how or whether the funds can be recouped. If they cannot be, even mainstream economists have begun to wonder whether the international financial structure can survive.

B. The IMF: Disciplining the Nations

In 1944, with the end of World War II in sight, leaders of the capitalist industrial world met in Bretton Woods, New Hampshire, to design the structures of an integrated economic order designed to prevent a slide back into depression and to facilitate postwar recovery. One of the principal institutions that grew out of those accords was the International Monetary Fund (IMF). Its chief function was to fix and maintain the exchange rates of various national currencies so that countries would not be able to devalue their money in order to make their products cheaper in the world market, thus gaining an advantage in international trade. The IMF also acted as a lender of last resort to countries having a temporary deficit in their balance of payments. This arrangement worked well for two decades after World War II. But in the early 1970s the U.S. abandoned the gold standard, and the Bretton Woods Agreement came to an end.

Except for the petroleum crisis and the financial chaos that it caused, the IMF might simply have gone out of business by the mid-1970s. Instead, it embarked upon a new career as overseer, adviser, and disciplinarian of economically troubled nations. There are some 140 countries that are members of the IMF. Representation is not based on the concept of one nation, one vote; it is determined by the amount of money each participant puts into the Fund. Thus the United States holds about 23 percent of the voting power, the European Economic Community 19 percent, and the ten richest nations over 50 percent. The thirty-seven poorest countries control just 6 percent of the voting power. Not surprisingly, then, the policies of the IMF tend to reflect the perspective and interests of the advanced, industrialized nations.

Most Third World nations spend more money on imports than they receive from exports. To make up the difference, a country may seek to borrow money from the IMF. The IMF will make such a loan only after a team of IMF experts has conducted an on-site study of the local economy. The goals of the study are simple and straightforward: to ensure that there is enough money to repay the loan when it comes due, and to prevent future balance-of-payments problems. Thus the IMF usually "recommends" that the country increase net foreign-trade earnings by decreasing imports and increasing exports. The country has little choice but to agree, because the IMF can withhold its seal of approval. This would not only deny the country the IMF loan but also close the doors to commercial credit, since most commercial banks have made their loans to troubled nations contingent upon compliance with IMF recommendations. Without the IMF's seal of approval, a country would likely be denied commercial credit regardless of the need for or the soundness of the specific project for which the loan was sought. As a result, the government is in a weak bargaining position and must essentially comply with whatever measures the IMF might "recommend."

Typically, a country seeking IMF approval must agree to do a number of things: devalue its currency (making its exports cheaper to other countries); reduce the growth in money supply (slowing the economy and cutting consumption); impose wage controls (which help keep costs of production down and make goods more competitive in the international market); reduce government spending (cutting subsidies for food and fuel, social services, and infrastructure investments); promote exports (diverting production away from domestic needs); raise taxes (so that the government will have funds to devote to debt repayment); raise interest rates (to encourage savings and investment); end trade barriers (in order to force national producers to be competitive); and encourage foreign investment.

Needless to say, such economic interventionism is reserved for poor and weak countries; the rich and industrially powerful are presumed wise enough to solve their own problems. Although the U.S. runs huge trade and budget deficits and is the world's largest debtor, the IMF has not attempted to impose its program here.

What follows is, in broad outline, the program instituted by Mexico. After five years of profligate spending of petroleum revenues, frantic industrialization, and unbridled consumption by the upper classes, Mexico had become the world's second-largest Third World debtor. (Only Brazil is more encumbered.) In 1982 the Mexican government instituted the draconian measures of the IMF's monetarist, free-enterprise program. Within three years the country had redeemed itself in the eyes of the international financial community, and Mexico was being touted as one of the success stories in helping to move the global banking system back from the edge of the abyss.

Such success in macro-level finance, however, comes at a very high human cost. It was estimated that the IMF formula instituted in Mexico would cut the nation's gross national product by 5 percent and reduce the living standards of 75 million people by 8 or 9 percent.[6] The poor bear the heaviest burden in any crash program to assure that banks get paid.

In 1982, when the IMF was pressing Chile to cut public spending by 50 percent, a measure sure to increase joblessness, unemployment already stood at 26 percent. When prices rise while wages are held in check, investors get richer, and the middle class have to postpone buying new cars, but the poor have food snatched from their tables. When a government cuts spending, it is the health care and education of the masses that usually suffer first and most. When more and more of the economy is turned over to market forces—ending food subsidies and seeking new exports—consumption by the already marginalized is further threatened.

So why don't countries just defy the IMF and default? That may yet happen, but other logic has so far prevailed. One answer lies in the fact that policymakers and politicians in these countries are, by and large, from the upper class, whose interests and perspectives coincide with those of the international financial community. A more fundamental answer, however, is that the alternatives have so far seemed worse than compliance. If a country were to default, it would likely mean that any assets the nation has abroad would be seized by the banks. All credit in international markets would likely be ended. All imports would probably have to be paid for in cash in advance. A trade embargo and other economic sanctions would probably be imposed. The country would thus have to finance its development from internal resources. The social strains of such an approach would almost certainly bring down whatever political structure tried to impose it. Consequently, most Third World countries bargain, complain, and resist, but ultimately go along with the basic requirements of the IMF formula until they simply can pay no more. Then, after a moratorium on payments, some type of emergency rescue package is hastily arranged so that the illusion of full payment will continue.

Now, after more than a decade of the IMF's functioning as the global economic policeman, serious doubts are beginning to emerge about the dangers implicit in the IMF strictures. First there was concern about the possibility of a "debtors' cartel," in which a consortium of nations would seek power through weakness by jointly threatening to default as a way of extracting basic changes in the global economic system. In recent years that concern has faded somewhat as Third World nations have shown more willingness to make sacrifices to honor their commitments to the system than anyone had reason to expect. Should they be pressed to the extreme by another deep global recession, however, such a cartel is still not beyond possibility. In 1986 Peru declared it would use only 10 percent of its export earnings to pay international debts. Other nations are now threatening similar action.

A more enduring concern is that the stringency of IMF requirements may cause a political explosion in less developed countries. Cutting deeper and deeper into the standard of living of the already impoverished in order to pay the profits of foreign banks is not something that can be done for long under a democratic system. A repressive regime is ultimately required. But even such governments cannot survive indefinitely against the will of a people who feel that their rulers are indifferent to their plight.

Increasingly, concerns about the economic effects of the IMF formula are not limited to Third World countries. The formula rests upon the twin goals of expanding exports and reducing imports. That can be very successful for any given nation, but it may result in failure if used as a model for the global system. The hard fact is that not every country can export more than it imports. Someone has to buy all those goods, and even the vaunted American consumer can absorb only so much. In that sense the export goals of the IMF may simply be unreasonable when multiplied by the hundred or so debtor nations. Furthermore, seeking dramatic reduction in the imports of less developed countries may lead to recession or even depression in the advanced industrial economies like those of the United States, Western Europe, and Japan. Gone are the days when the only trade that mattered was that among the industrial giants.

C. Is There Any Hope?

It is clear that the global debt crisis will not be solved by the "save-the-banks-whatever-the-cost" mentality. As Fritz Leutwiler, president of the Bank for International Settlements, put it, "There is no way the major banks can get out of the situation without writing down some of the debt." This may sound harsh, but it must be remembered that the banks are not innocent bystanders in the debt dilemma.

There are several steps that policymakers might take to begin addressing the debt crisis. Most obviously, the banks will have to modify the terms on outstanding debt to ease the load on Third World debtor nations. This may mean that banks will have to write off some loans and lower interest rates on many others. A further step would be to convert recalculated loans from private to public debt so that the loans would be held by some public or quasi-public entity, not by commercial banks, which look only to the bottom line in making decisions regarding loans. A step beyond this conversion would be to create an international lending authority charged with reviewing, approving, and keeping track of all international loans above a specified amount. Included in such review and approval should be a consideration of both the borrowing nation's ability to repay and the extent of total Third World exposure of the bank or banks proposing to make the loan. Of course, it will be complained that this is an infringement on free enterprise. The only answer to that complaint is that the present debt crisis demonstrates that global banking is too large, complex, and important to be left wholly to the mechanisms of private interests.

III. Values: Money as a Moral Matter

A. The Bible's Double Standard

At its root, biblical faith is not ascetic. Israel's faith was refined in the stark life of the desert, but the vision was always of a land flowing with milk and honey. Prophets may have worn sackcloth as a protest against ostentatious living, but destitution was never regarded as having spiritual advantage. Poverty was viewed as resulting from oppression and was thus a condition from which people were to be liberated. Barring the distortions of sin and injustice, a life of plenty was the goal of creation and the outcome of faith: "If you are willing and obedient, you shall eat the good of the land" (Isa. 1:19, RSV).

Nevertheless, biblical faith is deeply suspicious of money. According to Ecclesiastes 5:10 (RSV), "He who loves money will not be satisfied with money; nor he who loves wealth, with gain"; and 1 Timothy 6:10 (RSV) warns, "The love of money is the root of all evils." Money is not regarded as a gift from God or a sign of God's blessing. Rather, its possession is seen as a great spiritual risk.

To the contemporary mind, these seem like two contradictory perspectives. How can a vision of plenty be proclaimed while money, the modern store of value, is denounced? Clearly, because the good things that God provides for the human enterprise are to be used, not accumulated. Like the manna in the wilderness, God's daily plenty spoils when hoarded. The Scriptures treat money harshly because its accumulation seems to be an attempt to make oneself independent of God. So serious is the threat money poses that Jesus regarded it not as a mere passive instrument but as a demonic power. In mammon, money is personalized and competes with God for our commitment. Thus Jesus' dire warning, "You cannot serve God and mammon" (Luke 16:13, RSV).

The biblical concern, of course, is not with currency itself. It is accepted that goods may be bought and sold, paid for in silver, gold, and the coin of the realm. Yet the reality is that money loses its tie to exchange, to consumption, and becomes a value in itself because it gives the possessor power over the output, and therefore the lives, of others. It is this ability to manipulate people and to play God through money that the prophets so vehemently condemned: "I will not revoke the punishment; because they sell the righteous for silver, and the needy for a pair of shoes" (Amos 2:6, RSV).

The fact that money fuels the will to power is what makes it a spiritual problem. It drives a wedge into the life of the community, putting rich over poor and powerful over powerless. Likewise, money separates the possessor of wealth from God by giving the illusion of a life where God is superfluous. It is not surprising, then, that the announcement of Jesus' coming indicated a determination by God to challenge the values of a culture distorted by the exaltation of wealth and the power it imparts:

> He has shown strength with his arm,
> he has scattered the proud in the imagination of their hearts,
> He has put down the mighty from their thrones,
> and exalted those of low degree;
> he has filled the hungry with goods things,
> and the rich he has sent empty away. (Luke 1:51-53, RSV)

In no small measure, biblical faith is defined as a challenge to the temptations of a monetized culture. That does not mean that there is no place for currency in a society where people are both faithful and just, but it does mean that concern for the fullness of life for all people takes precedence over everything else. That is the perspective from which we must approach the present dilemmas of our monetary system. Monetary policy is not merely a technical issue; it is a struggle over power and competing values.

B. Moral Issues in Inflation

Writing as I am when the consumer price index shows an annual rate of increase of less than 3 percent, it might seem a bit strained to become exercised over the moral issues at stake in inflation. Still, just as economists are always concerned about it, so too should ethicists be.

By the beginning of this decade, when the nation had experienced historically high rates of inflation for a dozen years, peaking at 13.5 percent in 1980, all sectors were complaining. It seemed that everyone in the country was falling behind. Of course, that was not the case at all. Inflation produces winners as well as losers. To be sure, the massive shift in funds to foreign petroleum producers was a drag on the whole economy, and in some way it cost everyone. Still, between 1970 and 1980, per-capita real income increased by 29 percent, and in only three

Table 8.2

Distribution of U.S. Family Income, 1970 and 1980

Segment of Population	% National Income Received	
	1970	1980
Poorest 20%	5.4%	5.1%
2nd 20%	12.1	11.6
3rd 20%	17.6	17.5
4th 20%	23.8	24.3
Richest 20%	40.9	41.6

Source: U.S. Bureau of the Census, *Current Population Reports,* P-60 series, no. 145 (Washington: U.S. Government Printing Office, 1980).

of those turbulent years did the gross national product show even small fractional declines.

If all groups in society had been equally affected by the general rise in prices, their income shares would have remained essentially the same both before and after the period of high inflation. Table 8.2 (above) indicates that this was not the case.

In 1970 the inflationary pressures caused by U.S. involvement in Vietnam were just beginning to be felt. The year 1980 represents the peak of the inflationary period as well as the last year to be unaffected by the Reagan tax-cut program that redistributed income upward. The shift in income shares over the decade of the 1970s was not dramatic, but the pattern is clear enough. The three lowest income segments, representing 60 percent of all families, each lost ground, while the two top groups, representing 40 percent, both gained.

Such data must be interpreted with care, because other things besides inflation happened in the 1970s that helped to shape income distribution. Nonetheless, it seems fair to say that the burden of inflation rested more heavily on the poor and the near poor than upon those of greater means. Throughout the decade, the price of such basic items as food, fuel (for both heating and transportation), and housing rose more rapidly than inflation as a whole. It is not surprising, then, that the poor and the lower working class were hardest hit by inflation, since they must spend the majority of their income on such necessities.

Inflation reallocates the costs and benefits of an economy. When the poor and the powerless bear the heaviest burden, inflation becomes a moral matter and not merely a technical one. But even if income shares remained unchanged, a long period of high, sustained inflation should be an issue of concern to the faith community. Such inflation changes the way people look at life. It creates a mood of anxiety about the future that tends to reward the hustler rather than the worker, the spender rather than the saver, the speculator rather than the investor. Inflation encourages frivolous consumption out of the fear that money will be worth a lot less next month or next year. It encourages an equally distorted investment climate so that it may be more logical to purchase Persian rugs or stamp collections rather than risk resources in producing useful goods for an uncertain market.

Ultimately, the moral issue of inflation is that it fosters an attitude that the future is always worth less than the present. Such a distortion of economic life creates a world that is at odds with the biblical vision. For that reason, too, inflation assumes a moral and theological dimension as well as a social and economic dimension.

C. Consumption Ethics in Yuppie Culture

One of the characteristics of money is that it is a store of value. One of the realities of a period of inflation is that money is not a very reliable store of value. There are those horror stories about the hyperinflation in Europe after World War I—people pushing wheelbarrows of cash to the market to buy a couple of days' groceries, people rushing frantically from pay window to stores, knowing that if wages were not spent in an hour or two the money would be virtually worthless. Our recent bouts with inflation in this country during the 1970s were not anything like that, but a few years in the double-digit range were enough to convince most people that spending now was better than spending later.

Coming through adolescence and reaching adulthood in a culture that had suffered significant inflationary shocks is undoubtedly one of the factors that has helped to create the consumer psychology of the cultural subset we have come to call yuppies—young, urban professionals. They and their peers have had other names. They are the "baby boomers," that rich harvest of humanity given birth by our society from 1946 to 1961 after two decades of small families and reduced consumption due to depression and war. In another, less glorious war, the boomers became the Vietnam generation, the teenagers who fought the war, protested its horrors—or at least its threat to their own lives and plans—and then, too frequently, forgot or repressed it. They have been the hippies, the flower children, and the acidheads. But in whatever form, we have known them for twenty-five years, and they have been generators of styles and setters of trends. Now between the ages of twenty-five and thirty-nine, dominating the workplace and beginning to reach their peak earning power, they are out to show the world what it means to be truly self-conscious consumers.

Of course, yuppies are a minority in their generation. The median real income of all those in the twenty-five to thirty-four age group actually fell by 14 percent from 1979 to 1983. Yet the young, urban professionals have come to embody the spirit of the age. There is no clear agreement on the boundaries of yuppiedom, but if it is assumed to have a threshold of $40,000 a year in income from a profession or managerial career, less than 10 percent of the baby boomers qualify. Their small number, however, is almost irrelevant; it may even enhance their mystique. Their true importance lies not in their own buying power but in their ability to shape the perspectives and the values of the whole generation and perhaps of the whole society. It is not a matter of influencing people so that they buy one beer rather than another; football players do that! Yuppies have heard the higher calling to define what life as a consumer is all about in an affluent culture.

The gentry of this generation did not invent conspicuous consumption. Royalty, the robber barons and their more socially acceptable descendants, and the aristocracy of many cultures have well understood the special joys of public indulgence so that the envy of others is added to the actual pleasure of consuming. For yuppies, as for many more traditional elites, to have is to be.

The thirty-two-year-old president of a group of specialty clothing stores in Manhattan spends about $300 a month on wine. It's not that he overindulges; with his tastes for Niuts St. Georges at $47.98, that may amount to only a couple of bottles a week. The sudden taste for fine French wines by young people of means has caused a boom in Bordeaux. Exports from France in 1984 totaled $1.6 billion and were up 23 percent in just one year. The sudden surge is fueled in part by the strong dollar but mostly by American yuppies, who want the best in everything and who have now decided that means France's best vintages.[7]

The buying power of two-profession couples—determined to avoid the suburbs and live near the bars, theaters, restaurants, and stores that define their life—has made quarter-million-dollar condos converted from factory lofts a new prestige address in urban America. Typically, the kitchen may be equipped with a thousand dollars' worth of cookware and a larger-than-life spice closet for the preparation of the few meals a month not eaten in a restaurant. Style is everything, from the high-performance imported car used primarily to drive in bumper-to-bumper traffic, to the $125 running shoes that are the intentionally unstylish accent of a professional woman's $600 work ensemble, to membership in not one, not two, but three health clubs. Indeed, the health club may be the perfect symbol of the new elite consumer, who tends to believe that everything of value can be purchased—even health.

Advertisers, ever quick to capture and capsulize the spirit of an age, fashioned a hymn for the new elite in the verses of a beer commercial. "Who says you can't have it all?" You can have "pinstripes and rock-and-roll," you can "work for someone else and still be you," and, most important, you can "make it to the top without losing your soul." The elites of all ages have wanted the assurance that there is no spiritual danger in having vastly more than most others in society. And today, as almost always in the past, religion has accommodated. The quintessential religious voice of yuppie values was that of southern California's Reverend Terry Cole-Whittaker (who is now pursuing other activities). She regularly assured her affluent congregations that "you can have it all *now*" and that prosperity is a "divine right." Those for whom life is turned wholly in upon itself and for whom buying defines being are undoubtedly in need of such constant assurance. Religion without sacrifice, without challenge, and without commitment is the perfect companion of life without responsibility except to oneself. But the baptism of well-groomed hedonism is not a Christian ministry.

Consumption raised to a fine art ultimately rests upon two attitudes. First is that buying is freedom. This is not just an affirmation of unencumbered markets; it is much more than that. Every purchase that is beyond need can be regarded as a celebration of a life that is beyond necessity and obligation. In the moment of purchase, the buyer is truly sovereign. By extension of this logic, one might even argue that the more frivolous the good, the greater the display of freedom—the secularized version of "sin boldly that grace may abound."

The second underlying attitude of high consumerism is the assumption that there will always be more. That is not an unreasonable assumption for a generation of individuals who have no personal memory of the Depression years and who quite objectively see themselves as well-prepared to take a position at the top of the social order. Why shouldn't young, urban professionals expect more? Such natural optimism is strengthened by what they see happening. Two bright young law-school students graduate, marry, and find themselves beginning family life with an $80,000 to $100,000 annual income. A twenty-five-year-old associate producer for a Boston ad agency sees the value of her condominium go from $65,000 to $95,000 in a year's time, "which means she made more money going to sleep each night than she did at work each day."[8] Why wouldn't such people assume that "more and more" is normal if not inevitable, at least for themselves?

However, even if economics and limited resources do not intrude upon the world of the yuppie and those who share the vision of life defined by consumption, the convictions of biblical faith must. The biblical perspective measures the meaning of life less by the power to acquire and consume than by the ability to participate with God in the process of creation, less by what one can gain than by what one can contribute to the divine-human enterprise that is history.

The call to discipleship is never an invitation to embrace the dominant values and attitudes of the culture. It is an invitation to examine, challenge, and change the prevailing way of thinking about life. That is a needed message for the yuppie generation and for all generations.

Notes

1. "How to Cut the Deficit," *Business Week,* 26 Mar. 1984, p. 50.

2. "The New Shape of Banking," *Business Week,* 18 June 1984, p. 104.

3. Darrell Delamaide, *Debt Shock: The Full Story of the World Credit Crisis* (Garden City, N.Y.: Doubleday, 1984), p. 6.

4. *U.S. Foreign Policy and the Third World: Agenda 1985-1986,* ed. John W. Sewell, Richard E. Feinberg, and Valeriana Kallab (Washington: Overseas Development Council, 1985), p. 177.

5. *Managing Third World Debt* (London: All Party Parliamentary Group on Overseas Development Institute, 1987), p. 23.

6. "The IMF and Latin America," *The Economist,* 11 Dec. 1982, p. 69.

7. "The Year of the Yuppie," *Newsweek,* 31 Dec. 1984, p. 28.

8. *Newsweek,* 31 Dec. 1984, p. 14.

Chapter Nine

The Intentional Economy

I. Concepts: To Plan or Not to Plan—Is That the Question?

Is economics, after all is said and done, a gambler's art? Are the problems of economic life so many, so varied, and so unpredictable that chance, as mediated by market forces, represents the only hope? George Gilder concludes, "The most dire and fatal hubris for any leader is to cut off his people from providence, from the miraculous prodigality of chance, by substituting a closed system of human planning. Success is always unpredictable and thus an effect of faith and freedom."[1] Is Gilder right? Or is the economic mechanism so delicately hinged that we dare not leave it to the jarring slams of chance so characteristic of an unfettered market? Can economics be a science, however inexact, in which prediction and intervention represent a better way than the invisible hand? In a sense, these questions focus the economic debate of our time: Is an intentional economy necessary, possible, and desirable?

A. An Overview of Attitudes toward Planning

Among the advantages of laissez-faire economics is that it relieves one of all responsibility toward the future. History is treated, with fatalistic determinism, either as the best of all possible worlds or as something beyond the positive influence of rational intervention. However, most economists believe that keeping hands off the economy is not enough, that there are choices to be made about economic structure and performance that can make the future surer and perhaps better. Planning is at the heart of such an intentional economy.

There are few things that incite such strong reactions among those interested in economic issues as the matter of *national economic planning*. Those of the classical tradition tend to share the conviction of Friedrich Hayek that planning is not just inefficient but evil.[2] Hayek had observed at close hand the tragic experience of Central Europe between the two world wars as governmental economic interventionism degenerated into fascism that robbed people of their freedom in the name of necessity. Hayek's concern was that planning, once embarked upon, knows no limit until it engulfs the whole of society, and citizenship is reduced to slavery.

At the other pole are the idealists who look upon government planning as the way to ensure freedom in society. An exaggerated example of the perspective is the syllogistic series that appeared a number of years ago in a special issue of the *Indian Journal of Political Science:* "1) Planning increases production. 2) Production allows the satisfaction of more needs. 3) The satisfaction of needs is the condition of freedom. Hence, planning is the condition of freedom."[3]

The attitudes of most who consider the issue fall somewhere between these two extremes, according to their understanding of what national economic planning means. For many, the only images are of Soviet Five-Year Plans with the rigid allocation of resources according to bureaucratically determined goals. When planning is perceived this way, it predictably finds little place in the hearts and minds of most Americans or in the political arena in the United States.

B. Three Planning Models Abroad

Yet the postwar recovery of Japan, the nation regarded as our chief international competition, was built on just such mechanisms. Basic industries were revived under the aegis of strong central planning at the same time that the foundation was being established for a private enterprise economy. In the mid-1950s, the Five-Year Development Plan was established to cultivate the steel, textile, machine-tool, and petrochemical industries—except for the latter, competitors we now greatly fear. All this was done either under a U.S. military occupational administration or with the approval of American advisers.

Another understanding of planning involves the establishment of official developmental and social goals accompanied by extensive government record-keeping and reporting. The assumption is that a better-informed capitalism, advised by government of the direction in which it would like to steer society, will be able and willing to accommodate the vision because business too will benefit from a more intentional economy where public and private sectors are pulling together. This is a type of planning that has been adopted by numerous Third World countries in part because it is less resisted by the traditional power centers. What makes such planning possible, however, also makes it powerless and therefore pointless.

Somewhere between these two lies a third approach that is typified by the French program of indicative planning. France, of course, has a fairly large and powerful set of companies in several sectors—mining, railroads, petroleum, automobiles, and electrical power—that are owned and operated by the government. Official planning starts with a significant amount of government economic clout in the business sector. Indicative planning differs from traditional socialism in its ability to include major elements of the private sector in the setting and carrying out of national economic goals.

The effort begins with a comprehensive national plan developed by a government commission in consultation with leaders from business, labor, agriculture, various levels of government, and private organizations. The plan that results is not just a statement of overarching goals. It gets very specific—how much will be spent on roads, ports, and sewage systems; the amount, type, and location of housing construction; which social services will be increased and by how much; the amount and type of investment that will be made by government-owned firms; the volume and kind of anticipated government purchases. With such goals in mind, specific production targets are set for the industries involved.

The strength of this approach is not just the public relations value of its broad-based participation. Obviously, business and labor will be more likely to support a program they have helped devise. Equally important, however, is that firms are able to get a pretty clear indication of the sales they can count on, and they can begin to allocate their resources accordingly, without having to wait for market signals.

What the French system seeks to accomplish is a large measure of social and economic planning without resorting to extensive nationalization of enterprise or other forms of compulsion. Indicative planning is essentially voluntary and achieves its goals more by the carrot than by the stick. How successful it has been is a matter of dispute. Throughout the 1980s France has suffered from the effects of the global recession. Like other European economies, it has lagged behind the recovery experienced by the United States. This continued stagnation was a major factor in the triumph of Socialist President François Mitterrand, who came to office promising to get the economy moving again by instituting even more interventionist economic policies. Resistance to this approach by the international financial community together with an overvalued dollar during the early years of the decade caused a virtual collapse of the franc and a retreat of the government from a larger planning role that the succeeding conservative government has not been anxious to revive.

C. The American Experience

As noted earlier, citizens, businesses, and bureaucrats in the United States have generally been more suspicious of the whole idea of planning than have their European and Japanese counterparts. Forty years of Keynesian dominance and another seven of monetarism have had little to do with comprehensive planning. Policy has usually represented government reaction to impending disaster rather than leadership toward a preferred future. Furthermore, policy has almost always meant unilateral action by government rather than a consolidated effort with business and labor based on shared goals and strategies.

The fact that the economy in recent years has responded sluggishly, if at all, to governmental tinkering has given rise to the new *rational expectations school* of economic thought. It makes the none-too-startling assertion that individuals will seek their own best interest as dictated by what they perceive as the likely outcome of various economic options.

Its advocates eschew both Keynes and Friedman. They base economic analysis upon mathematical models so esoteric that they often puzzle and anger even many influential economists. Wassily Leontief, one of the profession's notable mathematicians, complains, "Page after page of economic journals are filled with mathematical formulas leading the reader from sets of more or less plausible but entirely arbitrary assumptions to precisely stated but irrelevant theoretical conclusions."[4] The purpose of these models is more to explain the economy than to remedy it. The central idea of the rational expectations school is that the people and institutions of society have become so adept at anticipating and reacting to changes in government policy that positive economic interventionism, and particularly planning, is no longer possible. Thus the philosophical underpinning of the new mathematical economics is a resuscitated classical viewpoint: the government that governs least, governs best. Adam Smith has been reborn as a computer jock!

Such a technical rejection of planning, however, rests upon the assumption that it is an exercise of government hatched by state functionaries ariesand foisted upon an unsuspecting and hostile public. But national economic planning does not necessarily mean turning over private purse strings to policymakers or abandoning business to bureaucrats. At its best, it means planning *with* people, not just *for* people, by involving in the process representatives of all sectors: agriculture, banking, business, consumers, labor, and federal, state, and local government.

In this country the planning debate is defined by the false premise that our choice is between planning and no planning. In fact, there already is a lot of planning, though not in the careful, systematic way such an important activity merits. We see governmental planning in every city, state, and federal budget and tax law. When tobacco and grain have federal price subsidies and peanuts have acreage allotments, that is national economic planning. When states give tax holidays to attract businesses and municipalities change zoning laws to accommodate them, that is national economic planning. When U.S. auto companies stop making small cars of their own design and opt instead for licensing agreements or joint ventures with foreign firms, that is national economic planning. When corporations are bailed out and banks are propped up by government funds, that is national economic planning.

To plan or not to plan is *not* the question. The question is, how best to plan? We can only ask, who will plan, how will the planners be chosen, and for whose benefit will planning be done? In the end those are not merely economic or technical matters but moral ones.

Some would say that tyranny always lies at the heart of planning, and therefore we dare not risk an intentional economy. But surely a people who can be trusted to govern themselves politically are also capable of establishing the necessary mechanism to guide their economic future. The issue before us is not whether we should imitate the French, the British, or the Soviets. The issue is that we should determine whether it is possible to make the economy function more efficiently and humanely in achieving the goals we have set for our society.

II. Realities: The Industrial Policy Debate

Although the idea of comprehensive national economic planning has never fared well in the United States, there has been lively debate in recent years over the related but more limited concept of a national *industrial policy.* Industrial policy acknowledges a new economic task for government beyond the Keynesian role of manipulating macroeconomic variables. It involves using the levers of government, in coordination with business and labor, to insure the viability and global economic competitiveness of key American industries.

Why has this issue rather suddenly emerged from classroom consideration to become a hot topic of news magazines, op ed articles, and political debate? Quite clearly because of the sagging and uncertain economy of the 1970s and 1980s. Almost no one wants to talk about changing anything as long as the economy is working well. However, a decade of rampant inflation, high unemployment, negative trade balances, and a reduced real standard of living is enough to make even the most loyal free-enterpriser ask what has gone wrong and what can be done to make things right. For the first time in living memory, American businesses seem seriously threatened by products from abroad. In the ten years following 1970, foreign automobiles jumped from 8 to 23 percent of the U.S. market, imported steel increased by over 50 percent, and consumer electronics from Asia and Europe multiplied their share of the American market by fivefold and accounted for half of all sales in 1980. In that year over 70 percent of all U.S.-made goods faced active competition from similar foreign products. Whole industries such as textiles and shoes now seem all but lost by U.S. producers. Feeling the hot breath of foreign competition on their necks, hundreds of firms have moved abroad in search of cheaper and more compliant labor and better profit margins. Millions of industrial jobs have been lost in the U.S. due to plants closing, subcontracting abroad, or relocating.[5]

Why is America losing out? Economists, bureaucrats, and business executives have focused on the slowdown in U.S. industrial productivity as a major cause.

A. The Productivity Dilemma

Labor productivity is generally defined as the real dollar value of all goods and services produced divided by the number of hours of all workers used to produce them. By that standard, growth in industrial labor productivity in the United States declined steadily from 1965 through 1980. The average growth in worker output averaged 3.22 percent per year from 1948 to 1965. From 1965 to 1973 the rate of increase fell to 2.4 percent, and diminished to just 1.1 percent during the next five years (from 1973 to 1978). Then, during the period from 1978 to 1980, for the first time since the Depression, American industry turned out less per hour worked than in the previous year.[6] The negative productivity rate has continued for most years since then.

The rate of productivity growth is important in an economy because the ability to produce more with the same effort is what makes it possible to give workers a raise, or to give investors greater dividends, or to increase the social expenditures of government without causing inflation. Decreasing productivity contributes to stagnating standards of living, inflation, or both—which is precisely what happened during the 1970s. Even so, there probably would have been no major call for a national industrial policy in the U.S. if all other nations had suffered the same fate. The occurrence would have been written off as a quirk of the economic system. But as a matter of fact, our chief trading partners in Europe and Asia continued to experience much higher rates of growth in industrial output.

It seemed that we were being left in the economic dust of the Japanese and the Germans. Actually the United States still has the highest overall labor productivity of any country in the world. Other nations, however, are closing the gap rapidly. While U.S. industrial productivity increased by 20 percent during the 1970s, Japan's leaped by 145 percent, France's moved up by 77 percent, and Germany's increased by 75 percent. More important, in some subsectors such as automobiles, steel, textiles, and shoes, the United States has fallen far enough behind other countries that our industry's products are not truly competitive in the market and would probably be forced out except for various forms of protection. The same situation exists for other product lines such as calculators, cameras, copiers, and color television sets.

It is clear that part of our country's international trade difficulty stems from a frequently overvalued dollar. But the productivity decline began back in the mid-1960s and has continued as a force largely independent from the vicissitudes of currency values. The question that confronts industrial America is how the trend of recent years can be stemmed.

In the early discussions of the productivity dilemma, editorial writers and self-appointed champions of free enterprise had a way of making the whole problem seem the fault of labor. Myths arose about the loyal and disciplined Japanese worker who always arrived an hour before starting time and always stayed an hour after the final whistle, who labored all day, hardly taking the time to breathe, much less to eat lunch. Meanwhile, parallel myths thrived about the American worker who, coddled by union contracts, wouldn't even give a fair day's work for a full day's pay. More reflective people, of course, knew all along that what workers can produce is determined more by the equipment they have to work with than by how much they sweat in the process. That is not to say that worker effort and attitude have no importance. Rather, it is to acknowledge the fact that even highly motivated workers cannot overcome the productivity drag of poor investment decisions and poor management.

B. A New Approach

The industrial policy debate begins with the assertion that the misallocation of resources—both capital and human—lies at the heart of the productivity problem and therefore at the heart of what is regarded as the American industrial crisis. In his book *The Next American Frontier*,[7] Robert Reich points to management's failure to recognize how rapidly the economic world has changed over the past fifteen to twenty years as the key factor in the nation's industrial decline. Until World War II, the U.S. led in the development of high-volume, standardized production—symbolized by the manufacturing assembly line. The ability to produce massive quantities of identical products by mobilizing vast amounts of capital and labor in inflexible systems was the hallmark of America's industrial success. The system served the country well for over half a century, and many of the machines that were installed at the beginning of the era were still functioning at the end.

Meanwhile, the Japanese and the West Europeans, whose industrial apparatus had been heavily damaged during World War II, were able to rebuild with the most modern and efficient equipment. This led to their initial productivity advantage over competing U.S. firms. At first that was hardly noticed in this country because most goods produced by Japan and Western Europe were designed for their own people, to meet the pent-up demand created by years of war and the austerity required for reconstruction. As that internal demand was met, however, Japanese and European production began to seek other markets. By the 1960s American firms that had for over fifteen years experienced something of a trade monopoly began to encounter competition abroad. But since only a small part of U.S. production went for exports, most American managers were not concerned. Even as foreign-made goods began to trickle into the homeland, the dominance of U.S. firms seemed unassailable. Management saw no need to change investment patterns, no need to seek greatly increased productivity by investing heavily in new generations of equipment while the old was still producing profits, no need to think about massive retraining programs for workers. But within a decade the trickle had become a flood of goods produced abroad, and U.S. managers realized belatedly that the industrial world had changed. An indication of the magnitude of that change is seen in the fact that from 1980 to 1984, a period that included a very strong economic recovery, twenty of the nation's twenty-five basic manufacturing industries experienced declines in total employment.[8]

The initial response of businesses was to try to make the world stand still so that American industry could catch up. Thus, by the mid-1970s, the managers of threatened industries joined an anxious labor force in calling for protectionist tariffs and quotas, for relaxed environmental, safety, and antitrust regulations, and for government subsidies and bailouts as well as lower taxes. Many of these pleas were honored during both the Carter and the Reagan administrations. However, managers often used the reprieve to rebuild company profits and to diversify into other activities rather than to risk more capital in highly competitive industries. The reaction exacerbated what Robert Reich calls "paper entrepreneurialism."[9]

Reich maintains, however, that the great failure of American management was not in its lack of dedication to recapturing lost market-share but in its tardiness in recognizing that the model of manufacturing that stressed the indefinite production of basic goods was no longer viable. The new model, advocated by Harvard Business School professor Raymond Vernon, maintained that innovations would be retained under the close control of the originating firm (or nation) only so long as the technical skills of the parent organization were necessary to make the production system work. Once the process was made routine, it could be expected to pass to less skilled hands and ultimately to less developed countries, which would have a labor cost advantage.[10]

Japan understood this, and responded accordingly. While American companies and labor organizations were lobbying for quotas on imported rolled steel, Japan was shifting its production toward specialty steels in anticipation of Korea's major expansion in output of the basic product. Reich maintains that the United States and other advanced industrial countries must also move away from assembly-line techniques dependent on high-volume, standardized production and toward the processing of precision-manufactured, customer-tailored, and technology-driven goods. This requires a flexible production system that rests on problem-solving skills and great adaptability by both labor and capital.

C. Do We Need an Industrial Policy?

Critics respond to this question with a resounding "no." Simply stated, their objection is that a policy of collaboration of business, labor, and government is not necessary, possible, or desirable. Airing the rationales underlying this view and responding to them is a fruitful way of getting at an answer to the question.

The critics say that an industrial policy is not necessary because the fundamental problem it seeks to correct—the decline in productivity—is already being solved. While few experts expect a return to the 3.2 percent growth rates of the period from 1948 to 1965, many foresee a near future with annual productivity increases of 2.7 to 2.9 percent. There is some support for this view. The labor force is aging. Older workers are, on the average, more experienced and more productive than younger ones. Energy costs have dropped dramatically due primarily to OPEC's inability to impose production controls. Productivity growth may also be expected to rise with an increase in the capital-to-labor ratio, as investment funds replace antiquated equipment and increase the number of machines per worker. In addition, research and development expenditures are up. This could be crucial for productivity growth, since increased knowledge accounts for more than 40 percent of all productivity gains. Finally, some claim that there is a new sense of cooperation between labor and management. As evidence they point not only to the number of labor-management productivity teams that have sprung up but also to the number of companies offering stock options and profit-sharing plans to their employees. What is not often mentioned in this regard, however, is that in a tight economy, business has been able to use the bankruptcy laws to break union contracts or force contract renegotiations, resulting in pay cuts and fringe benefit give-backs.

The problem with relying on these indicators as the harbingers of sustained productivity growth is twofold. First, they are projections based on the assumption that nothing negative or unexpected will happen. For instance, energy costs will stay down only if OPEC doesn't get its act together and there isn't a serious flare-up in the Middle East that would cause a major disruption in petroleum supplies. Second, the projections tend to ignore the rest of the world. All of these things might actually happen, but the United States would not be relatively better off if productivity growth rates in other countries increased commensurately. If energy costs decline for U.S. industries, they also decline for Japanese and European industries. Similarly, while the U.S. is increasing expenditures on research and development, so too are the other industrialized nations. In other words, productivity gains can be understood only in relative terms—those of the U.S. compared with those of the rest of the world.

Critics also say that an industrial policy is not possible. No one, they contend, can look into the economic tea leaves and identify the *sunrise industries*—new business activities that will dominate the future. It is impossible to know where and in what field the next technological breakthrough will come, and impossible to project with any certainty how human and economic resources should be allocated to meet or even encourage the breakthrough. These critics claim further that no planner can guess what consumer preferences will be.

The problem with this argument is that it ignores the fact that all of these dilemmas must be confronted anyway, even if things are left exactly as they are. Someone has to decide where investment funds will be channeled and what consumers are likely to buy. The question is simply whether it will be done ad hoc, leaving decisions largely to individual profit-seekers, or whether, given the complexity of the global economy, it will be done with some measure of rational planning.

Finally, the critics contend that an industrial policy is undesirable. They insist that any expanded role for government in society is objectionable on the grounds of ideology and efficiency. Increased government intervention, these critics argue, will curtail the freedom of action enjoyed by business. This is an ideological position that can be answered only with the moral assertion that freedom of action for business must be secondary to the elaboration of an economic system that meets people's need for employment and income and not just their need for products. The critics also contend that government intervention should be avoided because of government's poor track record in economic affairs. The best rejoinder here is to point to history, noting that it was government action that pulled the economy out of the nosedive of the 1930s, that the twenty years following World War II when government was increasingly involved in the economy was a period of business success and of general prosperity, and that a number of important businesses (e.g., Lockheed, Continental Illinois, and Chrysler) continue operating today only because government intervened to save them.

Nor should we allow the critics of an industrial policy to define the debate by insisting that the sole criterion for evaluating such a policy is whether it solves the productivity crisis. Productivity growth alone does not guarantee a healthy economy. There was an unqualified productivity gain in 1984 when the Wells Fargo Bank cut seven hundred employees from its force through the installation of automatic teller machines. Yet this does not mean that the economy as a whole is better off unless those seven hundred people found new jobs. If some or all of them remain unemployed, or must work at jobs below their skills or for much less money, the economy loses and people suffer. More broadly, we can imagine a future in which all of the goods and services we require might be produced by half of the present work force. This would be a productivity bonanza but a torment for the displaced and a real threat to an economy that could not find a way to share the benefits.

Do we need an industrial policy? The question should not be answered on the basis of the next quarterly dividend statement or even on the basis of a business upswing that may last five or ten years. Rather, the question must be answered by referring to a more distant planning horizon, one measured in decades and generations. It must be answered by deciding whether rational and coordinated action holds out more hope than the spinning roulette wheel of the market.

D. Elements of an Industrial Policy

The United States already has an industrial policy. The only problem is that it is unintentional, unimaginative, and inefficient in doing what needs to be done. A more effective policy will involve such elements as the following.

1. An Economic Civil Service

While adopting a more formal industrial policy does not mean a government-directed economy, it does mean a different and more active role for government in micro-economic affairs—that is, in the functioning of industries and firms. This does not have to mean huge new bureaucracies. Japan runs its Ministry of International Trade and Industry (MITI) with just 2,500 professional staff members. In the United States, people already employed in the Departments of Labor and Commerce, as well as the staff of the Council of Economic Advisors, could be shifted to a new organization and given new responsibilities.

2. An Industrial Policy Council

Perhaps this name is too formal. What is needed is a forum within which representatives of the various interests and perspectives of American economic society can meet to agree upon an appropriate industrial strategy and the way in which the costs and benefits of achieving it are to be shared. Who gets how much? Who pays how much? One example of such a group is the Economic Cooperation Council, which was the centerpiece of the 1985 congressional bill for a National Industrial Strategy Act. This called for a twenty-member council to be made up of equal numbers of representatives from government, business, labor, and the public interest. Congressman Stan Lundine, who proposed the legislation, envisioned members serving a maximum of two six-year terms in this body, whose authority would be only advisory.

3. Management of the Industrial Transition

Supporters of a more adequate and intentional industrial policy are often perceived as being divided into two camps: protectors of smokestack America, and promoters of the high-tech hope. The latter group, typified by Robert Reich and Ira Magaziner, begins with the observation that either labor-intensive, high-volume, standardized production will pass to the Third World with its cheap labor, or American industrial wages will drop dramatically in order to be competitive.

Reich and others who are perceived as pinning all their hopes on the rapid expansion of high-tech industry and services are accused of willingly abandoning traditional basic industries such as steel, automobiles, and textiles. Reich insists that this is not the case. What he seeks is a way of maintaining these industries by developing their more specialized products and functions without investing further in their most vulnerable elements. For instance, he advocates no further investment in production facilities for basic steel bars, sheets, and tubes, but a major investment in the production of special-formula and special-purpose products: high-tensile-strength steel, light enough to be used in fuel-efficient cars; steel mixed with silicon, designed to improve the efficiency of power transformers and electric motors; and corrosion-resistant steel.[11]

Those like Barry Bluestone and Bennett Harrison who are perceived as being defenders of smokestack industry begin with the concept that, in the narrow pursuit of profits, corporations have used viable businesses as cash cows without regard for the employees or the communities in which the plants are located. Financial managers have sought to milk every dollar of profitability from firms while reinvesting the minimum. The result has been a whole series of plants and industries rendered noncompetitive by avarice, by lack of investment, or by the decision to move to another state or country or to offer another product line on the basis of a fractional point of increased return on investment. This hypermobility of capital has left in its wake millions of unemployed workers and scores of scarred communities.

The concern of this group is not that a national industrial policy should protect every failing plant or industry but that mechanisms should be found to prevent the most narrow definitions of profit from being the sole determinant of investment patterns in the United States, and that mechanisms should be established that will ease the transition, for both workers and communities, from declining industries to those with greater potential.

Although the rhetoric of these two groups is somewhat different, their concerns are substantially the same. Both would likely include in the adequate management of our industrial transition such steps as the following:

- Requiring a corporation to give prior notification of its intention to close a plant.
- Assessing such a corporation some of the costs experienced by the community for a plant closing.
- Ending accelerated depreciation on plants and equipment on the grounds that it encourages investment that cannot be justified on the basis of business alone, and thus encourages the premature abandonment of facilities.
- Allowing interest deductions from corporate income tax only for actual

investment in new or renovated plants and equipment. (This would specifically disallow mergers and acquisitions providing a tax advantage greater than staying in business.)

- Providing federal support for the establishment of regional development banks to supply long-term, low-interest loans to firms that agree to invest in becoming more competitive and to remain in their present location or some other agreeable site in the region served by the bank.

4. Commitment to the Development of Human Capital

In considering the need to reorient American industry, the emphasis is usually placed on the reallocation of capital. In many ways, however, it is labor that is most seriously affected by problems of deindustrialization and therefore most needful of economic reorganization. Capital is both more mobile and more malleable than labor. A financial investment in an aging machine-tool company can be written off in a northeastern state today only to reappear next week or next month as an investment in an electronics firm in the Sunbelt or in Singapore. Transformation is not that simple with human workers. Gone are the days when labor was an indiscriminate mass force, when people were able to do virtually any job available. A person cannot leave work as a lathe operator on Friday and begin work on Monday as an etcher of computer memory chips. A considerable amount of lead time and retraining are necessary for workers to acquire the new skills involved. Establishing the mechanisms to do this more efficiently will benefit not only the unemployed but also business enterprises and the society as a whole.

Robert Reich suggests that, rather than establish an extensive network of government job-training programs, a government agency provide unemployed workers with vouchers to be given to companies in exchange for on-the-job training. Firms accepting the vouchers would be eligible to receive reimbursement from government for half their training costs during a maximum three-year period. Such an arrangement would benefit the company by allowing it to reduce its training costs while assuring it that the employees it was hiring would become well grounded in the specific technology and system it uses. Employees would benefit by gaining skills for jobs that already exist rather than for a general area of technology. And the government would benefit from lower costs since the workers would be employed while learning rather than receiving unemployment compensation. Reich suggests that such a program could be financed by a payroll tax paid by both employees and employers. However, it would not be necessary to limit the funds available to income from that source alone.

Reich also suggests using tax incentives to encourage greater corporate investment in employee and community development. The present situation is just the opposite. Companies that wish to relocate in search of lower taxes or a cheaper labor force are allowed to declare the moving expense as a business deduction, write off the value of the plant and equipment left behind, and receive accelerated depreciation on any machinery acquired for the new site. Investments in education and training costs, however, yield no tax advantage. To end or dramatically reduce the former while encouraging the latter would be a positive incentive for firms to stay in the communities where they now are and to contribute to the development of their present labor force rather than seeking greener pastures in other communities or countries.[12]

Such suggestions about how to reshape the industrial structure are important not because they are right in their every detail but because they encourage us to think in new ways about the nature of economic society. The success of a more adequate industrial policy, or of even more comprehensive economic planning, depends ultimately not only upon the technical matters of implementation but upon a loosening-up of ideological rigidity and upon the vision of society held by the planners and the people.

III. Values: The Creation of the Present

A. A Perspective on Progress

The closing years of the last century and the early decades of this one marked a period in this country of unparalleled confidence about history and the human condition. Progress seemed inevitable and social problems as malleable to the institutions of modern society as those of the physical realm were to science and technology. There was confidence that power was the servant of good intention. As Horace Bushnell put it, "Power moves in the direction of hope."[13] And hope—a social and historical hope rather than an eschatological one—was the hallmark of the age. Perhaps it was not really hope (which rests ultimately upon belief in a transforming interventionism) but optimism (which is possessed of mechanistic confidence) that was the true sign of the times.

The Social Gospel movement was the religious expression of this general optimism. To its adherents, the convergence of Christian vision and social institutions seemed at hand. In the words of Washington Gladden, one of the early voices of the movement, "Our laws are to be christianized; the time is coming when they will express the perfect justice and the perfect beneficence of the Christian law. . . . The administration of justice is to be christianized. . . . Doubtless this millennial perfection of state is a great way off, but it is the goal toward which we are journeying."[14]

In the wake of technological progress, it was simply assumed that social advancement and moral perfection would unite and follow closely behind. A wave of triumphalism swept the nation, and with it the conviction that America and all its institutions, including religion, would lead the world to a new order of being. Utopianism was no longer limited to novels and philosophy but became the stuff of theology and sermons as well.

The supposed harmony of this new order was soon fractured. Leaders of the Social Gospel movement were dismayed to find that class and economic interests did not fade away in the face of a bright economic outlook. Facing reduced profits, owners hired strikebreakers rather than give in to union demands for more money and safer jobs; urban areas continued to degenerate into slums, even when it was clear that the financial power existed to make them better; farmers had little relief from an economy warped against them by the weight of urban and industrial political power. When the flaws of the modern world would not go away, it was a crisis for those who believed that the age of inevitable progress had come.

World War I proved not to be the war to end all wars. The social idealism of the Russian revolution dissolved into the bureaucratic excesses of Leninism and the brutality of Stalinism. Depression proved foolish the hope that national wealth could finance the elimination of social ills without strife. And in Germany the revival of national pride gave way to racism, to the Holocaust, and to yet another war. During World War II, there was little thought of creating a better world, only of avoiding a worse one. Even before this final disillusionment came, a somber theological note had been struck that was discordant amid the trumpets of progress and optimism.

Karl Barth was the voice of neo-orthodoxy that expressed the most extreme reaction to the optimism of liberal utopianism and the Social Gospel movement. Liberalism emphasized the spectral character of life with an almost imperceptible shading from God to humankind, from faith to reason, from grace to works, and from science, technology, and government to the kingdom of God. Barth denounced all such supposed continuities and saw instead a God who was Wholly Other, where there was no intersection between the work of God and the work of human beings and human institutions. He insisted that history does not progress to the kingdom of God.

The radical discontinuity that Barth proclaimed led to a great indifference toward even the most important issues of public policy and politics. When he addressed the World Council of Churches assembly at Amsterdam in 1948, he declared that "God's design" is the establishment of the kingdom in Christ and does not refer to any work of the church "'for the amelioration of human life' or for establishing world peace and justice."[15] Nowhere is the depth of that indifference better glimpsed than in his comments about the East-West conflict that emerged after World War II. "As Christians it is not our conflict at all," he proclaimed. "It is not a genuine, not a necessary, not an interesting conflict. It is a mere power conflict. We can only warn against the still greater crime of wanting to decide the issue in a Third World war."[16]

Ultimately, so great was Barth's pessimism that he virtually abandoned the hope of resolving social problems and saw as the main role of Christians a retreat to giving dire warnings. Those closely following such a perspective could be expected to have little confidence in the success of a national economic-planning apparatus and even less interest in Christians or the church commenting on the issue. In such a view, the Christian task is to recall the society to the Christian vision but without expectation that social institutions will become useful tools in implementing that vision.

In the neo-orthodox critique of optimism and liberalism, Reinhold Niebuhr was no less adamant than Karl Barth in his conviction that there are no ultimate solutions to the problems of society. The rediscovery of sin and its pervasive influence over all human activity left no room for the expectation that some set of laws or group of social institutions would ultimately overcome the will to power. Nevertheless, Niebuhr did not trade progressive perfectability for individualism and indifference. Instead, he insisted that "the certainty of the final inadequacy of every form of human justice must not lead to defeatism in our approach to the perplexing problems of social justice in our day. The possibilities as well as the limits of every scheme of justice must be explored."[17]

Niebuhr sought a theological position that would make participation in the sociopolitical process the norm for believers without at the same time making absolute commitments to any one human system. Thus he became for over three decades a persistent moral critic of both liberalism and orthodoxy, capitalism and socialism, individualism and collectivism. His 1952 essay entitled "Christian Faith and Social Action" contains many insights relevant to our concern here about an intentional economy and the planning apparatus that it might entail. "The liberal Christian form of sensitivity overestimates the moral possibilities of man's collective life," he asserted, "while the more orthodox Protestant versions are usually overcome by a pessimistic overemphasis on the evils in collective life, thus consigning it to the devil." He also maintained that "the power of the state is not as dangerous as the liberal creed imagines and not as beneficent as collectivist theory assumes."[18]

Niebuhr was deeply concerned about the degree to which capitalist society had underestimated its tendency toward a lopsided distribution of economic and political power. Likewise, he was concerned about the degree to which collectivist creeds had failed to take seriously enough the moral perils of a system that merges political and economic power in a single entity. He maintained that Christians have a part to play in the hard decisions that must be made about competing systems and political philosophies even when they do not touch directly upon Christian doctrine or observance. Niebuhr believed that the faith community must seek a society that

> will recognize the necessity of guaranteeing human welfare in areas in which a market economy does not satisfy human wants as, for instance, in housing and medical services. But it will not assume that human desires are naturally ordinate and that they can be satisfied by government agencies without the necessity of some restraint upon inordinate, or at least disproportionate, demands. It will not assume that all government interference in economic process is either good or bad; but it will study the effect of each type of interference.
>
> In very specific terms [the law of love] would require that in the social struggle the business community should learn from the Gospel a certain uneasiness about its uncritical devotion to freedom, and that the industrial workers should learn to be less confident of the consequence of a policy of planning.[19]

Thus the main point is that pragmatism, not ideology, must determine the role that government, and particularly planning, should have in society. There can be no illusions about the ability to plan and establish the perfect world. But neither can there be any illusions about an unattended capitalism producing that result.

B. The Importance of Vision and Hope

In his book *Small Is Beautiful,* E. F. Schumacher imagines that when God created the world and the people to inhabit it, he might have reasoned something like this:

> If I make everything predictable, these human beings, whom I have endowed with pretty good brains, will undoubtedly learn to predict every-

> thing, and they will thereupon have no motive to do anything at all because they will recognise that the future is totally determined and cannot be influenced by any human action. On the other hand, if I make everything unpredictable, they will gradually discover that there is no rational basis for any decision whatsoever and, as in the first case, they will thereupon have no motive to do anything at all. Neither scheme would make sense. I must therefore create a mixture of the two. Let some things be predictable and let others be unpredictable. They will then, amongst many other things, have the very important task of finding out which is which.[20]

Probably all cultures have regarded the future as both opportunity and threat, and all have sought to know what it holds in store. The Chinese for over two millennia have consulted the *I Ching,* the Book of Changes; ancient Greeks turned to the Temple of Delphi; pre-Davidic kings called in prophets to cast Urim and Thummim; a few stockmarket analysts admit to seeking insight from astrology; and the *Farmer's Almanac* still publishes annually. But computers, with their endless variety of software, are increasingly thought of as the modern-day oracles. From stock prices to weather forecasts to personal health projections to global grain production, computer prediction has become a business aspiring to be a science.

It is a mistake, of course, to speak about computers projecting "the future" as though it is closed and predetermined by either divine or human action. What a computer model of the national or global economy does is to relate vast amounts of data in such a way that there is the possibility of previewing many futures. Potentially it offers the opportunity to choose among alternatives rather than merely to inherit what chance or market forces or the interplay of powers may produce.

The normal way of thinking about history is to regard the present as the product of the past, the working out through the ages of a myriad of decisions and complexities so that present reality is only the chance byproduct of what might have been. The biblical approach is quite different; from a scriptural perspective, it is the future that calls forth the present. It is not just the knowledge that God is committed to "the future" that motivates us, but the conviction that God is committed to a particular future. That does not mean that tomorrow's world is closed, foreordained and established. There are many futures that might be, but to the eyes of faith, there is only one that *should* be and will be. It is that vision of historical oughtness that is the ground of Christian participation in the concrete issues of public policy and economic life; it is the conviction that God's intended future will come to pass in the end that is the ground of our historical hope. There is, of course, the eschatological hope of perfectly fulfilled relationships with God and among humankind that lies beyond history. But the boundary between the historical hope and the suprahistorical hope is unclear to the believer. The degree to which the ultimate can be achieved within the penultimate is therefore the arena of faithfulness.

Believers are certainly not the only ones who make history. Indeed, we are often—perhaps generally—among the bit players in the drama. But our commitment to a particular history can be influential even when we lack power. For that reason, those of the faith community ought not to be easily dispirited by political realities. Public policies that move a society toward the vision of the world of plenty, justice, and peace are appropriate and worth working for even when they fall short of full realization. Ours is not a hope based on illusory optimism. We hope because we know that the God who stands before the beginning and after the end is also present among us in the fashioning of the now, seeking always a world that conforms to creation's original goal and ultimate purpose. In the economic sphere, that means a society that produces abundantly and shares equitably in the context of a global concern for the environment and for all people of this and succeeding generations.

Notes

1. Gilder, *Wealth and Poverty* (New York: Bantam Books, 1981), p. 313.

2. Hayek, *The Road to Serfdom* (Chicago: University of Chicago Press, 1944).

3. Cited by Jacques Ellul in *The Technological Society* (New York: Vintage Books, 1964), p. 178.

4. Leontief, quoted by Robert Kuttner in "The Poverty of Economics," *Atlantic Monthly*, Feb. 1985, p. 78.

5. Barry Bluestone and Bennett Harrison, *The Deindustrialization of America* (New York: Basic Books, 1982).

6. Ira C. Magaziner and Robert B. Reich, *Minding America's Business: The Decline and Rise of the American Economy* (New York: Vintage Books, 1983), p. 31. These figures were compiled by the authors from various U.S. government sources.

7. Reich, *The Next American Frontier* (New York: Times Books, 1983).

8. "Do We Need an Industrial Policy?" *Harper's*, Feb. 1985, p. 37.

9. Reich, "The Next American Frontier," Part I, *Atlantic Monthly*, Mar. 1983, pp. 50, 52, 56.

10. Vernon, *Sovereignty at Bay: The Multinational Spread of U.S. Enterprises* (New York: Basic Books, 1971).

11. Reich, "The Next American Frontier," Part II, *Atlantic Monthly*, Apr. 1983, p. 104.

12. Reich, "The Next American Frontier," Part II, pp. 105-6.

13. Bushnell, quoted by Martin E. Marty in *The Search for a Usable Future* (New York: Harper & Row, 1969), p. 26.

14. Gladden, quoted by Liston Pope in "Can Social Problems Be Solved?" in *Christian Faith and Social Action,* ed. John A. Hutchison (New York: Scribner's, 1953), p. 218.

15. Barth, quoted by Roger L. Shinn in "The Christian Gospel and History," in *Christian Faith and Social Action,* p. 35n.13.

16. Barth, quoted by Reinhold Niebuhr in "The Church between East and West," *Cross Currents,* Winter 1951, p. 67.

17. Niebuhr, quoted by Liston Pope in "Can Social Problems Be Solved?" p. 220.

18. Niebuhr, "Christian Faith and Social Action," in *Christian Faith and Social Action,* pp. 242, 230-31.

19. Niebuhr, "Christian Faith and Social Action," pp. 233-34, 238.

20. Schumacher, *Small Is Beautiful: Economics As If People Mattered* (New York: Harper & Row, 1973), pp. 224-25.

Questions for Discussion

Chapter One:
Economics as Struggle, Freedom, and Responsibility

Concepts

1. In what sense is the market system efficient? What are the advantages and disadvantages of such efficiency?

2. Why is competition so important to the functioning of the market system? What moral dilemma does competition present?

3. Why is economic growth so important to the functioning of the market system?

Realities

1. Why is economic growth both a threat and a necessity?

2. In the face of limits to sustainable growth, do you agree or disagree with the author's summary of the characteristics of permissable growth?

Values

1. According to the author, what was Calvin's principal contribution to economic thought? How does this differ from the traditional Weberian view? How significant is this difference in defining the role of faith in the economic arena?

2. Contrast the economic perspectives of Reinhold Niebuhr with those of George Gilder and Michael Novak. Which perspective seems to have more influence in today's church?

Chapter Two:
The Role of Capital in the Market System

Concepts

1. Why is the savings rate so important in economic society? Do the author's comments about the myths of capital accumulation in the early days of capitalism have any relevance in understanding the global economic picture today?

2. How significant is the transformation of the savings and investment function brought about by large, modern corporations?

Realities

1. The Youngstown situation is pictured as a natural result of autonomous decision-making by owners and managers of a corporation. Should workers and elected officials have any control over corporate decisions that affect employees and communities? What could and should have been done differently in Youngstown to avoid the crisis?

2. Was the religious community's involvement in the attempt to rescue Youngstown Sheet and Tube appropriate? Why was the effort unsuccessful? How do you evaluate the author's comments about the reasons behind the opposition of both business and government to worker-community ownership?

Values

1. Which of the concepts of the early church fathers about money and ownership provide a useful framework for the thought and witness of the church today? Are any of their concepts flawed from a scriptural, theological, or moral perspective?

2. How does the stewardship concept affect the way believers approach economic issues?

3. If the economic perspective of the prophets and early church fathers is "avowedly interventionist," how does that affect the church's attitude toward a laissez-faire philosophy?

Chapter Three:
The Role of Labor in the Market System

Concepts

1. How serious is the problem of worker alienation in our society, and to what degree does it result from an increasingly refined division of labor?

2. Is there a significant racial bias in the employment patterns of U.S. society? If so, what does that portend?

Realities

1. What has brought an increasing number of women into the paid work force?

2. Do you regard the fact that more women work for pay as a positive or a negative factor in economic society?

3. Which do you regard as embodying the greatest sense of

economic justice—"equal pay for equal work" or "equal pay for comparable worth"?

Values

1. Does work define life theologically in a way that other human activity does not?

2. Is the author right in contending that (a) labor is supreme over capital, (b) full employment is the only acceptable national labor policy, and (c) "bread-and-butter" unionism is not enough? If not, how would you phrase a summary statement on each of these subjects.

Chapter Four: Big Business and the Transformation of Capitalism

Concepts

1. Why have corporations become the dominant factor in business over the past century? What benefits do they offer that other forms of business organization do not?

2. How do conglomerate mergers of corporations differ from other forms of merger, and why do they represent a special social and economic concern? Why do the size of corporations and the concentration of markets matter?

Realities

1. Why, according to the author, does big business have a structural bias toward inequality of income?

2. Overall, do you regard foreign investment as a help or a hindrance to less developed countries?

Values

1. Explain your response to the logic and theology of John D. Rockefeller's assertion, "I believe the power to make money is a gift from God. . . . It is my duty to make money and still more money and to use the money I make for the good of my fellow men according to the dictates of my own conscience."

2. When religious institutions urge their members who are influential in corporate management to change the corporation from within, are they being realistic? fair? responsible? Consider the case of Eli Black. What can and should religious organizations do to support their challenge to believers who are corporate managers?

3. If the corporate responsibility movement has the drawbacks noted by the author, is it worthwhile for churches to participate?

Chapter Five: The Old-New Economics and the New-Old Economics

Concepts

1. What are business cycles and why are they important to people who are not in business?

2. What was the principal contribution of John Maynard Keynes to economic thought, and why was it so important?

Realities

1. What does the Laffer Curve propose to demonstrate? How well does it succeed? What is the main problem with the concept?

2. The author argues that the goals of supply-side economics are more ideological than economic. How do you assess that judgment?

3. Is government in the United States too large? What economic danger exists in making a government too small?

Values

1. In discussing the economic drain of very high levels of military spending, the author concludes, "[Peace] conversion has thus become an economic as well as a theological concept." What is the argument behind that phrase, and how valid is it?

2. The closing section of this chapter seeks to document the charge that the shift in government from human-welfare spending to military spending is a sign of moral bankruptcy. Do you agree?

Chapter Six: Sharing in Economic Society: The Problem of Distribution

Concepts

1. On what grounds did David Ricardo conclude that capital owners had received less than their fair share of income? What is the social significance of that observation?

Realities

1. Is economic inequality necessary to the functioning of our economic system? If so, why and how much?

2. Does the United States tax structure tend to diminish economic inequality? Should it?

Values

1. How important is economic growth in avoiding social conflict in the United States?

2. How crucial is greater economic equality to our future as a nation?

3. Is accepting class struggle as both a reality and a necessity in achieving economic justice reconcilable with biblical faith?

Chapter Seven: The Trading Game: The Economy Goes Global

Concepts

1. The comparative advantage model makes several important assumptions. Which of these do you regard as posing the most serious limitation in applying the model to the real world of international exchange?

2. Why has the balance of payments problem brought changes to the contemporary trade environment? How significant are such changes for the future of international trade and trade theory?

Realities

1. Why has protectionist sentiment revived in recent years despite the obvious theoretical advantages of free trade and a 25-year record of benefit from an open trading environment? What are some of the difficulties and dangers facing the advanced industrial economies if restrictive, protectionist policies are imposed?

2. Why are the deteriorating terms of trade for primary products a special problem for less developed countries? What needs to be done about this, and why should the richer countries be willing to make necessary adjustments?

Values

1. How did Thomas Aquinas's doctrine of the just price differ from the attitude of earlier Scholastics toward economic exchange, and how did that shift contribute to the development of the market system?

2. How does the economic perspective of liberation theology differ from perspectives that have dominated in the church since the time of Aquinas? Do you regard liberation theology as a legitimate expression of biblical faith?

3. Does the socialist orientation of most liberation theology constitute a different and more difficult dilemma for those of biblical faith than the capitalist orientation of traditional theology? Why or why not?

Chapter Eight:
Banking on Money

Concepts

1. Why is the supply of money available such a crucial factor in the economy?

2. What is the principal conviction of the monetarist school, and what is the chief flaw in its logic?

3. What are some of the factors that contributed to the last inflationary spiral?

Realities

1. What part did banks play in the creation of the Third World debt crisis?

2. What is your evaluation of the role of the International Monetary Fund in dealing with Third World debt?

3. Do the author's suggestions for new approaches to resolving the global debt dilemma seem reasonable and acceptable? Why or why not?

Values

1. How should we deal with the Bible's suspicion of money in a modern, monetized culture?

2. What are some of the moral issues at stake in a period of high inflation?

3. What are the consumption values that most concern you in what the author describes as "yuppie culture"?

Chapter Nine:
The Intentional Economy

Concepts

1. How do you respond to George Gilder's defense of "the miraculous prodigality of chance" as a critique of economic planning?

2. Of the various planning models discussed, which seems most relevant to U.S. circumstances?

Realities

1. Why is labor productivity so important in the economy, and why has there been such concern about it in the United States in recent years?

2. What is a national industrial policy, and what are the pros and cons of having one?

3. What are some steps that might be taken to increase U.S. productivity?

Values

1. Which of the three perspectives discussed—that of Social Gospel liberalism, Karl Barth, or Reinhold Niebuhr—is most helpful to the church in defining a position in the debate on economic planning? Why?

2. To what extent does the doctrine of Christian hope help shape the believer's attitude toward economic planning and the commitment to a preferred future?